IMAGES
of America

Albuquerque's Huning Castle Neighborhoods

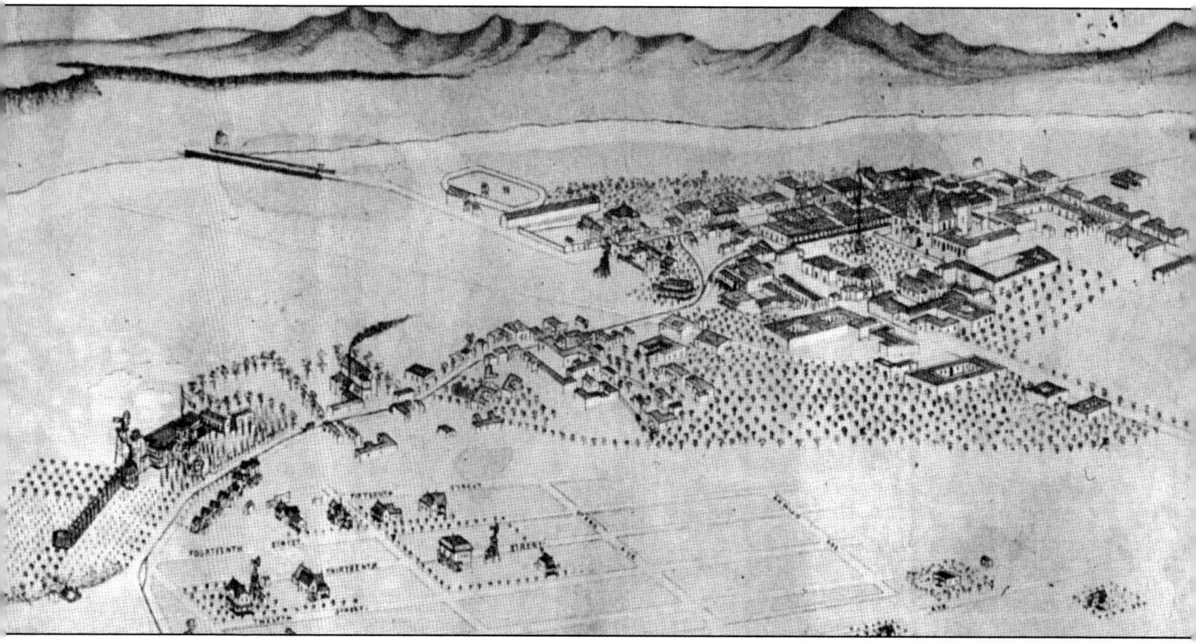

This detail from 1886 "Bird's Eye View Map of Albuquerque" by Augustus Koch is of Old Town, pictured at top right. Railroad Avenue ran along the front of Franz Huning's Molina de Glorieta flour mill (see smoke plume). The mill and Huning Castle are on the far-left side of the sketch, as are the castle's orchards. On the other side of the road is La Glorieta, Huning's first home in Albuquerque's Old Town. La Glorieta is now part of Manzano Day School. (Courtesy of the Valliant family through Dorothy Keleher Valliant.)

On the Cover: This 1880s photograph shows a southeast side view of Huning Castle, the Italianate-style home of Franz and Ernestine Huning, completed in 1883. Franz Huning stands outside the 14-room mansion, a marvel of three-foot-thick terrone (adobe sod) blocks covered by a wood sheathing carved to resemble bricks. Midway between Albuquerque's original Old Town and the New Town that developed as a result of the arrival of the railroad, Huning Castle remained a landmark until its demolition in 1955. (Courtesy of UNM CSWR, Huning-Ferguson Collection, 000-194-0009.)

IMAGES
of America

ALBUQUERQUE'S HUNING CASTLE NEIGHBORHOODS

Jane Mahoney

ARCADIA
PUBLISHING

ISBN 978-0-7385-9677-8

Published by Arcadia Publishing
Charleston, South Carolina

Printed in the United States of America

Library of Congress Control Number: 2012955499

For all general information, please contact Arcadia Publishing:
Telephone 843-853-2070
Fax 843-853-0044
E-mail sales@arcadiapublishing.com
For customer service and orders:
Toll-Free 1-888-313-2665

Visit us on the Internet at www.arcadiapublishing.com

To my husband, Rod, whose endless patience, support,
and computer assistance made this book possible

Contents

ACKNOWLEDGMENTS

Many historians, neighborhood residents, and organizations helped me along this journey to Huning Castle, which was once a real Albuquerque palace but is now only a memory. The castle may be gone, but builder Franz Huning's legacy lives on in the neighborhoods that previously surrounded the castle and later were associated with the Albuquerque Country Club. I thank the many residents of these neighborhoods and the Huning Castle Neighborhood Association for sharing stories, family photographs, and tours. Special thanks go to the Center for Southwest Research, part of the University Libraries at the University of New Mexico; Nancy Tucker for her amazing postcard collection; Mo Palmer for sharing her broad historical knowledge; Judy Cook for her photography; Manzano Day School; Middle Rio Grande Conservancy District; New Mexico BioPark Society; Albuquerque Country Club; Albuquerque Little Theatre; Andrew Hebenstreit; William B. Keleher; Frances Haussamen; Ellen Ann (Lembke) Ryan; Susan Palmer for her research records within the Huning Castle Neighborhood Association archives; Diane Schaller and Historic Albuquerque, Inc.; Ed Boles; city preservation planner, Albuquerque Museum of Art and History; Brad Tepper; Caroline Oxnard Meade; Arcadia Publishing editor Stacia Bannerman; and local Arcadia authors for their encouragement.

Many images in this book are provided courtesy of the Center for Southwest Research, University Libraries, University of New Mexico, which is hereafter listed as UNM CSWR.

INTRODUCTION

Once upon a time, there was a "castle" in Albuquerque, a two-story mansion blending German, Italian, and territorial New Mexican influences. Called "Castle Huning" by its builder Franz Huning and "Huning Castle" by nearly everyone else, the unique home with its three-foot-thick adobe/sod walls, squared towers, and lushly maintained estate grounds was considered a landmark structure from its completion in 1883 until its demolition 72 years later in 1955. While seven decades is not a long life for a castle, this grand home, located between present-day Fifteenth and Sixteenth Streets on the south side of Central Avenue (now home to the Huning Castle Apartments), was a silent witness to the growth of a city and the melding of diverse cultures.

Tucked close to the Rio Grande, halfway between Old Town with its centuries-old Spanish and Mexican influences and the bustling New Town (present-day Downtown Albuquerque) that boomed with the arrival of the Atchison, Topeka & Santa Fe Railway in 1880, the castle was home to Franz and Ernestine Huning. They were German immigrants who made their way by oxen train to Albuquerque from St. Louis by braving the challenges of the 900-mile Santa Fe Trail. Franz came to New Mexico at the end of 1849, living first for some months in Santa Fe, then in San Miguel. Ernestine arrived in New Mexico in 1863, accompanying her new husband along the trail. The couple's first home together was an old home known as La Glorieta near Old Town. This residence presently is the cherished older portion of the private Manzano Day School at 1801 Central Avenue NW. It was in this large old adobe home that the Hunings raised their son and three daughters before Huning Castle was constructed.

One of pioneer Albuquerque's most entrepreneurial businessmen, Franz Huning played a pivotal financial role in securing Albuquerque for the depot and shops of the incoming Atchison, Topeka & Santa Fe Railway. A well-experienced businessman, Huning had already built and was operator of the nearby Molina de Glorieta flour mill, a 15-horsepower steam engine complex that produced 15,000 bushels of cornmeal annually. The mill, near the site of present-day Central Avenue and Laguna Boulevard, burned in 1904, and Franz Huning died a year later. His granddaughter Lina Fergusson Browne wrote of the old German's increasingly reclusive years spent, by choice, at his beloved mill.

The neighborhoods that eventually filled in and grew around the Huning Castle estate, estimated between 300 to 700 acres, possess a charm and presence unique to Albuquerque. The magic is part location with the nearby proximity of the river and its thick forest of cottonwood trees and willows. The magic is also part man-made—this once-swampy river land was transformed into the lush greenery of the Albuquerque Country Club and the adjacent land that became the Rio Grande Biological Park. A diversion channel at the river became a mile-long lake known as Tingley Beach. It was a recreational swimming beach where Albuquerque residents gathered under the watchful eyes of lifeguards. Swimming lessons were taught, a diving platform was built, and there was the occasional marvel of a water-skier pulled by a speedboat. The neighborhoods' eventual northern boundaries became the thoroughfare through the city, first named Railroad

Avenue and then Central Avenue. This east–west arterial became part of the famed cross-country Route 66 highway that ran through the heart of downtown after 1937.

The creation of the Middle Rio Grande Conservancy District in the mid-1920s brought renewed life to the Huning lands. Once-productive farmland next to the river, the land had become heavily silted and alkali-tainted by the time Huning died in 1905. By then, the river flooded with frequency, destroying at least one time the steel Barelas Bridge a couple miles south of Old Town, as well as a pontoon bridge at Old Town. The encroaching marshland delayed the development of a residential neighborhood even after Huning's son, Arno, began dividing and selling parcels of the Huning property by 1913. In 1916, the memorable Aldo Leopold, an employee of the US Forest Service, arrived in Albuquerque with a message of conservation of natural resources. In Albuquerque, he is honored with a two-block-long Aldo Leopold Historic District, which includes his family home at 135 Fourteenth Street SW.

In 1928, after the Middle Rio Grande Conservancy District's stabilization of the river, the bulk of the Huning estate was platted into the Huning Castle Addition, a development that promised elegant and diverse homes. Property lots were larger and lusher than most found elsewhere in the city. Streets were wide and interesting with elegant "Laguna" gaining both a boulevard designation and a tree-filled median. With bustling downtown less than a mile away, well-heeled professionals, businessmen, and their wives found the former Huning property a convenient and prestigious place to live. As the memories of Huning's old castle faded after its demolition in 1955, the neighborhoods in the vicinity gained a second descriptive name—the Albuquerque Country Club area.

Although the first Albuquerque Country Club was founded in 1914 on property adjacent to the University of New Mexico, club members made the decision to build a new club on former Huning grounds in the late 1920s. The new location next to the Rio Grande included the remnants of an irrigation ditch, hog farm, and stables. The clubhouse design by George Williamson was a California Mission style greatly admired and duplicated throughout the residential development. Red clay tile roofs, towers, white stucco, arched windows, and wrought-iron details were common embellishments on neighborhood homes. Large Ranch-style homes and Territorial-style homes were also popular.

The two developers of the Huning Castle Addition, attorney William A. Keleher and former city manager and contractor A.R. Hebenstreit, purchased land from the Hunings and made their own homes in the neighborhood. A litany of well-respected builders and architects followed. The crash of the stock market in October 1929, followed by the Great Depression and World War II years, slowed construction, however. Homes built after the war years, in general, were smaller.

Lean times in the 1930s brought government funds for the construction of some of the neighborhood's most beloved institutions, thanks to Mayor Clyde Tingley's friendship with Pres. Franklin D. Roosevelt. Tingley Beach thrived until about 1951. The Albuquerque Little Theatre at 224 San Pasquale Avenue was built with Works Progress Administration (WPA) funds on land donated by the Huning Castle Addition developers. In later years, nearby Old Town became a magnet for many of the city's museums, most being within walking distance or bike range of residents in neighborhoods around Huning Castle. The city's botanic garden and aquarium took root nearby, as well.

Each Christmas Eve, merchants and church members in Old Town and residents in the Huning Castle neighborhoods fill small brown paper sacks with sand and candles for a holiday tradition that attracts bus tours, drivers, and pedestrians. The soft glowing sacks, known as luminarias, are set out by the thousands at dusk along sidewalks, driveways, rooflines, and walls. The Hebenstreit home at 201 Laguna Boulevard, one of the first homes built after Keleher and Hebenstreit subdivided the Huning estate, marks the occasion not only with luminarias, but thousands of tiny blue electric lights.

One

Franz Huning
The Man and His Times

German immigrant, Santa Fe Trail pioneer, mercantile owner, flour mill operator, railroad colonist, land speculator, publisher, farmer, and civic leader—these titles and more describe the entrepreneurial Franz Huning, born in 1827 as the sixth of 13 children to a prominent farming family in Dielingdorf, Germany. Following his childhood dream of immigrating to America, Huning and his brother Charles took passage on a sailing ship bound for New Orleans in 1848. He was just 21 years old when he stepped off a steamer in St. Louis. Although a tenderfoot, Huning signed on as a bull whacker for a wagon train headed down the Santa Fe Trail. He earned $30 a month plus food.

The villa of Albuquerque, New Mexico (still 63 years from becoming a state), would never be the same. Beginning work in Albuquerque in 1852 as a clerk in Simon Rosenstein's Old Town mercantile, Huning soon established his own store, the first of numerous business ventures.

Huning's memoir, *Trader on the Santa Fe Trail*, recounts numerous trading trips to St. Louis along the famed trail, none quite so memorable as that of 1863 when he brought back a German-born bride, Ernestine Franke. Huning built his pride and joy—the steam-powered Molina de Glorieta gristmill in 1864, a place where he found refuge in his reclusive final years.

Although Huning is best known today for his grand but now demolished Huning Castle home and two neighborhoods that bear his name (the second is Huning's Highland on the sandhills east of the railroad), the man's impact on Albuquerque was far-reaching, particularly his financial role in bringing the railroad's shops and depot to New Town. The development that resulted from the presence of the AT&SF Railway became the foundation for Albuquerque's downtown.

Franz Huning died at the age of 78 in 1905. He did not live long enough to see New Mexico achieve statehood.

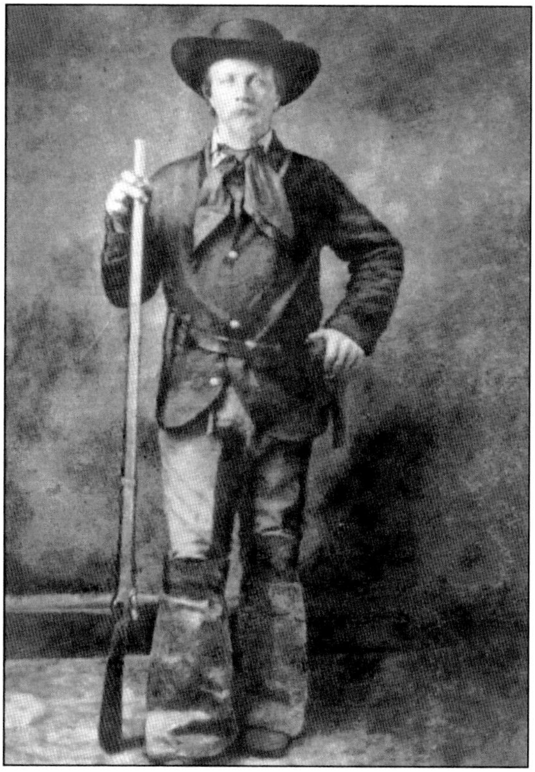

Franz Huning, shown here in Santa Fe Trail clothing in his 20s, made the trip across the plains dozen of times to support his mercantile and grain mill businesses in Albuquerque and elsewhere. The well-educated German immigrant learned to speak, read, and write Spanish in less than a year after his arrival in New Mexico. (Courtesy of UNM CSWR, William A. Keleher Collection, 000-742-0479.)

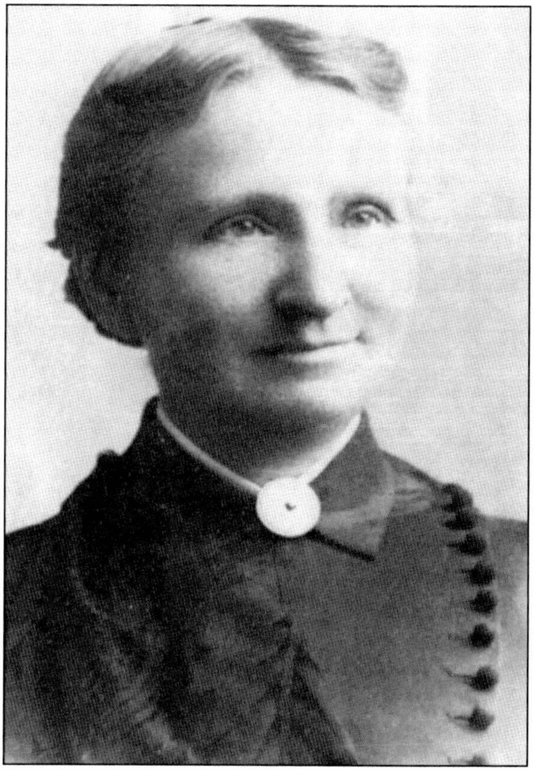

Franz Huning's bride, Ernestine Franke (1837–1923), traveled the Santa Fe Trail from St. Louis to Albuquerque with 10 caged canaries in her wagon. She became a social leader among Albuquerque's dozen English-speaking women in the early 1860s and hosted a coffee and sewing group each Thursday afternoon. Her mother and brother were killed in an Indian attack on the Santa Fe Trail in 1867. (Courtesy of the Horn family/Calvin Horn Publishing, from *Trader on the Santa Fe Trail.*)

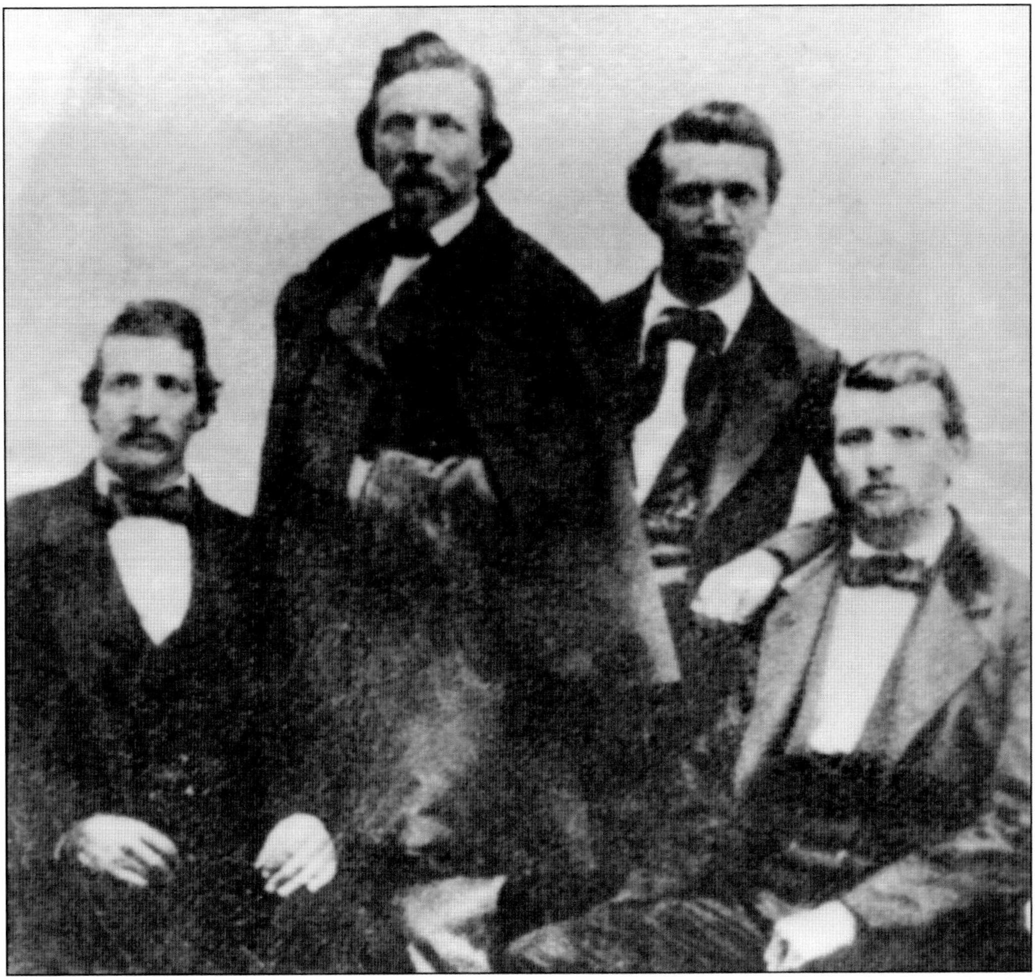

Four of the German-born Huning brothers immigrated to New Mexico, although Charles (sometimes known as Carl) eventually returned to his European homeland. Franz first clerked for Simon Rosenstein in Albuquerque; later he and his brother Charles built their own thriving F&C Huning mercantile businesses in Albuquerque and other outposts as distant as Zuni Pueblo. By the end of the 1850s, Franz had established himself as a leading merchant in Albuquerque's Old Town. The US census of 1860 valued the property of the Albuquerque Huning brothers at $30,000. Huning brothers Louis and Henry went to the Los Lunas area and opened several successful mercantile stores over the years. Henry eventually became a rancher in Arizona. From left to right are Louis, Franz, Charles (Carl), and Henry. (Courtesy of UNM CSWR, Robert Gish Collection, 000-645-0040.)

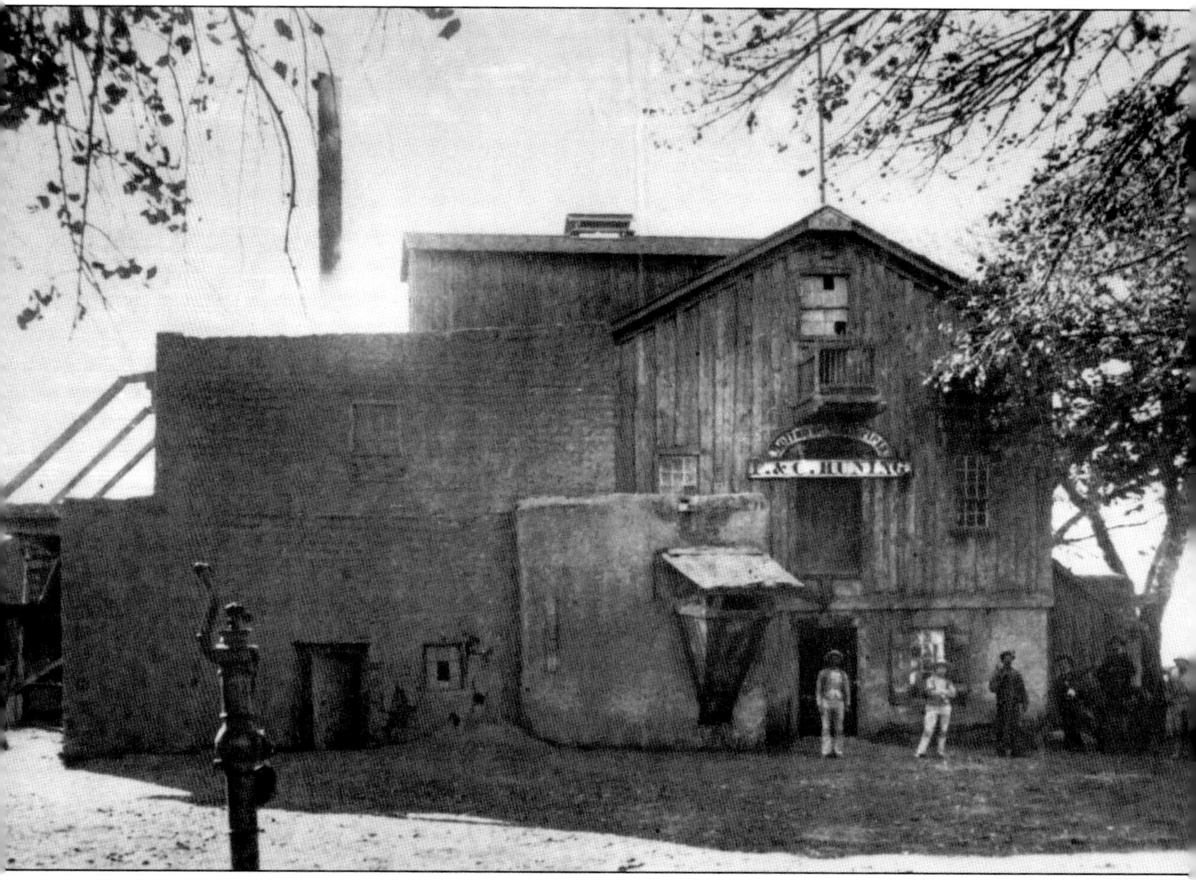

Franz Huning built the Molina de Glorieta flour mill in 1864, bringing in much of the equipment from Europe and then down the Santa Fe Trail. Until the arrival of the railroad in 1880, the mill was considered the largest industrial complex in Albuquerque. The mill, powered by a 15-horsepower steam engine located on Huning's property near current-day Central Avenue and Laguna Boulevard, produced an annual output of 15,000 bushels of corn flour. It burned 45 cords of wood yearly. The tall gabled building was just a short walk from Huning's first home at La Glorieta and close to Huning's second home, Huning Castle. Franz Huning became more reclusive as he aged and opted to spend much of his time at the mill after closing his hardware store in New Town. His granddaughter Lina Fergusson Browne speculated that Huning found New Town rushed and competitive after spending decades working in slower-paced Old Town. The mill burned in 1904, and Huning died one year later. (Courtesy of the Albuquerque Country Club.)

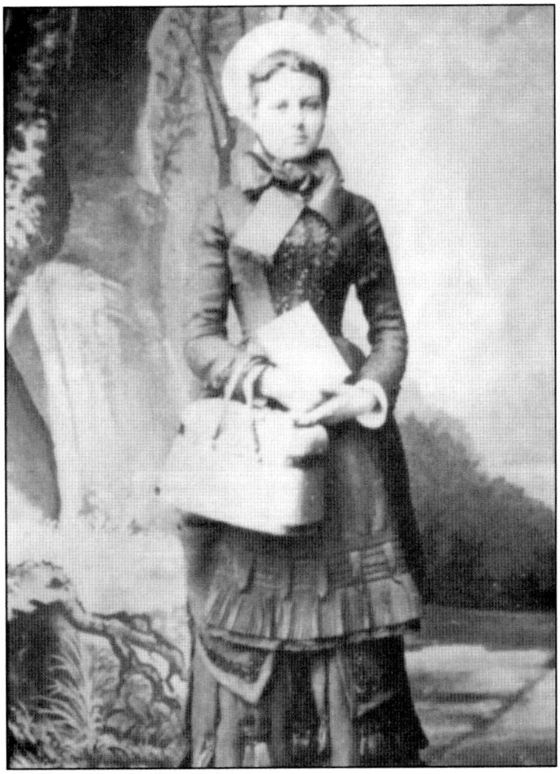

Clara Huning, born in 1865, was the eldest daughter of Franz and Ernestine Huning and, by some accounts, the first Anglo baby born in Albuquerque. She married Southern lawyer and aspiring politician Harvey Butler Fergusson (below) in 1887. He was elected to serve as the US representative to Congress after New Mexico became a state in 1912. The Fergussons raised their family at La Glorieta, her girlhood home. In a 1930s interview, Clara Fergusson recalled her childhood in the old adobe home. She described buffalo robes on the floor and white-washed walls tacked with calico. (Both, courtesy of Manzano Day School.)

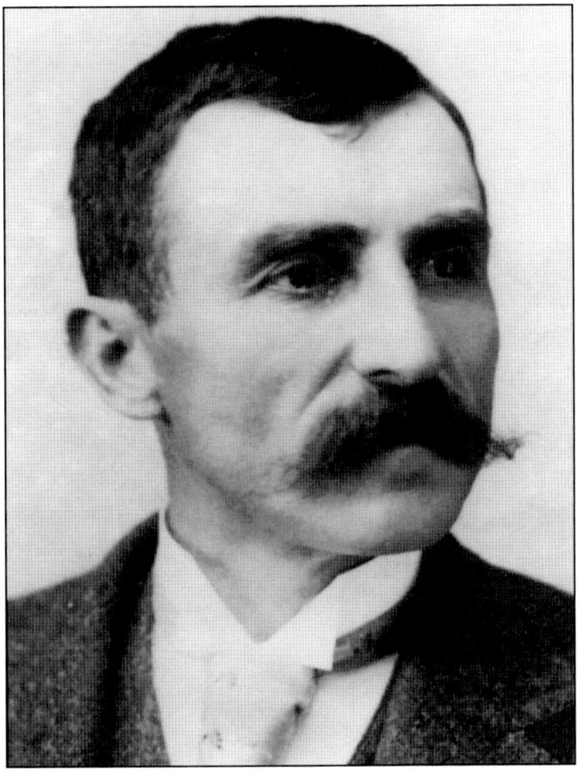

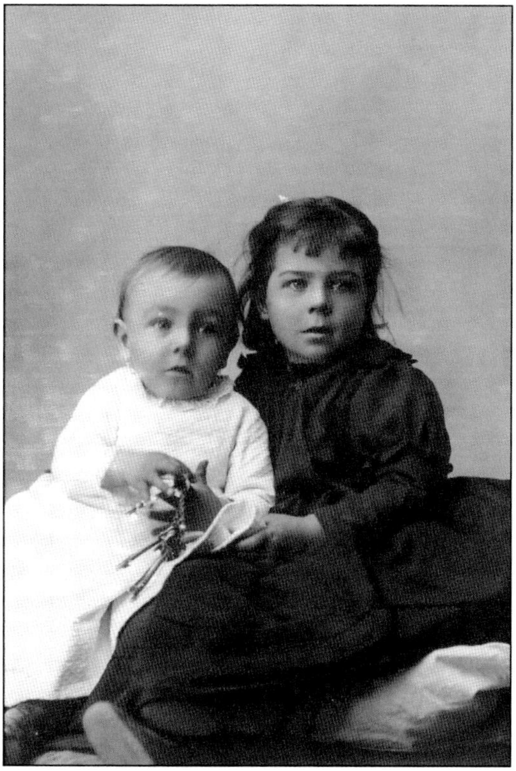

Erna Fergusson was one of four siblings raised by parents Clara (Huning) and H.B. Fergusson in the original family home known as La Glorieta. The first photograph shows Erna as a young girl holding her brother Harvey. Both siblings became well-regarded authors in adulthood. Harvey Fergusson wrote several books, including *Rio Grande*, a classic on the river and its influence on events in New Mexico. (Courtesy of UNM CSWR, Cobb Memorial Collection, 000-119-0324.)

Franz and Ernestine Huning had four children: Clara Mary (1865–1950); Arno (1869–1936); Lina (1873–1894); and Elly (1876–1881). The birth and death dates for the younger daughters vary by a year or two depending on the sources. This family portrait included elder parents Franz and Ernestine Huning seated alongside part of Clara's family, including husband Harvey Fergusson and children Harvey and Erna. Standing behind her father (far right) is Lina Huning, who would die at the young age of 21. (Courtesy of Manzano Day School.)

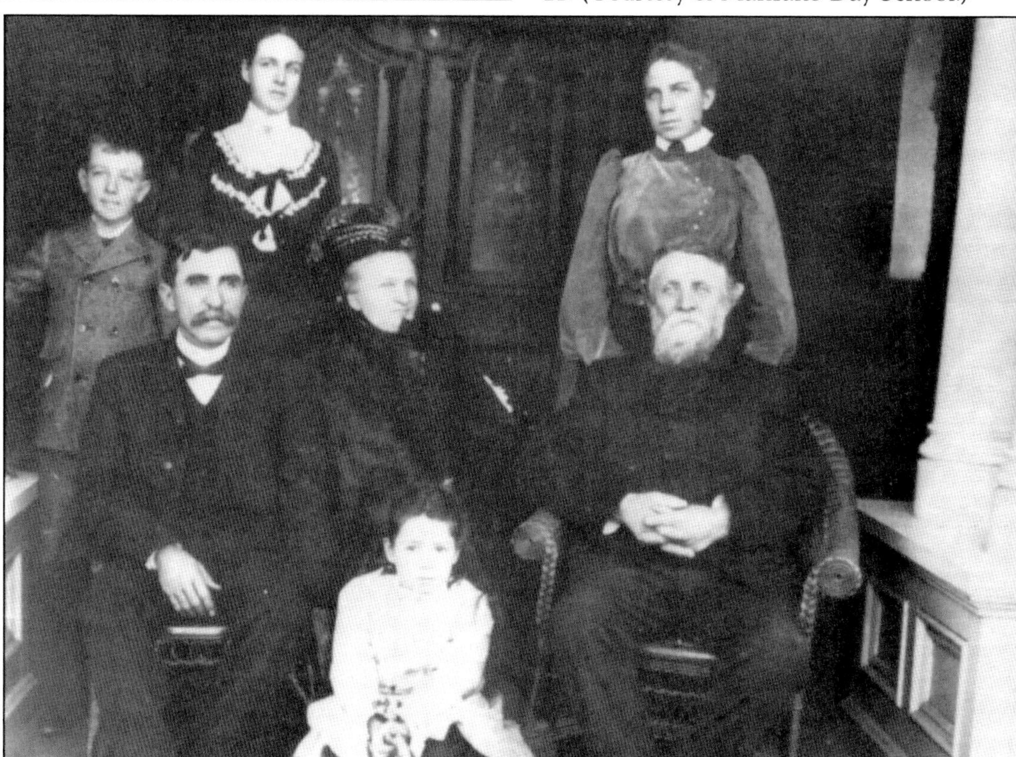

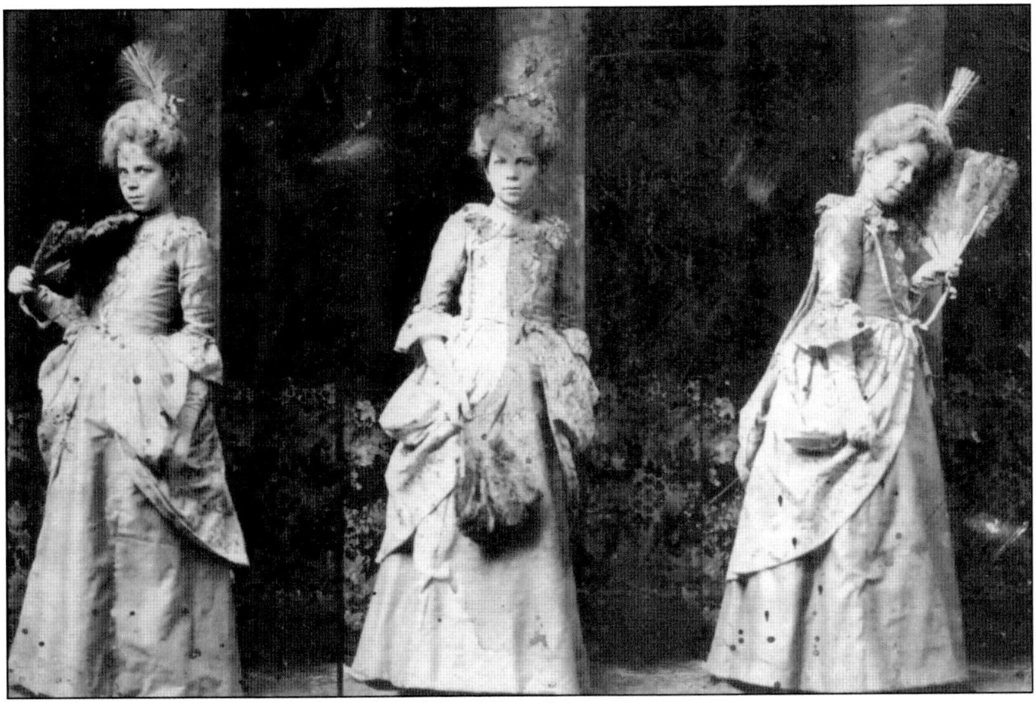

Erna Fergusson (1888–1964), the granddaughter of Franz Huning, is pictured above in costume for President Washington's birthday holiday in 1898. She was one of the earliest literary figures from Albuquerque. She had a variety of work experiences such as teacher, American Red Cross supervisor, newspaper reporter, and tour company operator. Her first book, *Dancing Gods*, was published in 1931 and established Fergusson as an authority on the Southwest. (Above, courtesy of UNM CSWR, Cobb Memorial Collection, 000-119-0044; right, courtesy of UNM CSWR, Huning-Ferguson Collection, 000-194-3000.)

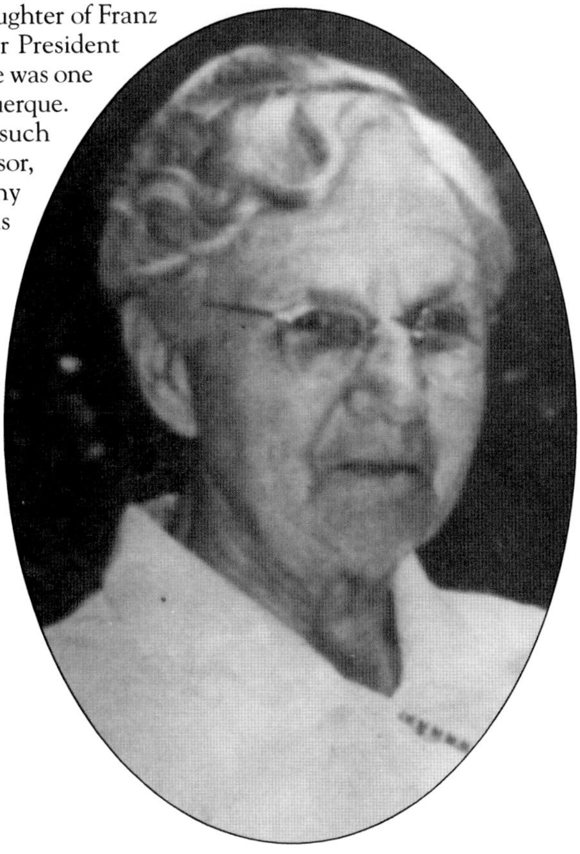

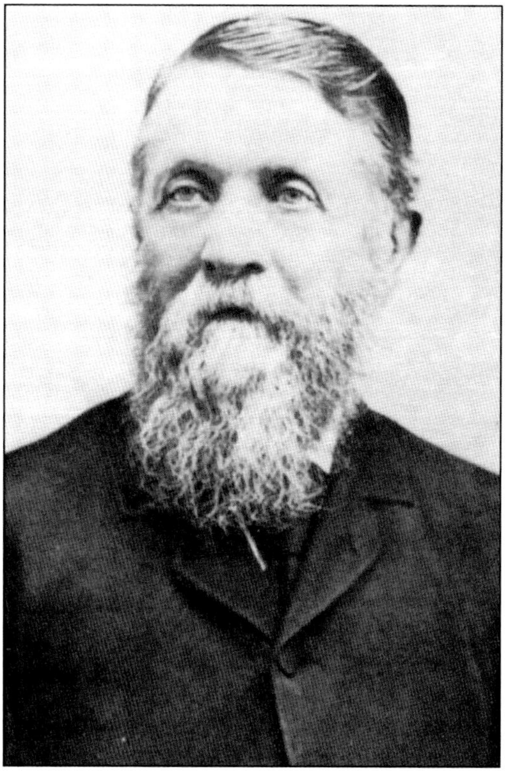

Franz Huning, described in *Germans in the Southwest* by Tomas Jaehn as a freethinker and atheist, left instructions in his final will: "I direct my remains to be cremated, the ashes put into an urn and deposited alongside my children Lina and Elly. And I strictly forbid any and all religious nonsense." (Courtesy of the Horn family/Calvin Horn Publishing, from *Trader on the Santa Fe Trail.)*

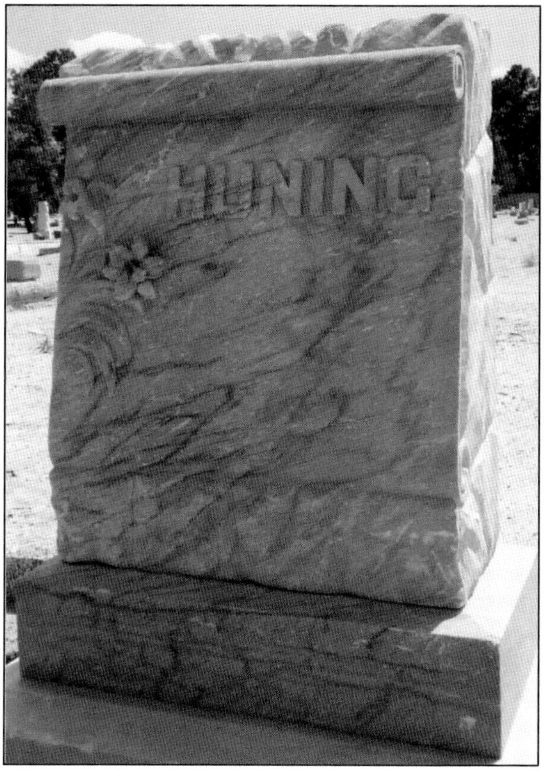

Franz Huning, his wife, and two daughters who preceded him in death are buried in a family plot marked by this simple headstone at Albuquerque's Historic Fairview Cemetery. Franz Huning died in 1905 at age 78 and left behind an estate valued between $200,000 and $300,000, according to newspaper accounts at the time. The original family cemetery was on the grounds of Huning Castle. (Photograph by the author.)

Two

La Glorieta
The Old Town Home and Manzano Day School

A low-slung adobe hacienda was the first family home for Franz Huning and his expanding family. The home, now the private Manzano Day School, is still in existence at 1801 Central Avenue NW.

Historians are not sure of the age of Huning's first home, known as La Glorieta and located southeast of the Old Town Plaza, but popular lore dates the home's beginnings to colonial times and possibly to original ownership by Diego de Trujillo whose family fled during the Pueblo Revolt of 1680. Without question, the home was built prior to 1821. Early records show Huning bought the old adobe home and land in 1861, then deeded the house to his bride, Ernestine, two years later as a wedding present. It was here that the couple's four children were raised, as were several of their grandchildren.

Eventually, Huning expanded the home to create a traditional *placita*, or courtyard. This area was shaded by a massive cottonwood that was planted as a sapling by Huning. He later claimed the tree grew especially large because the courtyard grounds were deeply fertilized by the blood of cattle slaughtered to feed an occupying regiment of Texans led by Confederate general H.H. Sibley in 1862 during the Civil War. Huning was in St. Louis at the time of the brief occupation.

La Glorieta has a rich history of promoting education, much of it instigated by Ruth Hanna McCormick Simms, a congressional representative from Illinois who immersed herself in Albuquerque's culture after marrying Albert G. Simms and moving to New Mexico. Since the 1942 school year, La Glorieta has been the permanent home of the private Manzano Day School. The three-foot-thick adobe walls and grand fireplaces are reminders of earlier times.

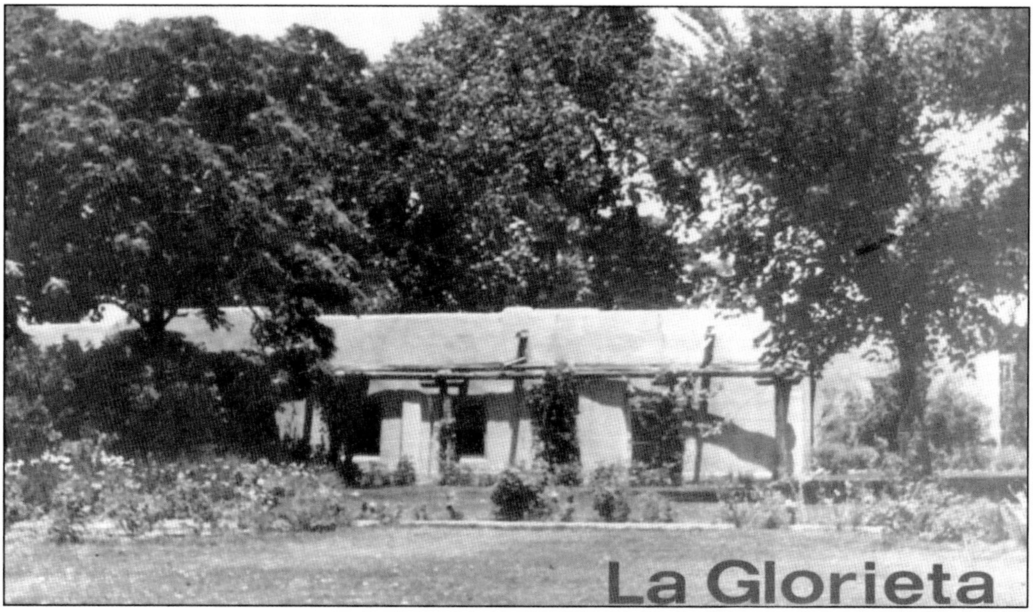

La Glorieta has long been a focal point for Albuquerque politics, culture, and history. Franz Huning acquired the home in 1861 and raised his family in the old home. Later, daughter Clara and her politically active husband, Harvey Fergusson, lived there with their children, Erna, Harvey Jr., Lina, and Francis. Early records indicate the home had eight rooms prior to the addition of new wings added by Huning to create a courtyard. The photograph below gives a glimpse of the shady portal that extended the length of the house. (Both, courtesy of Manzano Day School.)

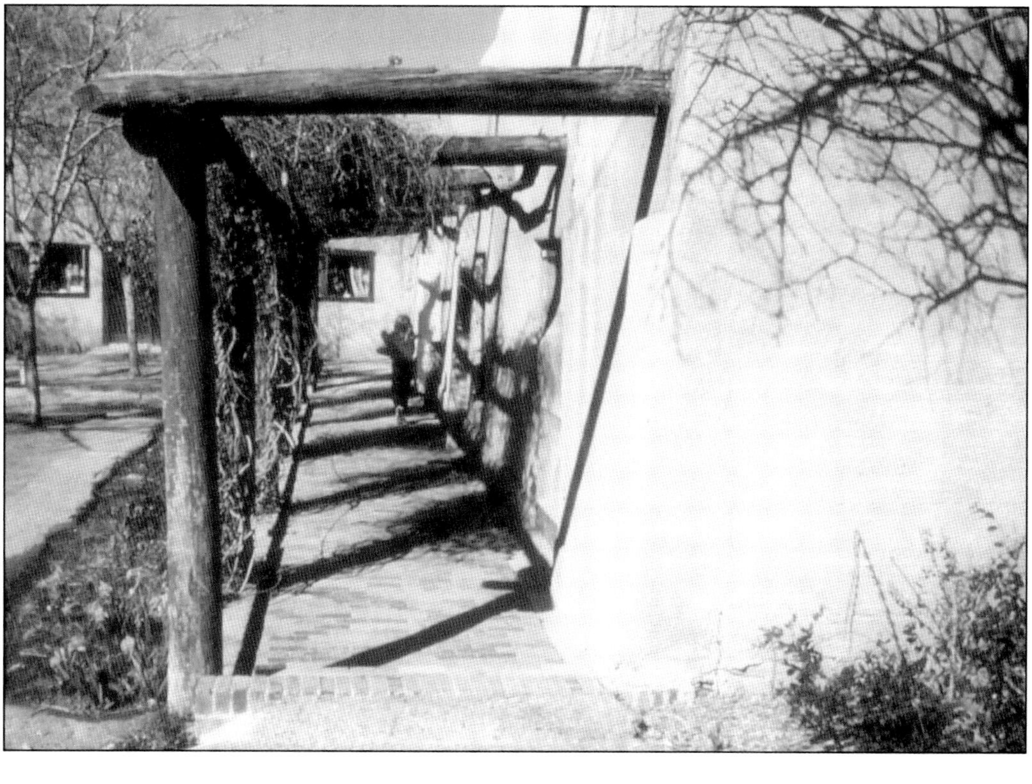

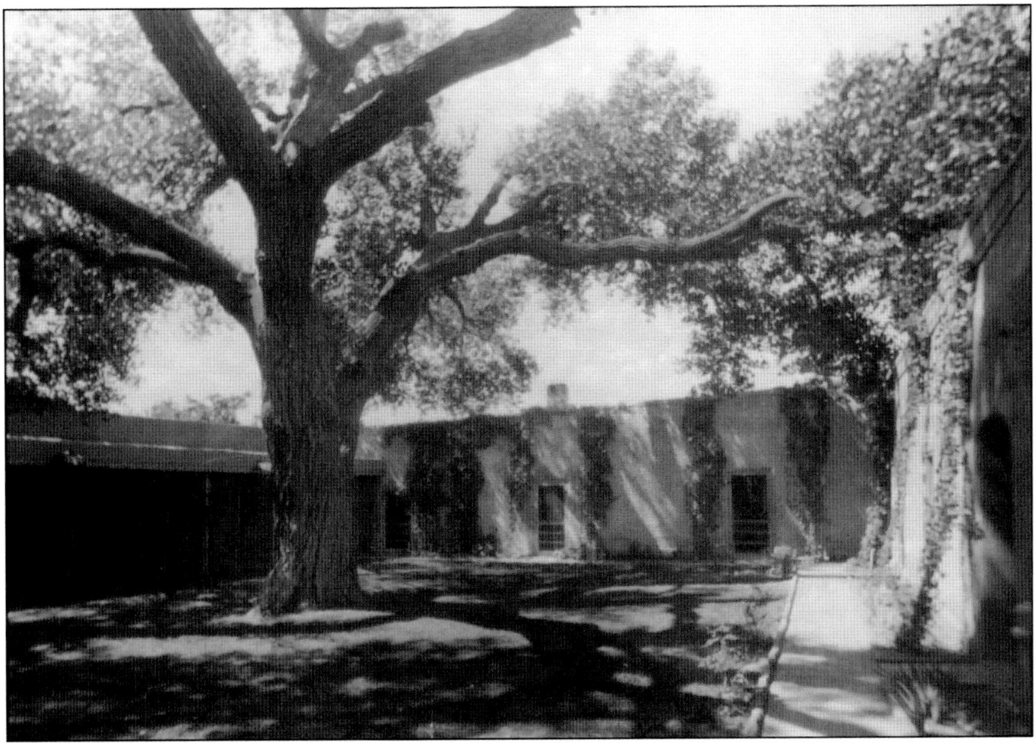

The cottonwood planted as a sapling in the courtyard when Franz Huning acquired the home in 1861 survived until 1984, when disease brought it down. Huning claimed the tree grew to 17 feet in circumference because it had been fertilized by the blood of animals slaughtered when Confederate general H.H. Sibley (pictured) briefly occupied the home during the Civil War in 1862. (Above, courtesy of Manzano Day School; right, courtesy of UNM CSWR, William A. Keleher Collection, 000-742-0139.)

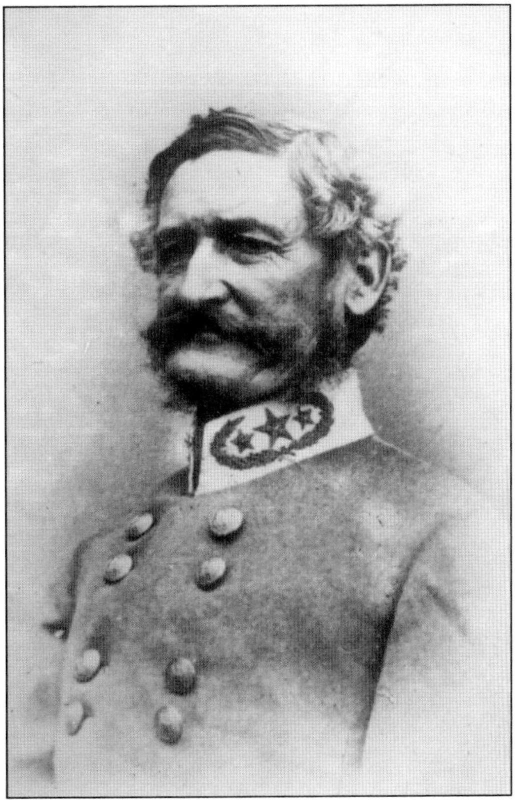

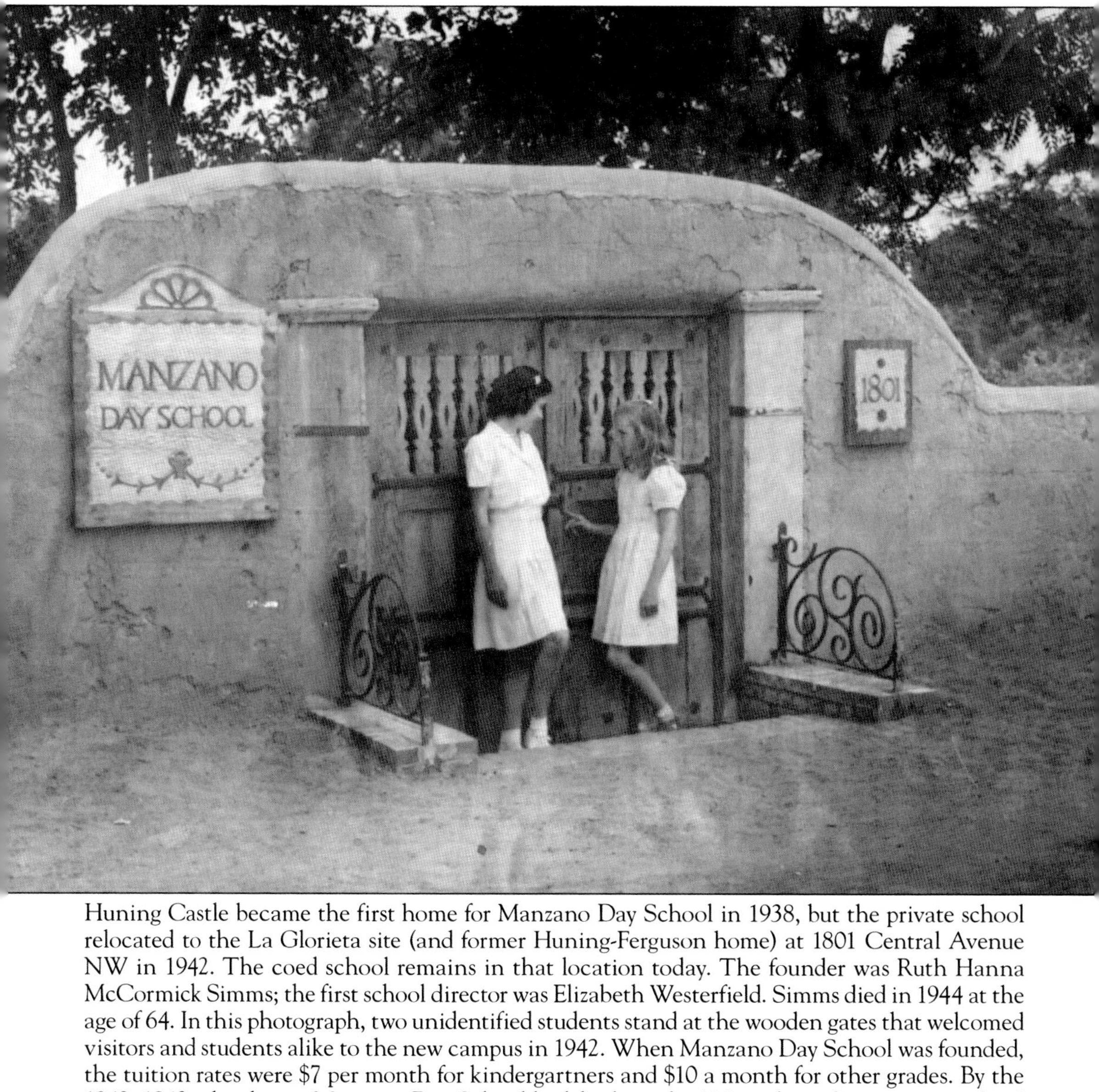

Huning Castle became the first home for Manzano Day School in 1938, but the private school relocated to the La Glorieta site (and former Huning-Ferguson home) at 1801 Central Avenue NW in 1942. The coed school remains in that location today. The founder was Ruth Hanna McCormick Simms; the first school director was Elizabeth Westerfield. Simms died in 1944 at the age of 64. In this photograph, two unidentified students stand at the wooden gates that welcomed visitors and students alike to the new campus in 1942. When Manzano Day School was founded, the tuition rates were $7 per month for kindergartners and $10 a month for other grades. By the 1942–1943 school year, Manzano Day School had facilities for 100 students from nursery school through eighth grade in its La Glorieta location. (Courtesy of Manzano Day School.)

Ruth Hanna McCormick Simms (1880–1944), a congressional representative from Illinois, moved to Albuquerque with her second husband, Rep. Albert G. Simms. She was a great promoter of education and founded the Sandia School in 1932. The girls' school originally met in a home on West Roma Avenue before moving to a 124-acre campus on the mesa east of the city. The lower school students from Sandia School were relocated to Huning Castle in 1938, and the school was renamed Manzano Day School. In 1942, Manzano Day School made its final move to La Glorieta, the old Huning/Ferguson home, which still had its lovely courtyard and huge cottonwood tree, as seen in the photograph below. Sandia School, which had accepted boarding students, closed because transportation availability for out-of-state students was uncertain during World War II. (Both, courtesy of Manzano Day School.)

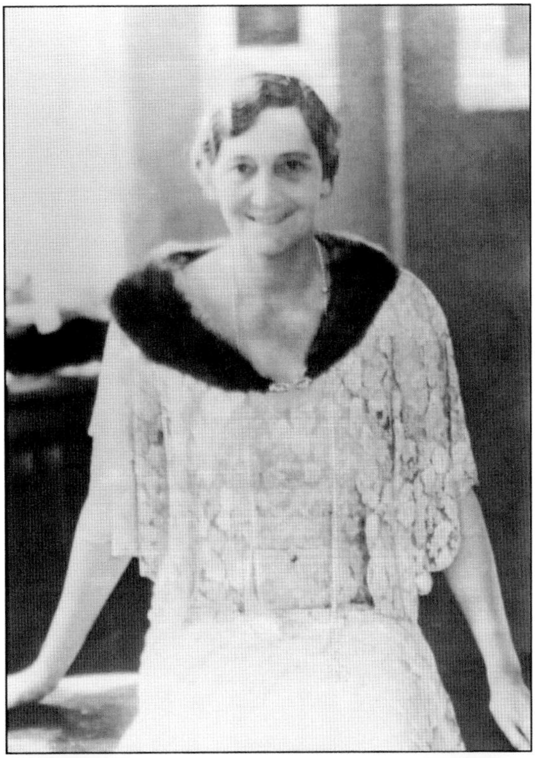

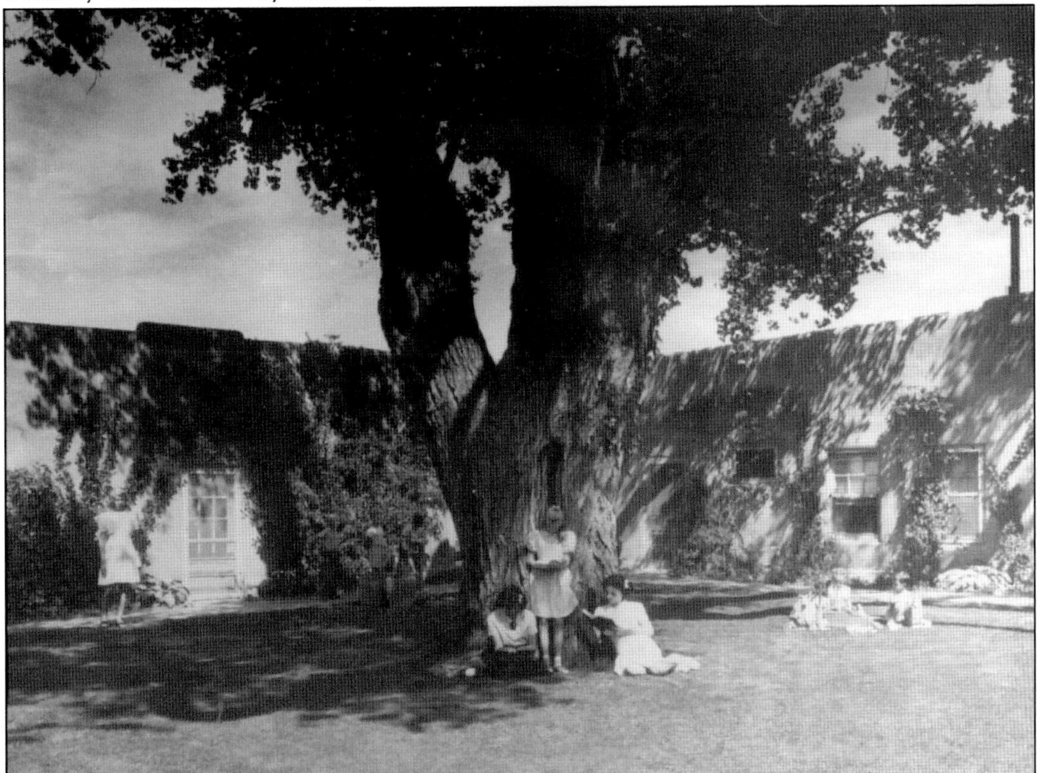

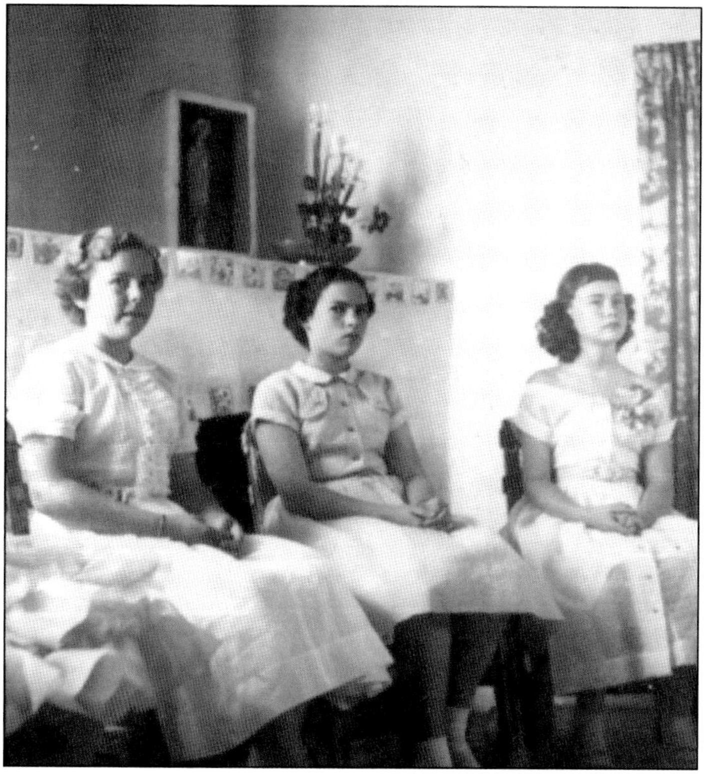

Pictured from left to right in 1952, students Joe Ann Crisp, Joan (Dreyer) Allen, and Judy (Claridge) Killough sit in the administrative offices of Manzano Day School, once the heart of the former Huning-Fergusson home. (Courtesy of the Dreyer family.)

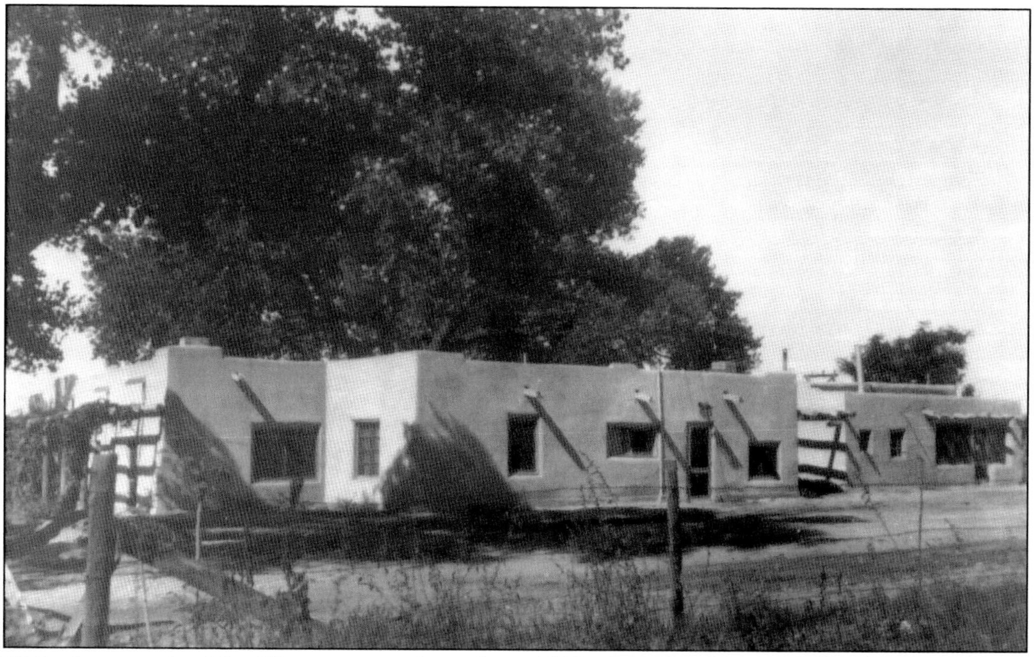

This photograph of La Glorieta was taken about 1910 when the Fergusson family still called it home. The adobe walls were so thick that Lina Fergusson Browne later wrote that her mother used the deep window sills as a playpen by barricading the baby in with chair backs. (Courtesy of Manzano Day School.)

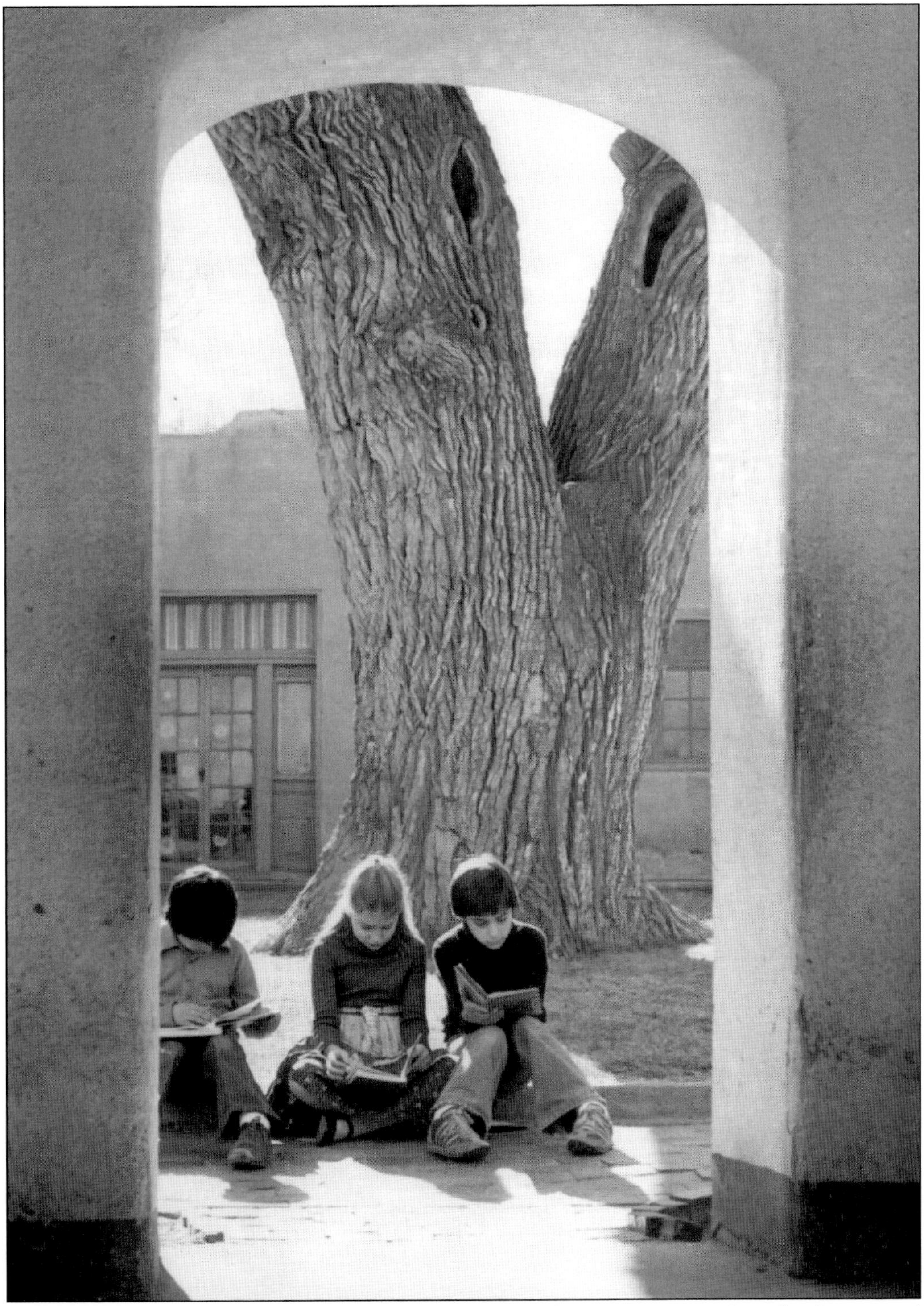

Not even the stump of La Glorieta's massive cottonwood tree remains in the school courtyard today. The tree provided a shady retreat for students through 1984, including these unidentified children attending Manzano Day School in the mid-1970s. (Courtesy of Manzano Day School.)

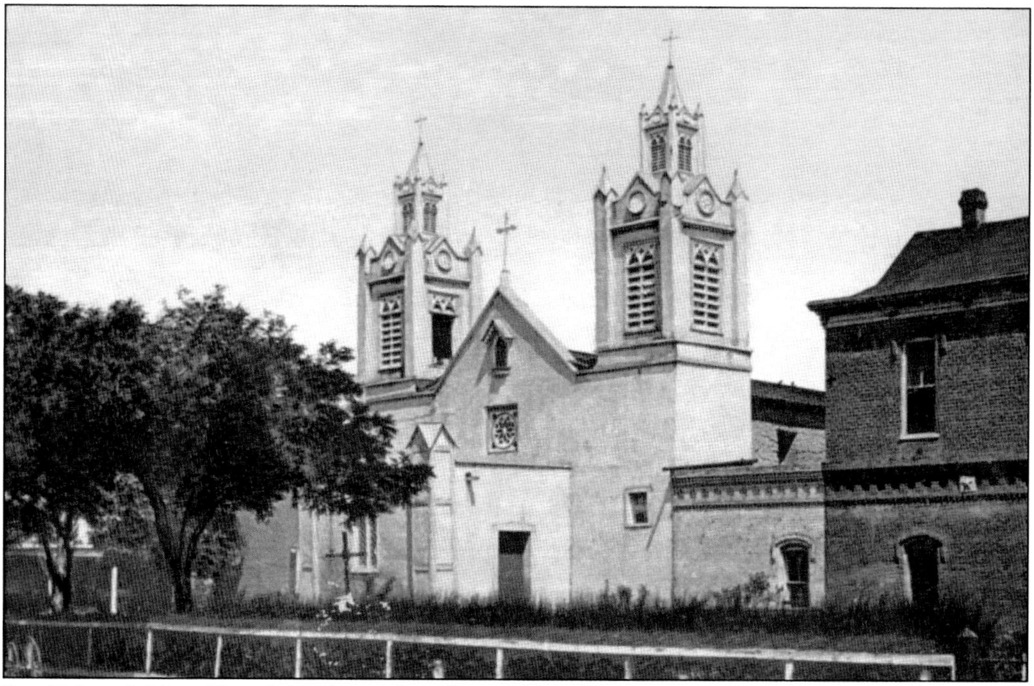

San Felipe de Neri Church has been the religious heartbeat of Albuquerque's Old Town since the founding of Albuquerque in 1706. It remains an active congregation today. The postcard of the church exterior is dated 1902 and shows the twin wood spires and the brick rectory. The second postcard shows the church's interior. The Gothic hooded pulpit, altar, and chapels are constructed of wood painted to look like marble. The original flat roof has been replaced with a low-pitched roof with a stamped tin ceiling. Much of the latter work was done by the Jesuits who wanted to change the Old Pueblo style established by the Franciscans. (Both, courtesy of Nancy Tucker.)

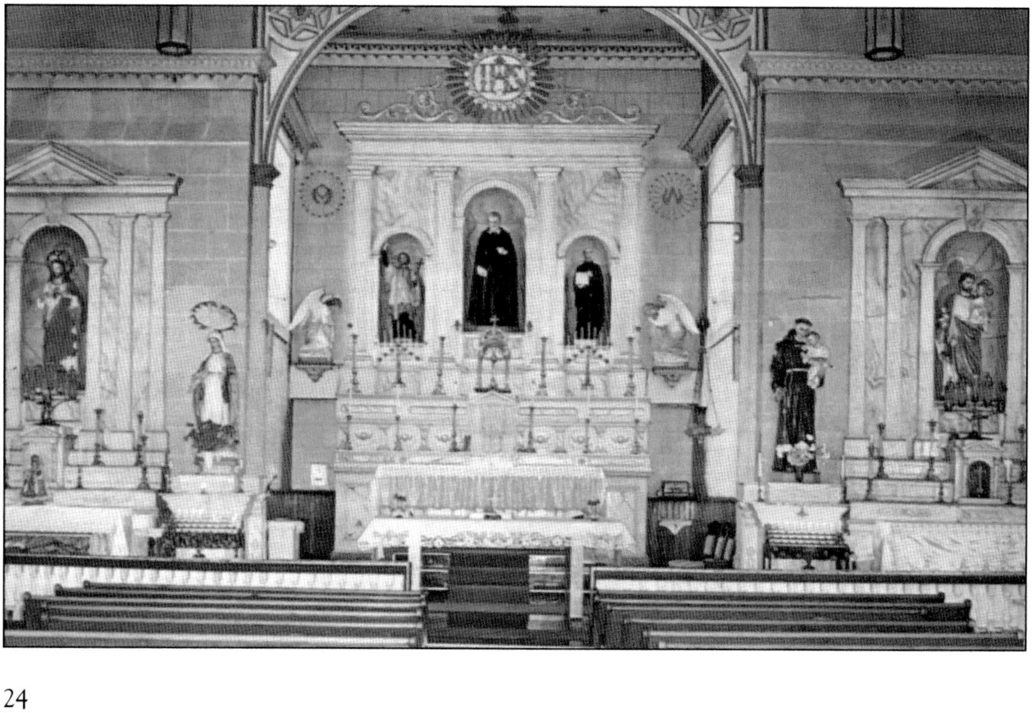

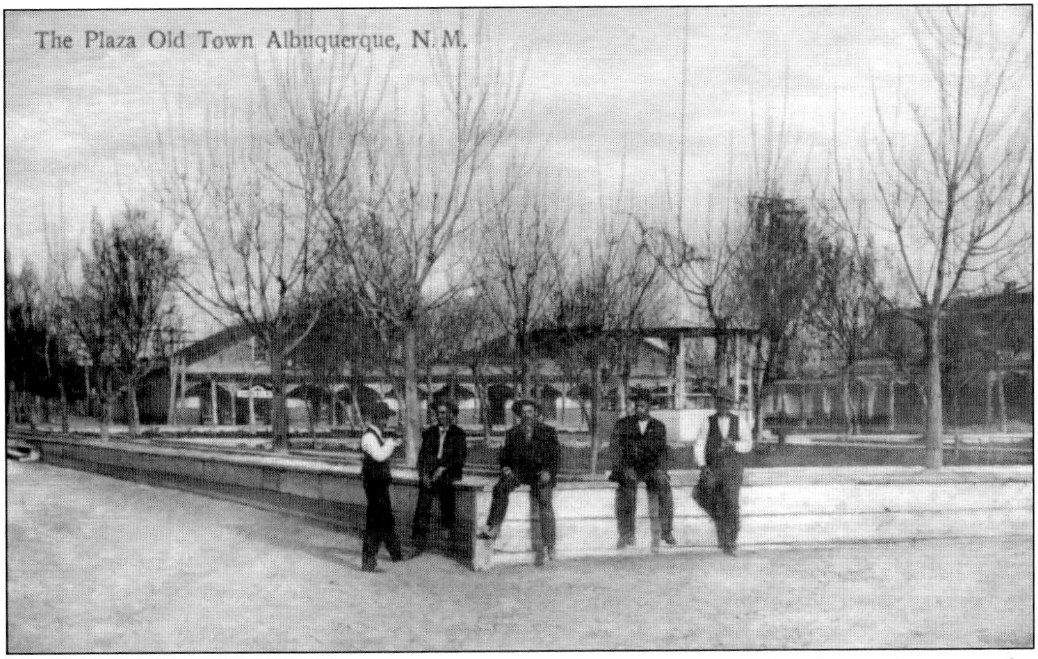

Two undated postcards show Old Town's shady plaza. The Old Town area bustling with mercantiles and homes was once several acres larger than it is today, according to Marc Simmons's book, *Albuquerque: A Narrative History*. Traditionally, the plaza was used for processionals, market days, and military drills. One card shows the flagstaff in the center of the plaza; the other depicts a later bandstand. Huning wrote in 1856 that the plaza's low elevation caused ponds to form after rainstorms. "I could have shot wild ducks from the store door," he claimed. (Both, courtesy of Nancy Tucker.)

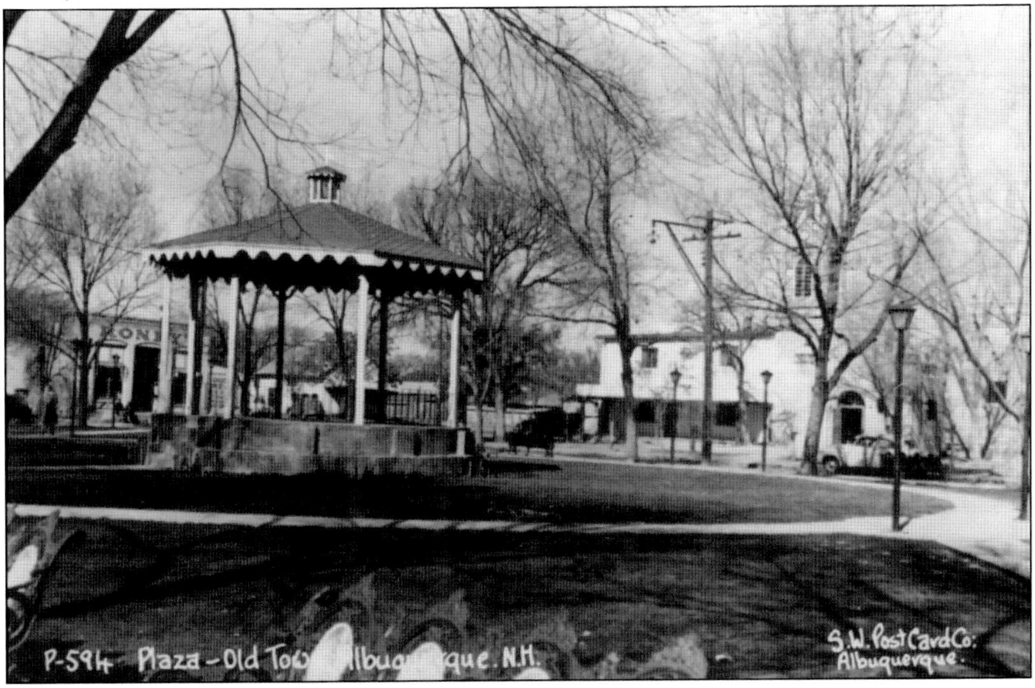

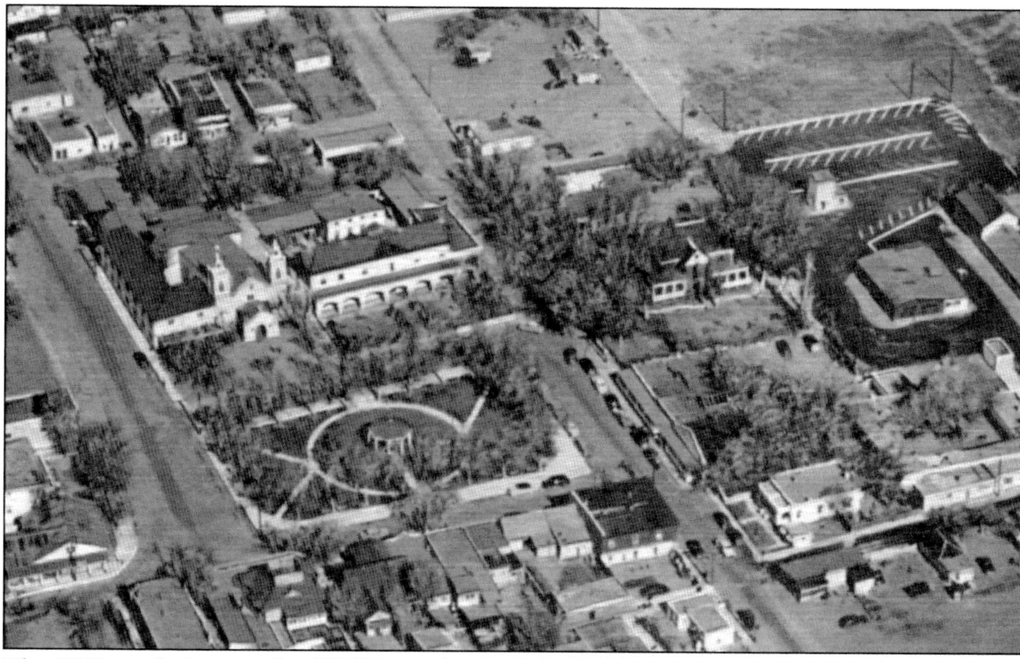

The 1952 aerial photograph of Old Town shows adobe buildings and narrow streets. The plaza and San Felipe de Neri Church are in the center. By the turn of the century, however, Albuquerque's boom area was New Town, home of the railroad. Old Town reinvented itself into a tourist enclave during Route 66's glory days and is still a popular destination. (Courtesy of Nancy Tucker.)

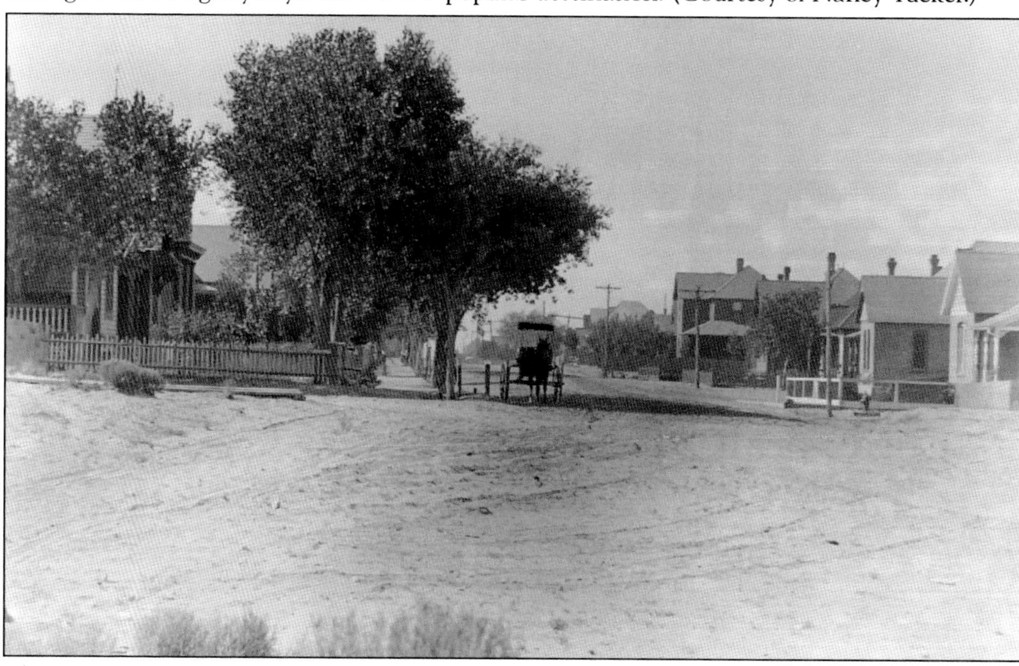

This view of Railroad Avenue in the early 1880s reveals a quiet day on the Old Town portion of the roadway. After the arrival of the railroad, this street (later known as Central Avenue) became a main east–west arterial connecting Old Town and the new downtown. Eventually, the avenue extended through the entire city. (Courtesy of UNM CSWR, Toulouse Collection, 997-001-0015.)

Three

The Railroad Arrives
The Beginning of New Town

The fact that Albuquerque became more than a whistle stop on the Atchison, Topeka & Santa Fe Railway in 1880 can, in part, be traced to the high land prices demanded by property owners in Bernalillo that were ultimately rejected by the railway.

A more favorable response was found in Albuquerque, thanks to the speculative nature and business acumen of the quietly formed New Mexico Town Company, headed by Franz Huning, William C. Hazeldine, and Elias S. Stover. The trio, thinly veiled as a real estate company, worked with railroad officers to buy large tracts of land near several proposed rail routes. Ultimately, the final location for the chief division point on the line was a mile east of the Old Town Plaza. A town-wide celebration was held on April 22, 1880, with the arrival of the first passenger train.

While much of the recently acquired land was deeded for the sum of $1 to the New Mexico Town Company—and eventually the Atchison, Topeka & Santa Fe Railway—the trio received a generous profit from the sale of the railroad's surplus properties and their own purchase of town lots to sell. By 1880, Albuquerque's population had reached 2,135.

Even before the last rail was laid at Albuquerque's new depot on April 5, 1880, Huning had already started improvements on the road that would connect Old Town with what would soon become New Town. Railroad Avenue (later Central Avenue) ran adjacent to Huning's home and flour mill. Horse-drawn trolleys connected the one-mile distance between Old Town and New Town. In 1937, Central Avenue became a segment of Route 66.

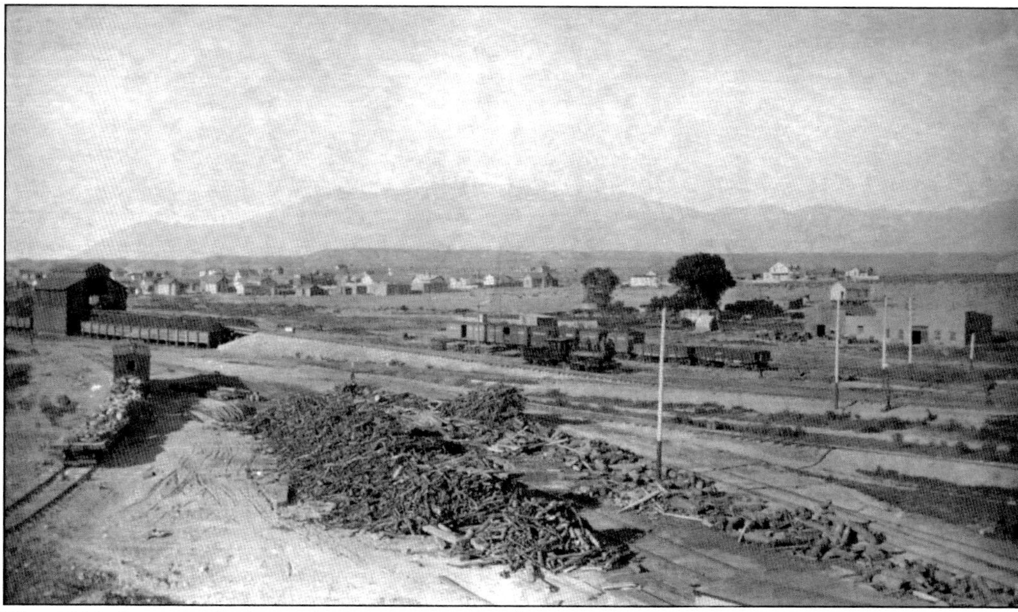

The 1880 photograph shows the beginning of rail construction in New Town. Track construction continued south of Albuquerque to link the AT&SF with the Southern Pacific Railroad, according to journalist Howard Bryan's book, *Albuquerque Remembered.* The Atlantic & Pacific Railroad Company, owned by AT&SF and the St. Louis & San Francisco Railway, also established its headquarters in Albuquerque in 1880 and began building west to California from a point 15 miles south of Albuquerque. (Courtesy of UNM CSWR, Atlantic & Pacific Railroad Collection, 000-083-0003.)

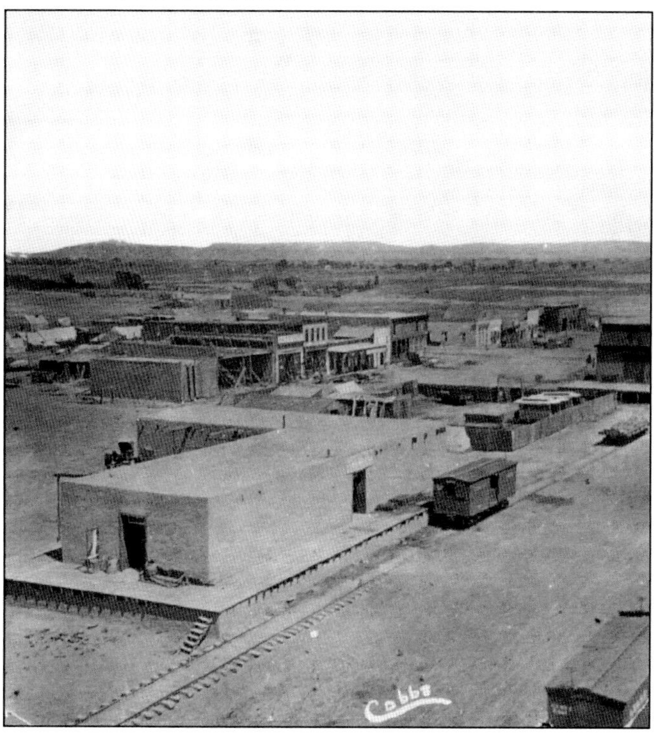

An 1880s bird's-eye view of New Town shows a makeshift railroad depot in the foreground. The AT&SF's repair shops and offices soon became the most significant local industry. By 1900, the AT&SF Railway employed 575 men, 60 engineers, and 60 firemen. (Courtesy of UNM CSWR, Cobb Memorial Collection, 000-119-0564.)

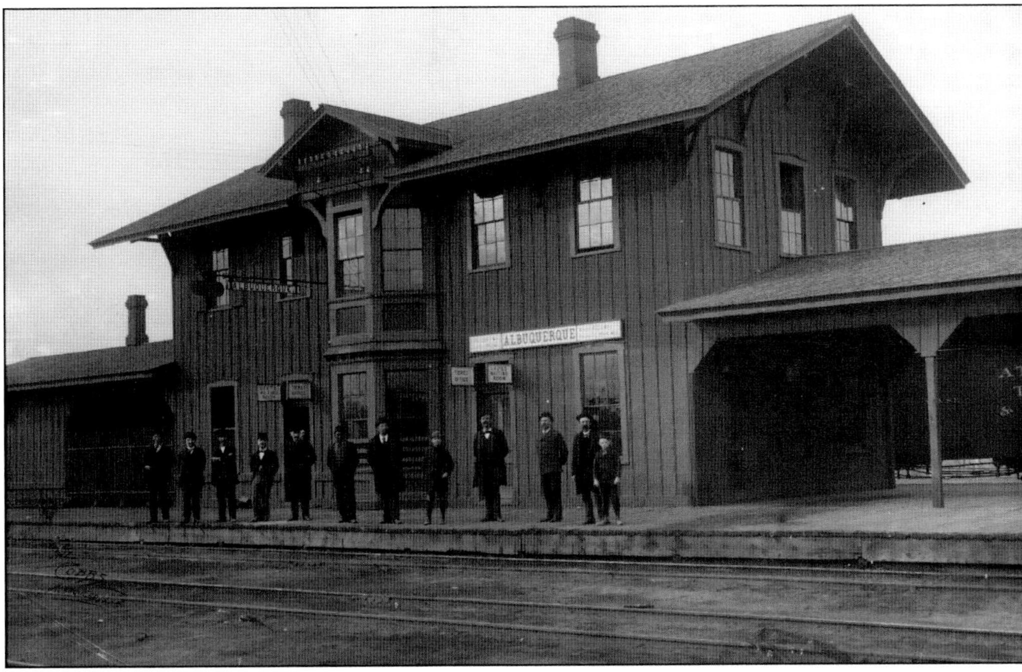

Before Fred Harvey built his attractive Alvarado complex to welcome rail arrivals, this was the AT&SF depot, shown here in about 1890, with separate waiting rooms for "gents and ladies." The railway's decision to make Albuquerque a division point with the depot, repair shops, and offices was a major coup for Albuquerque and jump-started the town to city status. (Courtesy of UNM CSWR, Cobb Memorial Collection, 000-119-0608.)

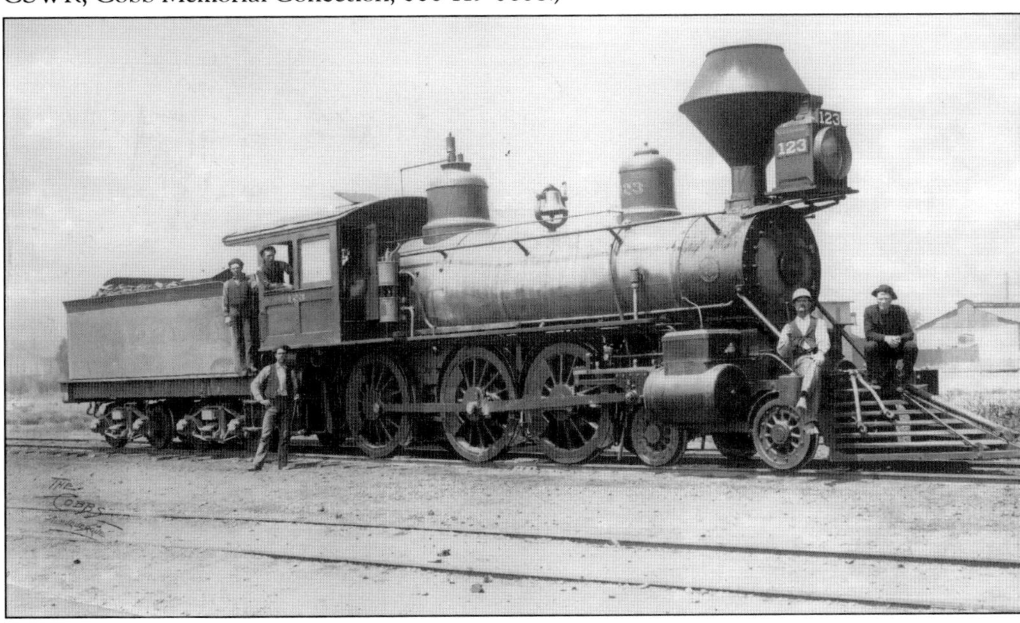

Steam Engine No. 123 was a typical sight at the rail yards about 1890. The railroad's impact created not only rail-related jobs but also spurred the growth of foundries, the wool industry, breweries, ice companies, and lumberyards. (Courtesy of UNM CSWR, William A. Keleher Collection, 000-742-0620.)

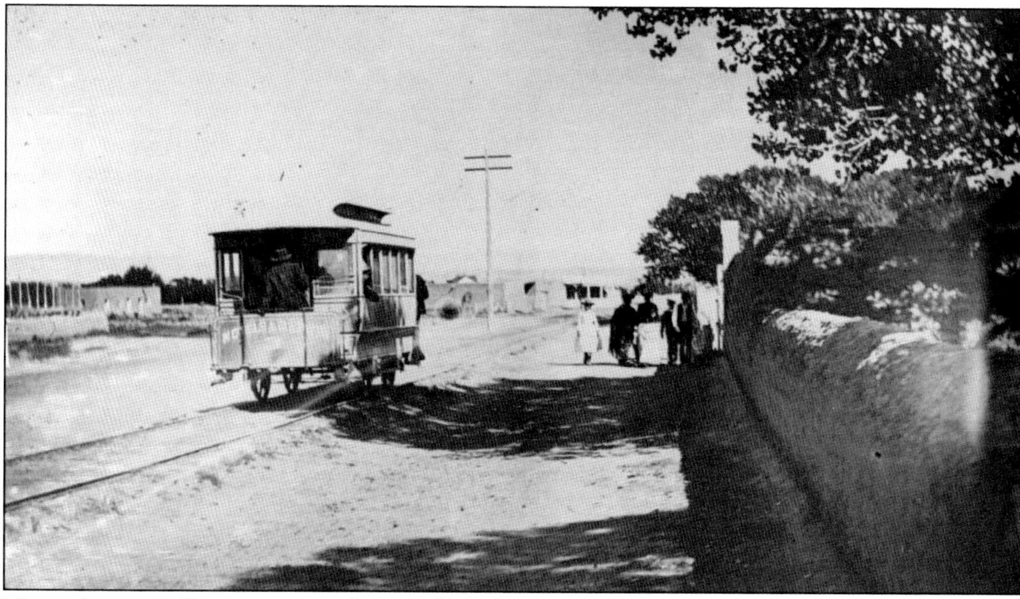

Horse-drawn trolleys ran on tracks installed along Railroad Avenue in the early 1880s, keeping visitors, commerce, and families connected between Old Town and New Town. By 1904, the trolleys ran on electricity. (Courtesy of UNM CSWR, Atlantic & Pacific Railroad Collection, 000-083-0134.)

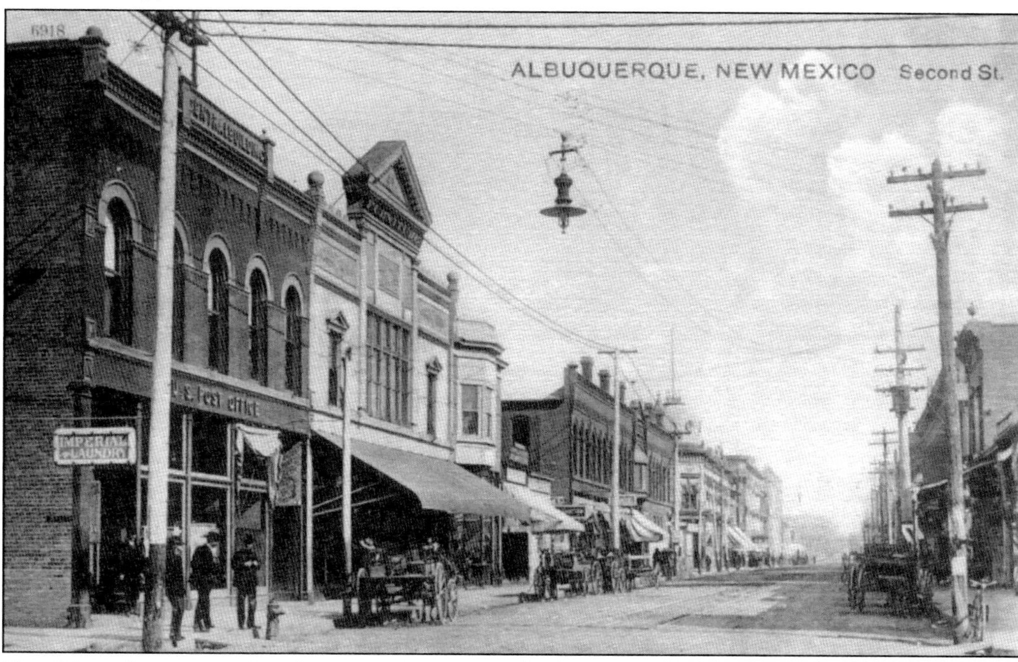

New Town (or present-day downtown) began with the railroad's decision to build the depot and repair shops a mile east of Old Town. These early street scenes along Second Street show the city's changing architecture as new arrivals from the East and Midwest began replicating their familiar hometowns. The low adobe buildings of the Old Town era gave way to two-story frame businesses in New Town. Building lots sold from $200 to $2,000 each, according to Howard Bryan's *Albuquerque Remembered*. (Courtesy of Nancy Tucker.)

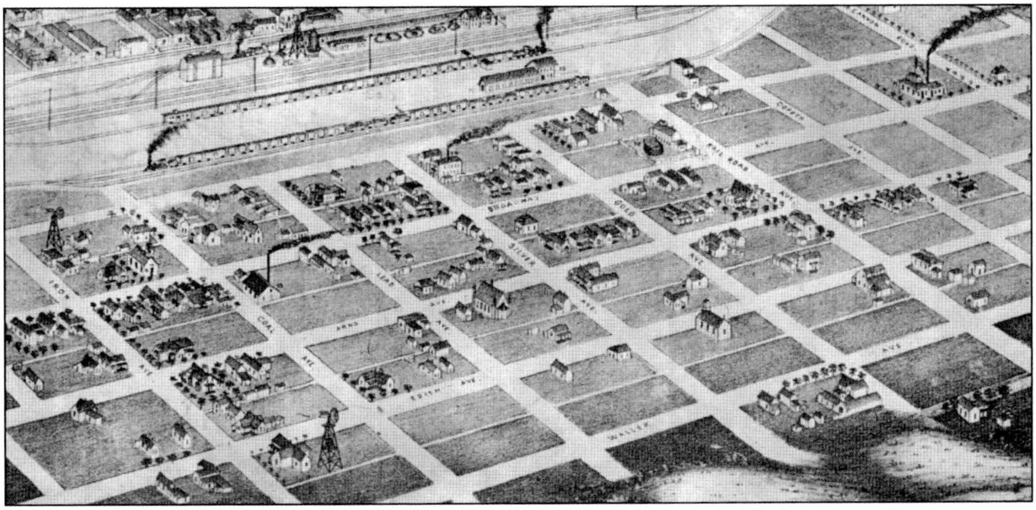

This detail from the 1886 "Bird's Eye View Map of Albuquerque" by Augustus Koch shows a rendering of the Huning's Highland neighborhood looking west and downtown from the sandhills east of the railroad tracks. This diverse area contained a variety of homes ranging from bungalows for the railway laborers to several of the city's largest and most elegant mansions. The district was named after developer Franz Huning. It remains an enclave of charming Victorian homes today. (Courtesy of the Valliant family through Dorothy Keleher Valliant.)

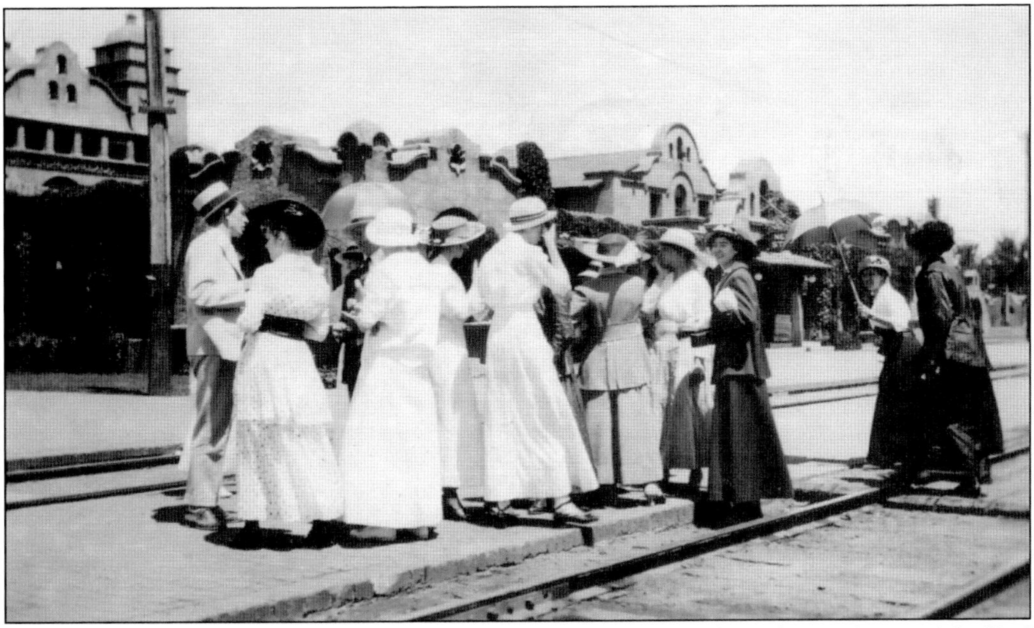

A group of women is pictured at the train station about 1910. The Alvarado Hotel, part of the Fred Harvey network, is in the background. It was an elegant place to shop, eat, and mingle for townsfolk and travelers. (Courtesy of UNM CSWR, William A. Keleher Collection, 000-742-0624.)

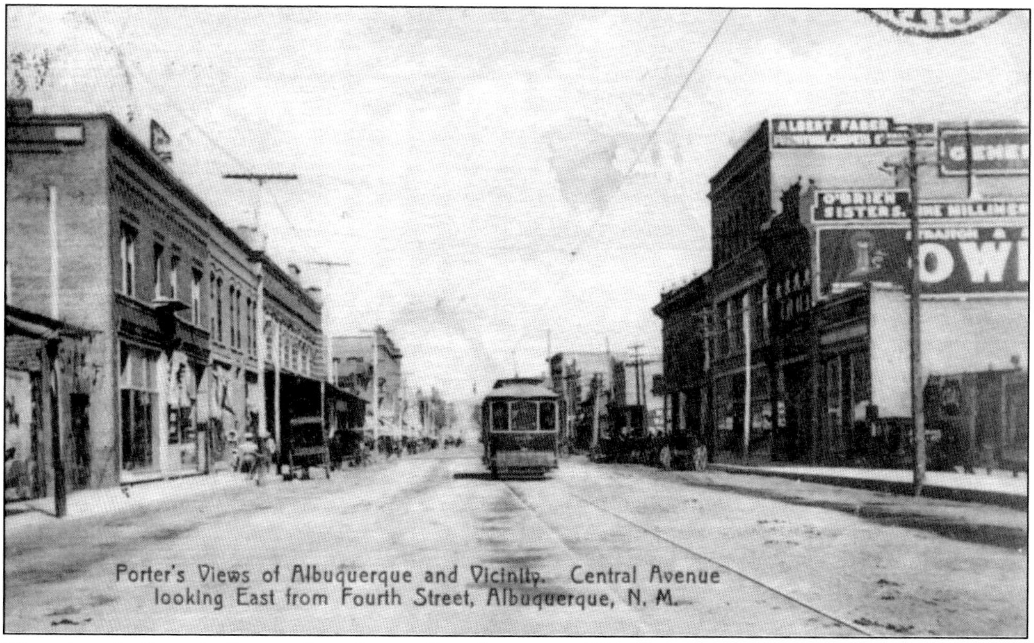

The electric lines indicate that the trolleys between Old Town and New Town were powered by electricity by the early 1900s. This postcard shows Central Avenue looking east from Fourth Street. (Courtesy of Nancy Tucker.)

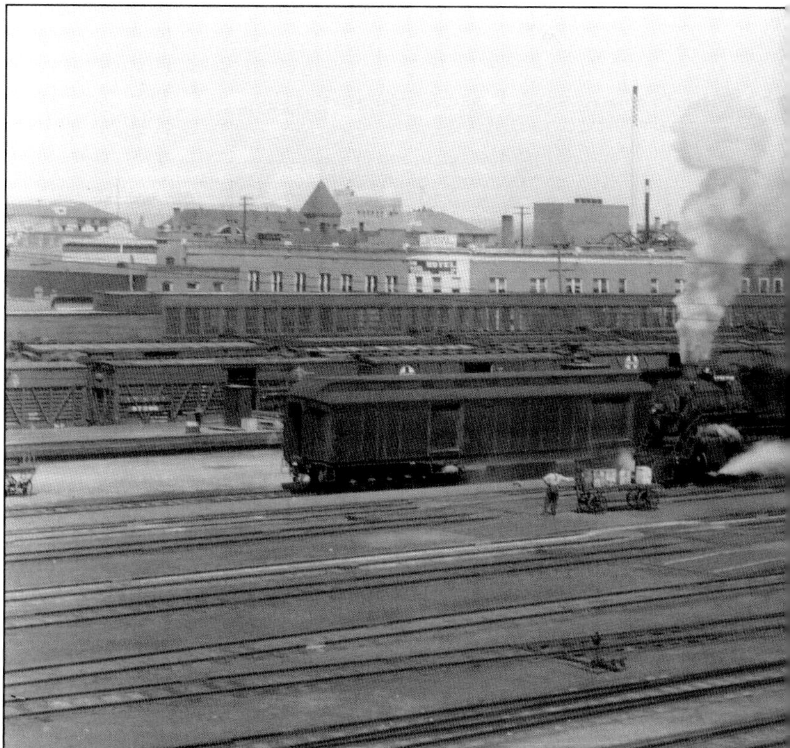

By 1931, the Santa Fe Railway was a major industry and employer in Albuquerque, as evidenced by the quantity of rolling stock. By this time, the railway was also bringing patients to Albuquerque's tuberculosis sanatoriums. (Courtesy of Middle Rio Grande Conservancy District.)

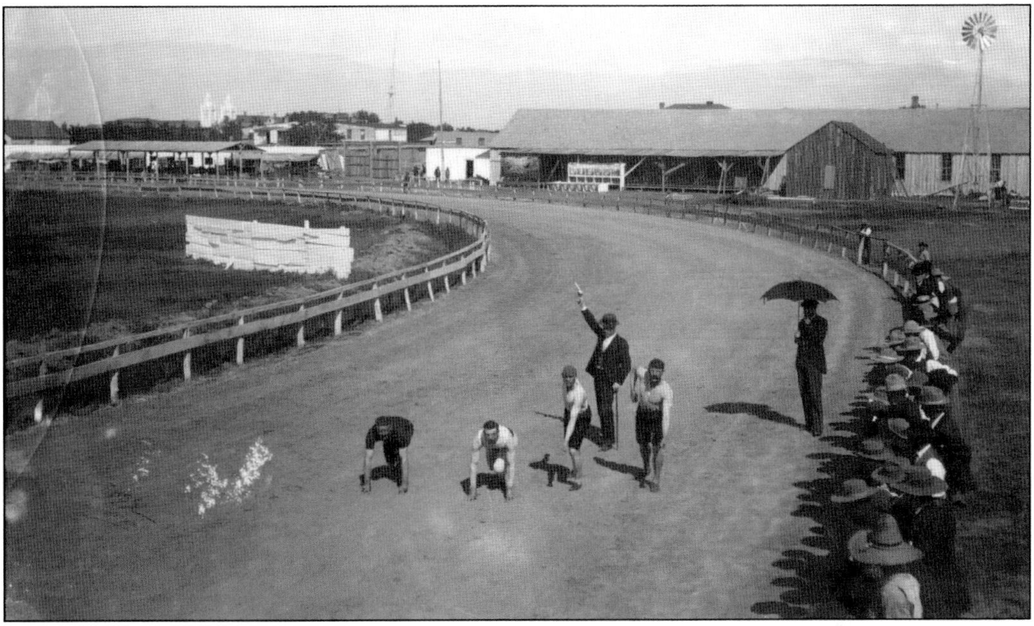

Territorial fairs at Traction Park near present-day Rio Grande Boulevard and Central Avenue drew crowds to Old Town in the 1890s. Participants in this footrace were members of the volunteer fire department. As an official holds the starting gun aloft, the racers wait in starting positions. (Courtesy of UNM CSWR, Cobb Memorial Collection, 000-119-00765.)

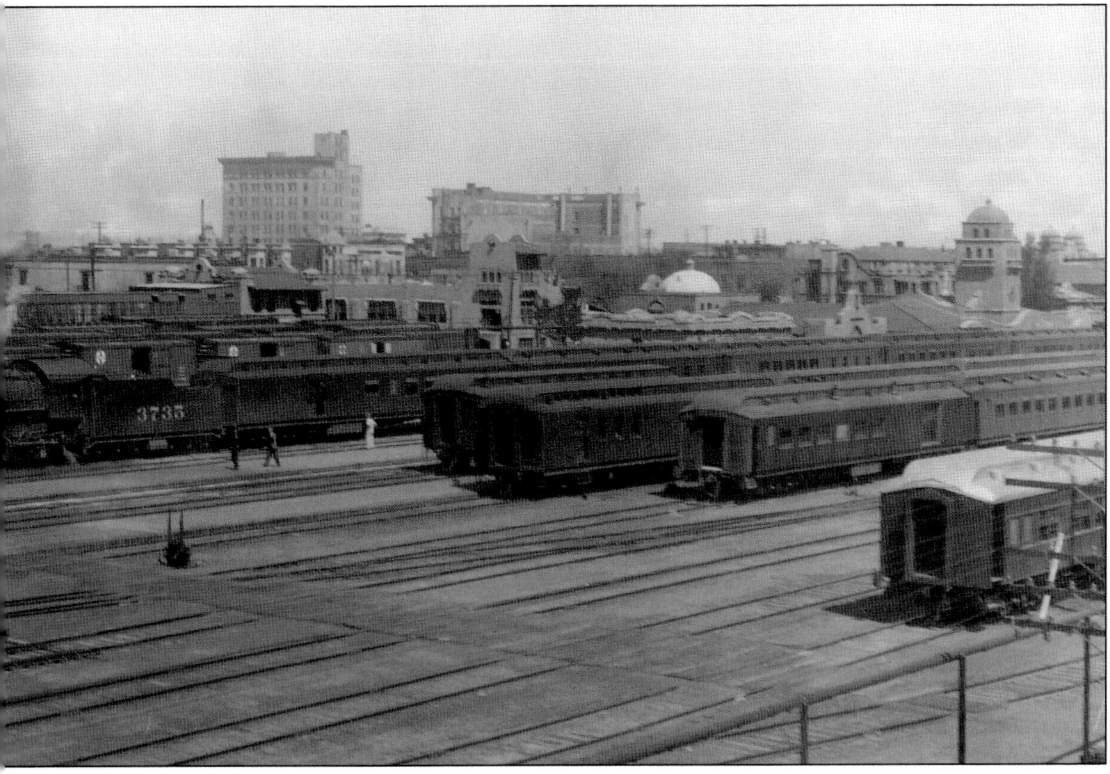

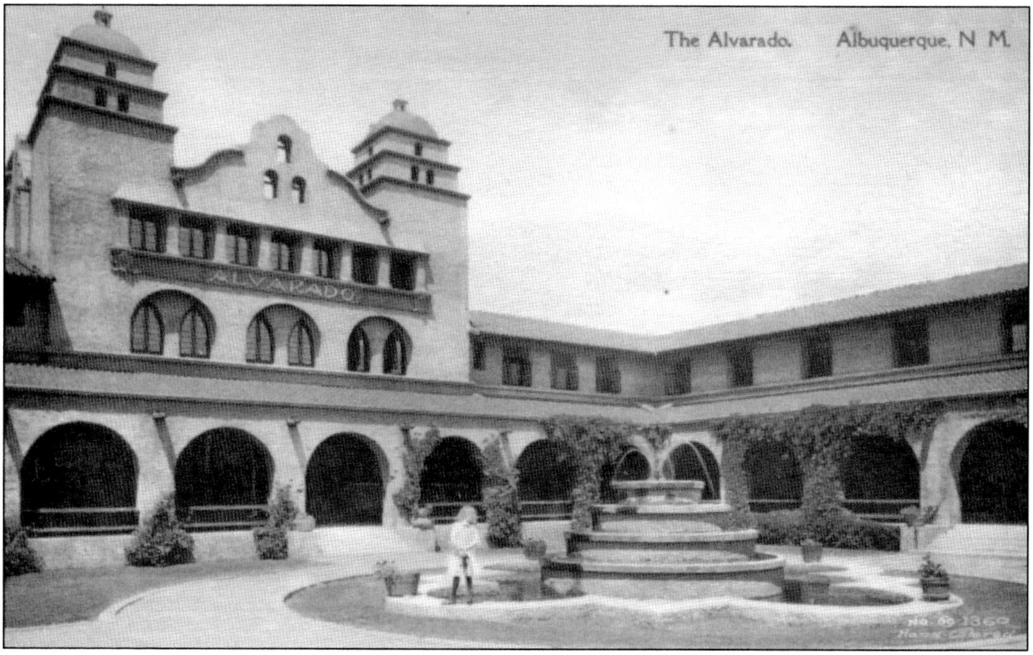

Fred Harvey's Alvarado Hotel and its complex of depot, restaurants, and galleries opened in 1902. It contained a fabulous display of Native American arts and crafts. Rail passengers had the unique experience of walking through walled gardens and beckoning porches lined with rocking chairs before entering the building for fine dining and shopping. The building was designed by Charles Whittlesey in the California Mission style. These postcards depict the outdoor fountains and the interior lounge. Albuquerque historians seem united in the opinion that the Santa Fe Railway's demolition of the Alvarado in 1970 was Albuquerque's most lamentable loss of an iconic landmark. (Both, courtesy of Nancy Tucker.)

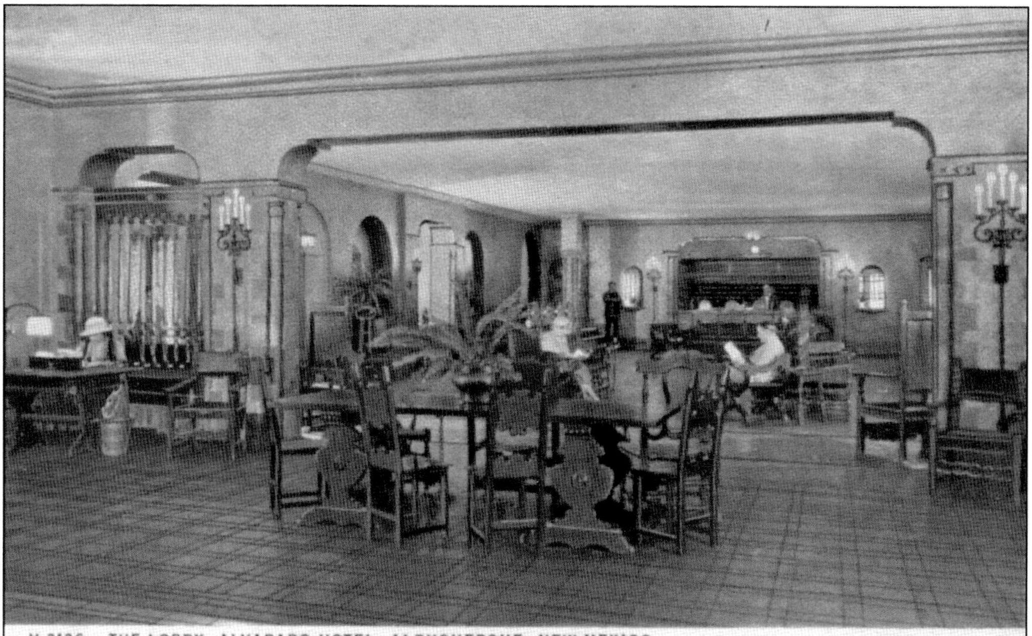

Four

Huning Castle

The Rhine along the Rio Grande

More than a half century after its demolition in 1955, the photographs and stories of what Franz Huning named his "Castle Huning" still provoke wonderment. Some say the 14-room mansion in frontier Albuquerque resembled a castle along the Rhine in builder Franz Huning's native Germany. Others point to the Italianate styling.

Whatever its style, eclectic "Huning Castle" was long known as Albuquerque's grandest private home and grounds. The mansion with its distinctive towers was completed in time for Christmas 1883 after two years of construction. According to later neighborhood codeveloper William A. Keleher, the estate grounds comprised about 700 acres that Huning had obtained in anticipation of the railroad's arrival. The property extended from Central Avenue on the north to about Seventeenth Street on the west and Tenth Street on the east. The river marked the southern boundary.

Using *terrones* (adobe sod) cut from his meadow, the home's three-foot-thick walls were sheathed with wood veneer on the exterior, then shaped and beveled to resemble stone. Huning left a note about the expense: "These terrones are just now the cheapest building material, especially for me since I own the meadows and labor being cheap. They cost $1 to dig and $2.50 to haul also $1.50 for the soil to be used as mortar and $6 for labor. That sums up to $11 in the walls per MM (thousand brick). It took 250,000 terrones for the whole house."

The castle was demolished in 1955 after it was declared unsafe and a fire hazard. According to newspaper accounts at the time, the city declined the donation of the old building because of the expense of restoration. Today, the Huning Castle Apartments stand in its stead.

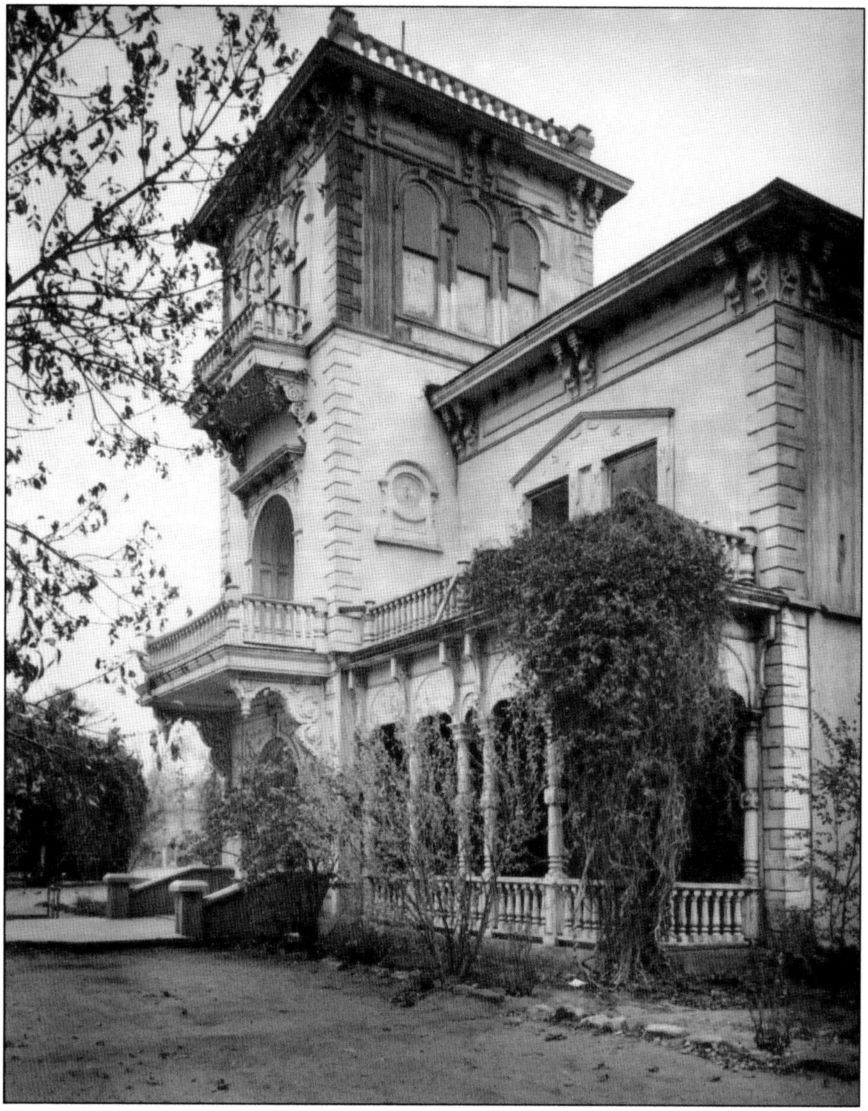

Set 100 feet back from Railroad Avenue (now Central Avenue), Huning Castle's entrance was situated precisely on the dividing line that separated Old Town from New Town. A distinctive three-story square tower (one of three) rose over the entry of the two-story, 14-room home. Doors and bay windows were brought from Chicago, and ornate jigsaw wood carvings arrived from St. Louis. Balconies, bay windows, lacy iron railings, and architectural moldings were part of this grand home that also included a library, a ballroom, a 16-foot-high ceiling, a two-story screened porch, a veranda, and two bathrooms with inside plumbing. Expensive furnishings included walnut paneling, a grand piano brought by oxcart from St. Louis, a pipe organ, and crimson velvet draperies. In Huning's memoir, *Trader on the Santa Fe Trail*, granddaughter Lina Fergusson Browne described a main bedroom furnished with a huge four-poster bed, dressers, and wardrobes, as well as an "elaborate bath" with a long marble counter holding two sinks. The grounds were equally impressive. Within walking distance of his Molina de Glorieta flour mill, Huning created an agricultural oasis with park-like gardens, an aviary, fountains, numerous specimens of bushes and trees, vineyards, a pond and island, and even a family burial ground. (Photograph by Walter Haussamen in 1955, courtesy of the Haussamen family.)

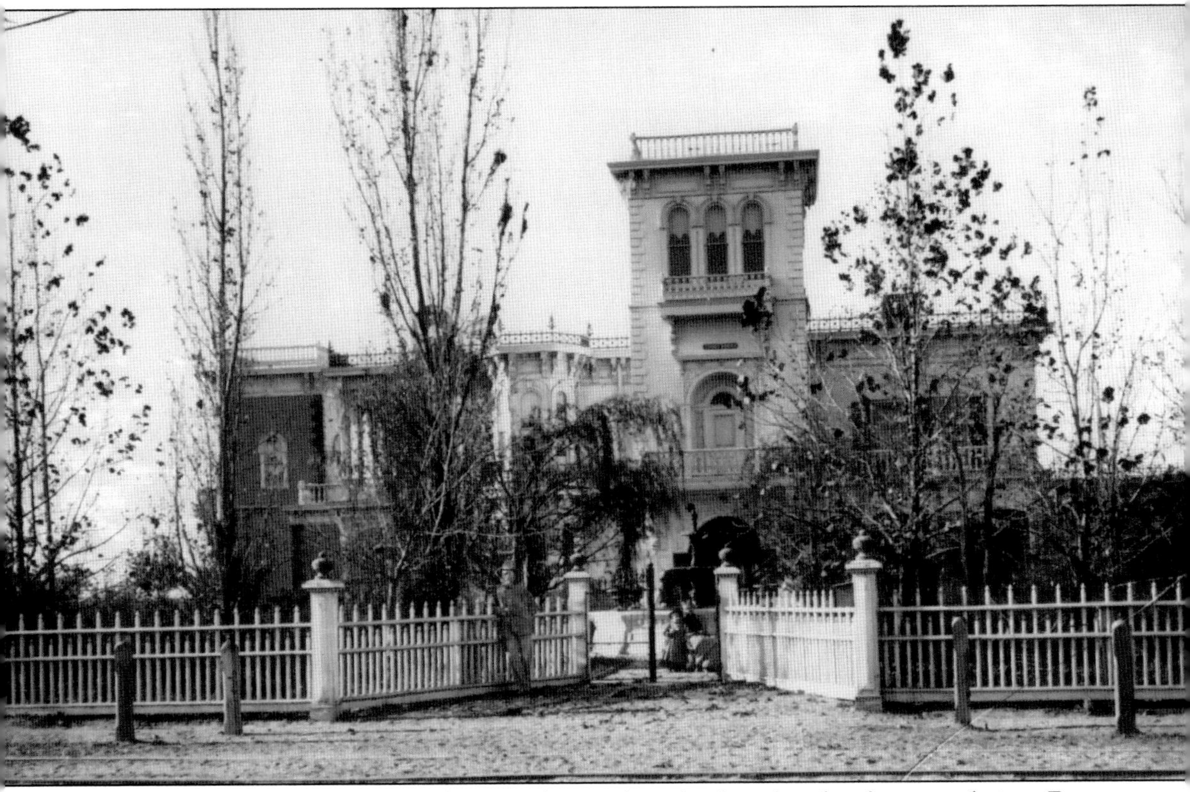

This photograph of Huning Castle was taken within the first decade of its completion. Franz Huning leans against the front picket fence, and his wife, Ernestine, tends grandchildren inside the courtyard near the fountain. Several features in the home made housekeeping easier here than in the older La Glorieta home. A cement foundation ensured all floors were level. The exterior sheathing required occasional repainting but not extensive replastering. Wood panel walls in the home's interior were topped with easy-to-care-for wallpaper. (Original photograph by William Henry Cobb and restored by Walter Haussamen, courtesy of the Haussamen family.)

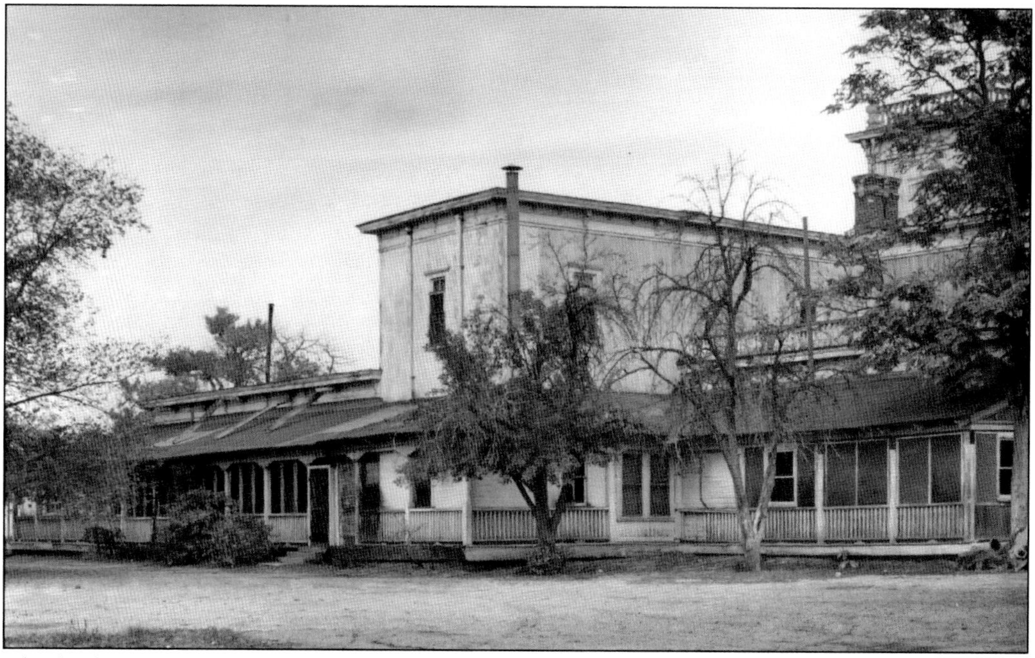

The back acreage of Huning Castle was planted with orchards, vineyards, and dozens of tree species. Across the back of the house were storage rooms for household supplies and coal, two kitchens, and the end of a 14-foot-wide hallway that extended 60 feet from the front to the rear of the home. (Photograph by Walter Haussamen in 1955, courtesy of the Haussamen family.)

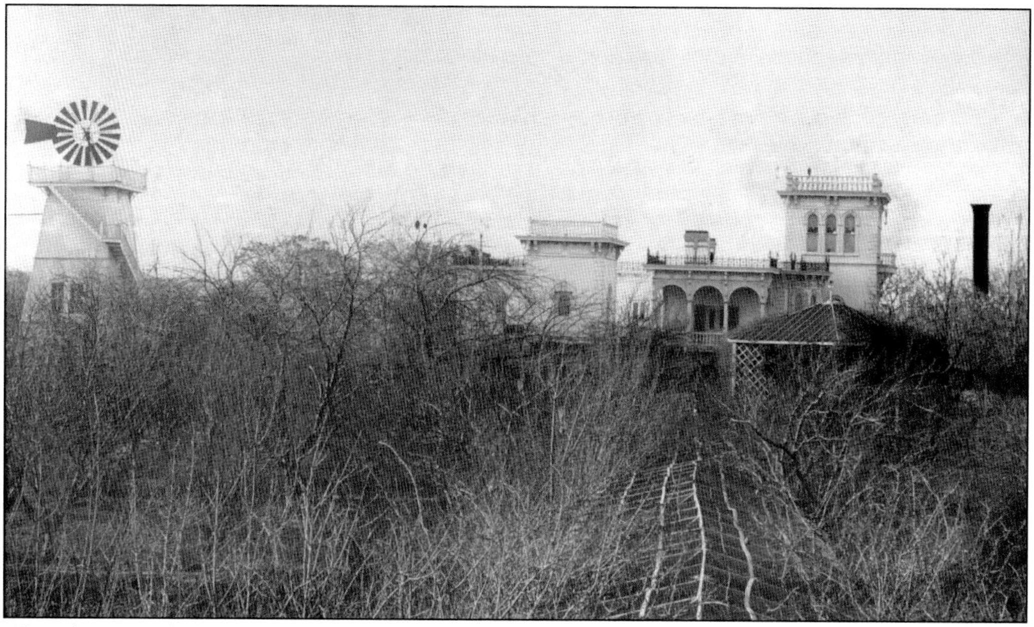

This photograph shows the increasing agriculture problems along the Rio Grande that impacted Huning Castle at the turn of the century. Intensive farming throughout the river valley and Colorado turned once-fertile fields into silt-swollen swamplands. Flooding was a common occurrence. The distance of the river from the castle was estimated at a half to three-quarters of a mile. (Courtesy of UNM CSWR, Huning-Ferguson Collection, 000-194-0011.)

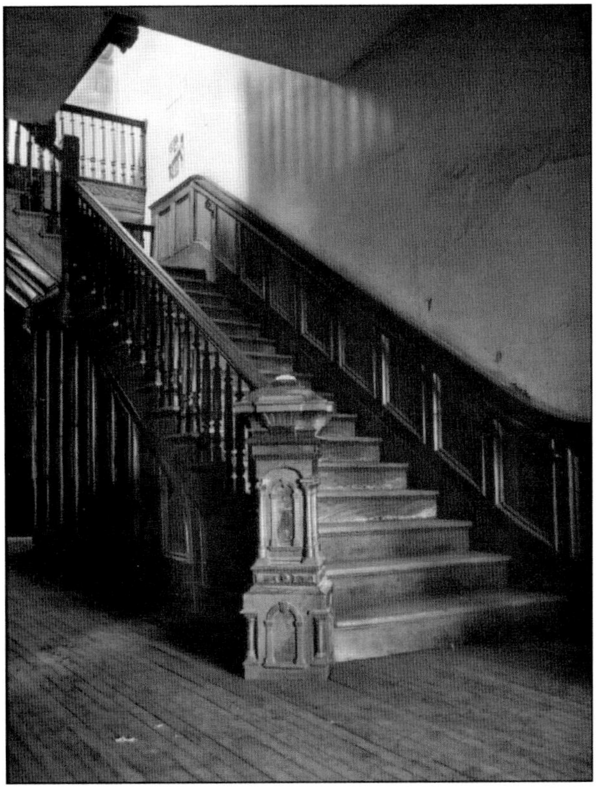

Shortly before Huning Castle was torn down in 1955, the home's staircase remained intact, as did a fireplace and a bin for fuel. Franz Huning died in 1905 and his son, Arno, remained with his own family in the castle for another 25 years. Eventually, the family began selling off parcels of acreage. One of the first portions to leave the family's ownership was a two-block stretch of Fourteenth Street in 1913. The magnificent Huning Castle was demolished in 1955, a half century after Franz Huning's death. (Both photographs by Walter Haussamen in 1955, courtesy of the Haussamen family.)

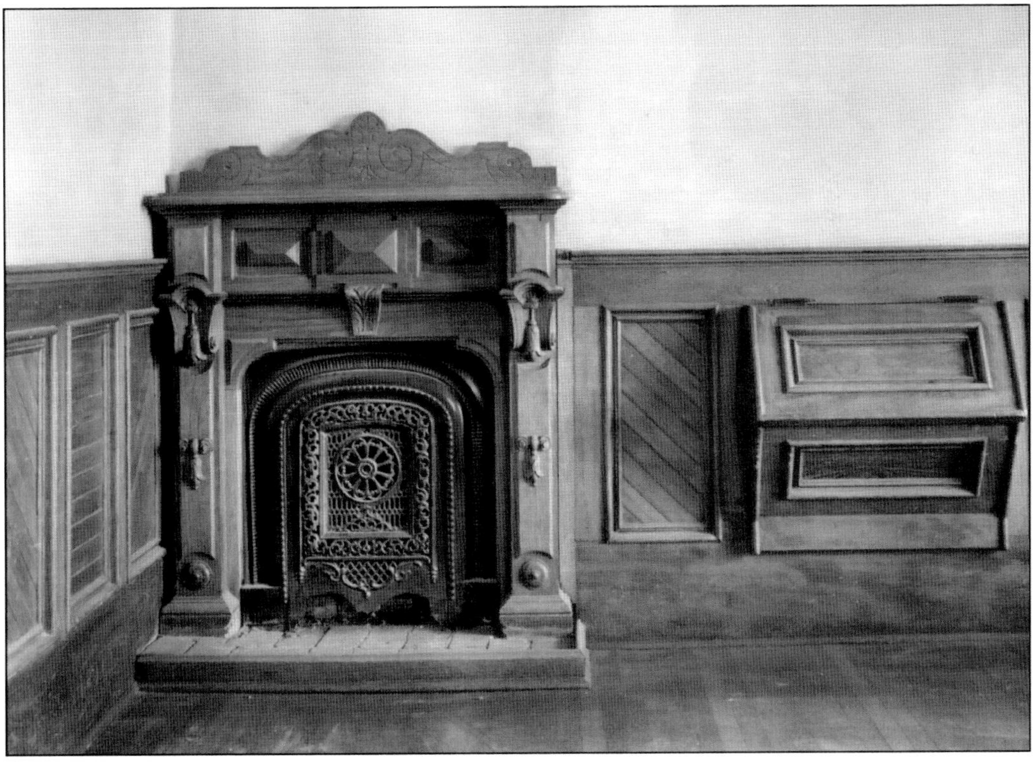

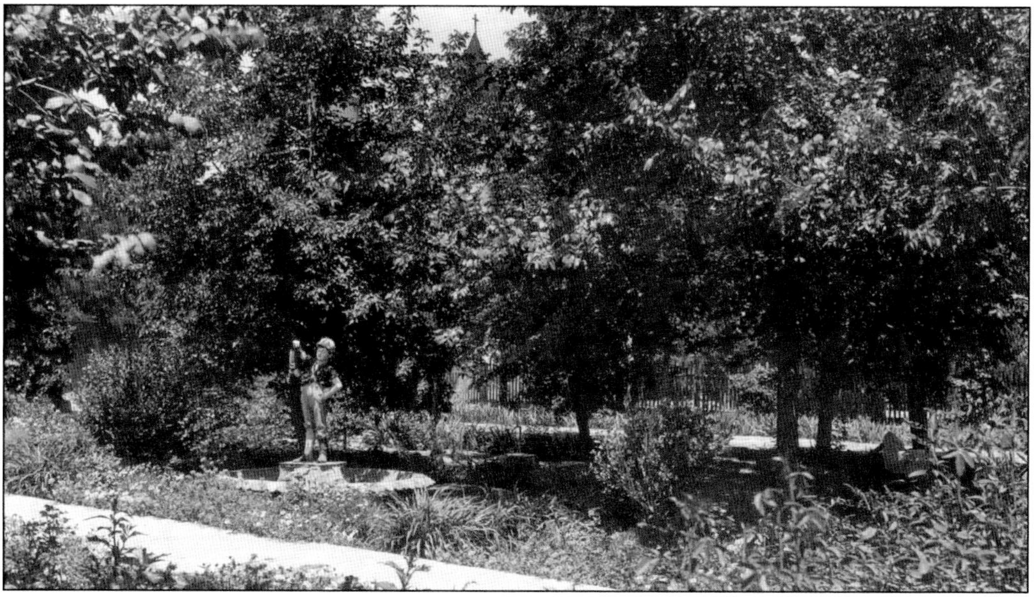

The photograph shows a garden at Huning Castle between 1900 and 1909. In her book *Old Houses of New Mexico and the People Who Built Them*, Sytha Motto described a pond stocked with German carp, stables, fountains, ornamental iron benches, and a carriage house. (Courtesy of UNM CSWR, Cobb Memorial Collection, 000-119-0602.)

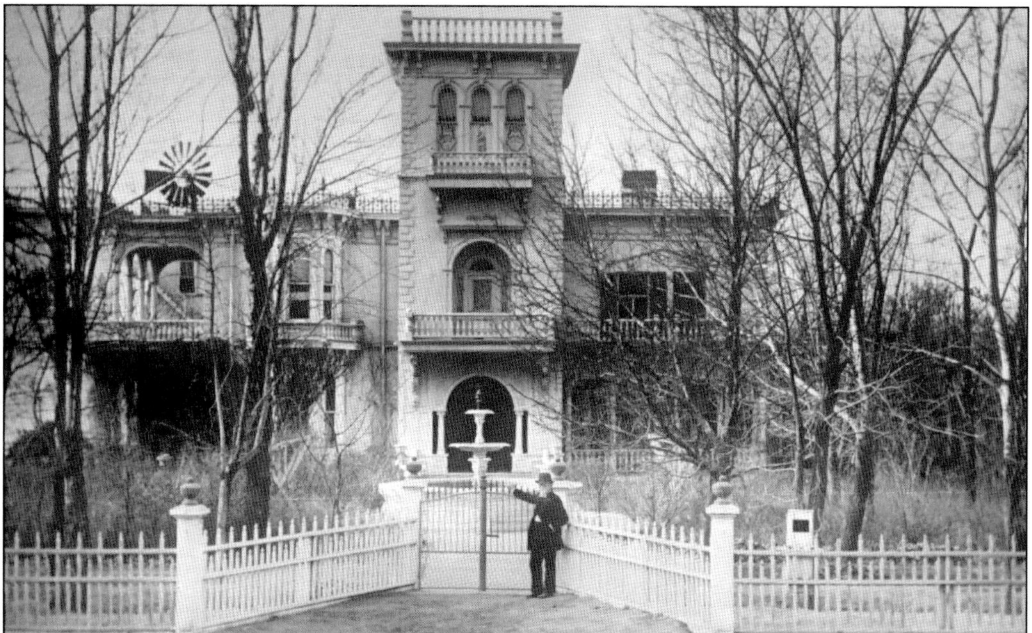

Huning Castle's double front door straddled the dividing line separating Old Town and New Town. William A. Keleher, who later developed much of the Huning acreage, was a Western Union messenger boy in his youth and learned quickly to make his deliveries to the side where the telegram originated for a good tip. Franz Huning's daughters were allowed to attend school in New Town after it was determined their bedrooms were on the east side of the home. (Courtesy of UNM CSWR, William A. Keleher Collection, 000-742-0480.)

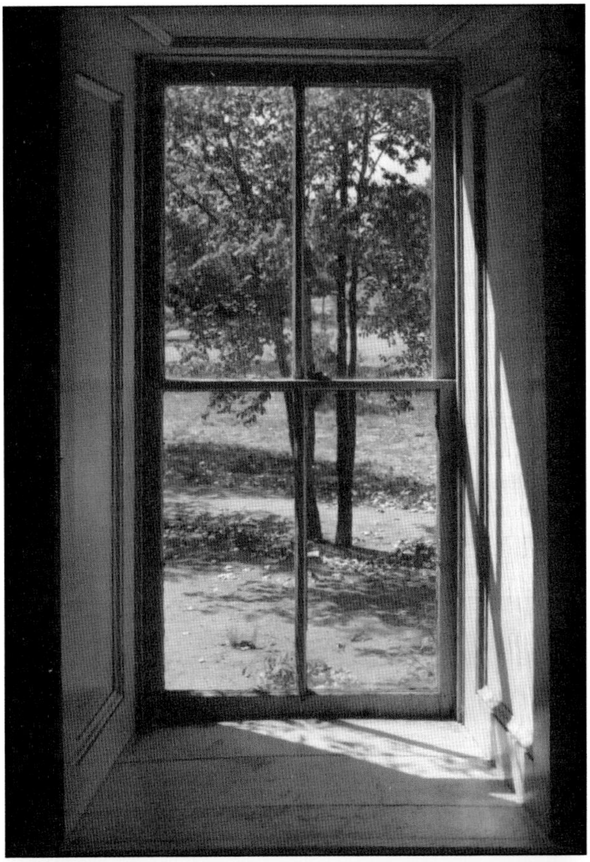

The terrones or sod building bricks for Huning Castle resulted in walls and window sills that were nearly four feet thick. In his memoir, *Trader on the Santa Fe Trail*, Franz Huning's granddaughter Lina Fergusson Browne wrote that a visitor's first sight upon entering the castle was a five-foot statue that a cousin identified as a likeness to Bois-de-Guilbert, a Templar knight from Sir Walter Scott's *Ivanhoe*. It was mounted on the newel post of the staircase. In 1960, the University of New Mexico's architectural historian and professor Bainbridge Bunting wrote a description of the castle's features recalled from previous visits. His detailed work has provided much of the information known about the castle today. (Both photographs by Walter Haussamen in 1955, courtesy of the Haussamen family.)

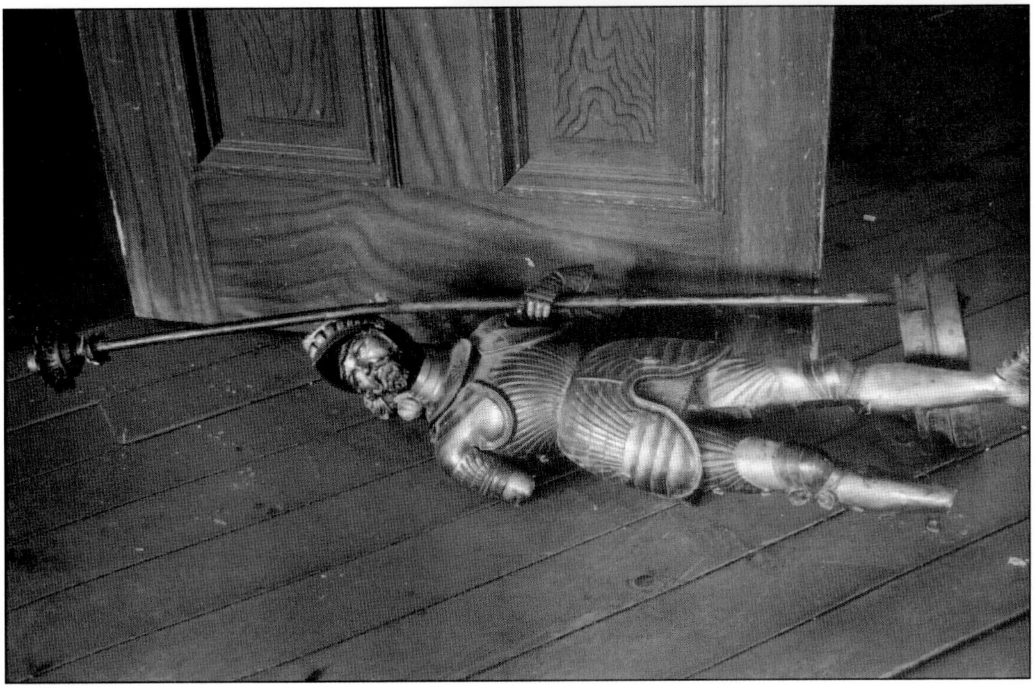

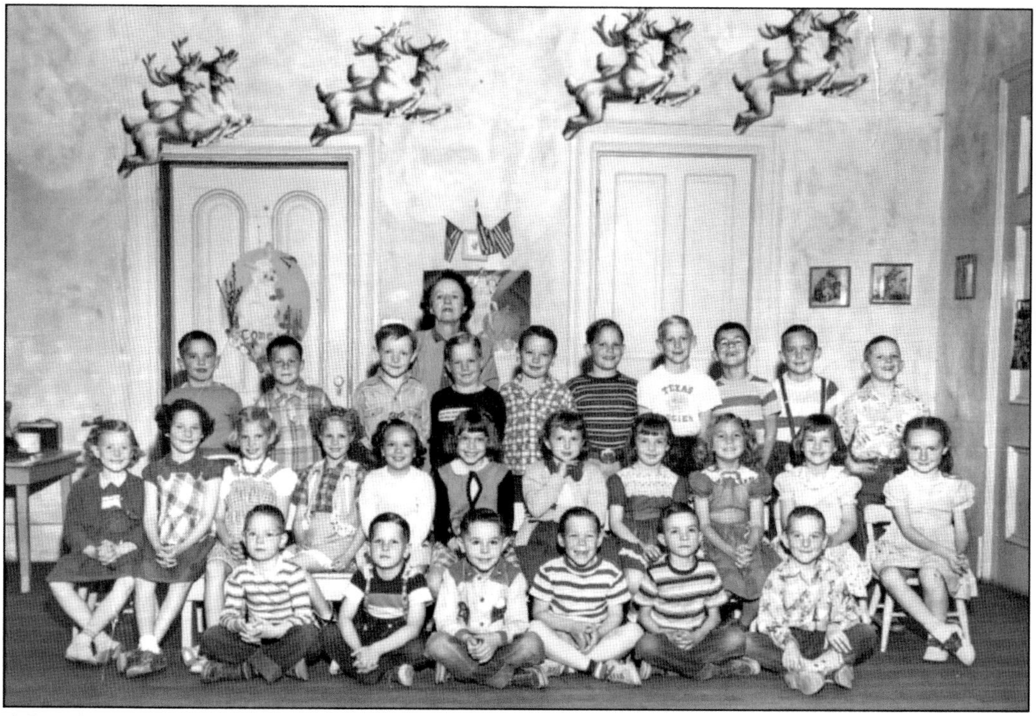

After Arno Huning's death in 1936 and before the home was demolished in 1955, the castle was home to two schools. Ruth Hanna McCormick Simms started Manzano Day School, an offshoot of Sandia School, at the castle in 1938 before it moved in 1942 west to La Glorieta, the old Huning-Fergusson home at 1801 Central Avenue NW. Mary Trudelle, pictured in the back row in the above photograph, ran a kindergarten from her home and later moved the Trudelle School to the Huning Castle after Manzano Day School vacated the premises. The undated class photographs depict students from Trudelle's School, including a rare glimpse of the castle's interior. (Both, courtesy of Rowena Hobby and Kathryn Bennett.)

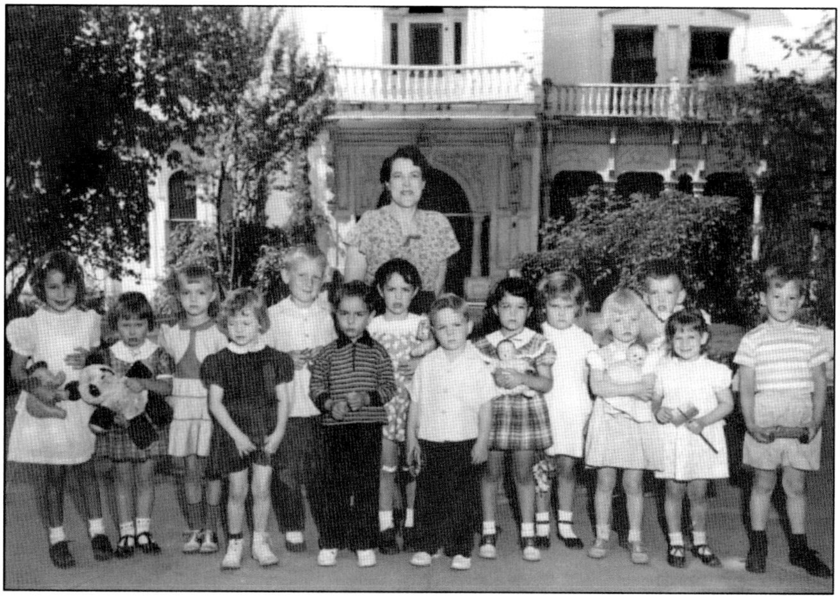

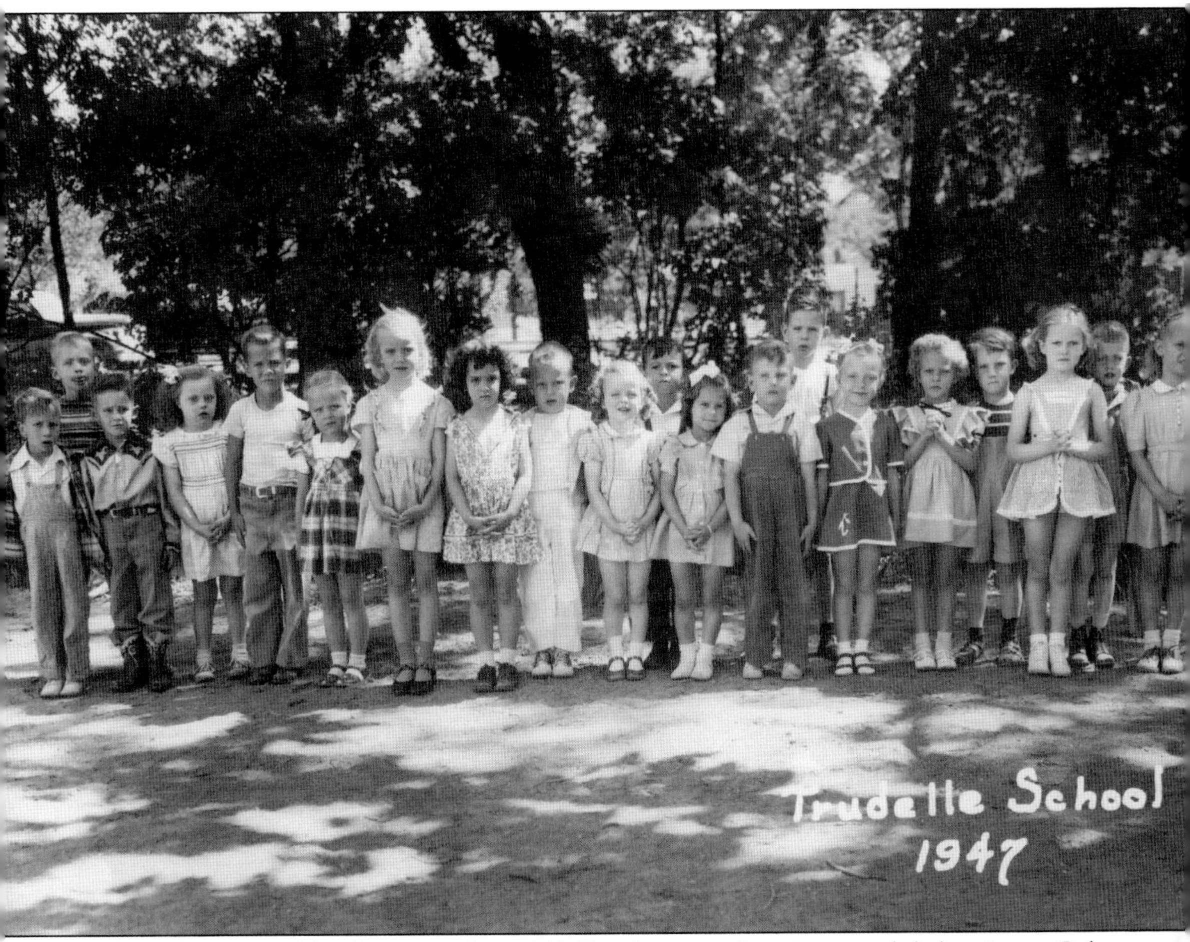

The Trudelle School kindergarten class of 1947 is shown in this photograph belonging to Gale Williams Doyel, sixth from the left in a plaid dress. Other identified students include Allan Taylor and Pat Carnes (first and second from left); Sally Barnett, Duff Walker, and Nancy Hebenstreit Kozikowski (eighth, ninth and tenth from left); Dorothea "Dottie" Howard, Suzanne Soker, and Sally Marsh (first, third, and sixth from right); and Stephen Wright Dinkle (the tall boy behind Sally Marsh). Mary Trudelle was a neighborhood teacher for more than 20 years. (Courtesy of Gale Williams Doyel.)

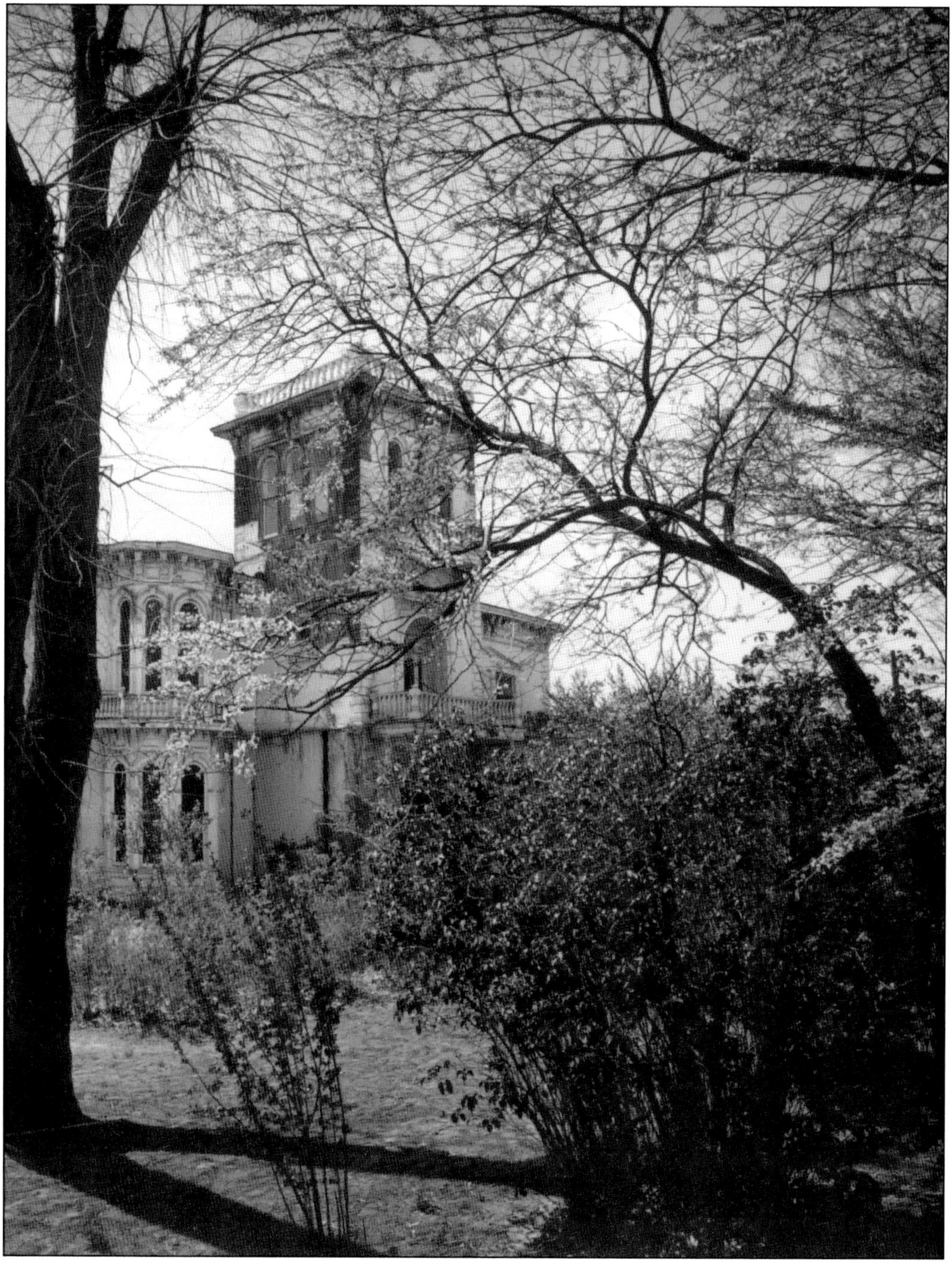

The grand old castle, owned by William A. Keleher and A.R. Hebenstreit at its end, was torn down in 1955. Hebenstreit noted that it would cost $2,810 to give the rambling structure even a single coat of paint. The city declined the donation of the castle, citing estimated restoration expenses of $400,000. After the castle was demolished, the land remained vacant until the construction of the Huning Castle Apartments in 2004. (Photograph by Walter Haussamen in 1955, courtesy of the Haussamen family.)

Five

Draining the Swamp
The Conservancy District and Tingley Beach

By the turn of the 20th century, the once-fertile agricultural fields along the Rio Grande were in distress. The gravity-fed irrigation systems perfected by the Pueblo peoples and early settlers along the river valley no longer functioned well. Farming and irrigation upriver in Colorado's San Luis Valley devastated New Mexico's croplands. The flow of water slowed, silt built up, and much of the valley's land suffered seepage that turned agricultural fields into marshlands or alkaline flats.

Agriculture productivity at the Huning estate, and indeed all along the Rio Grande, dropped dramatically. Floods were common. By the time Huning died in 1905, most of the family's swampy acreage could not be used for farming or development despite its convenient proximity to a growing downtown.

By the mid-1920s, there was a push to establish a Middle Rio Grande Conservancy District. The rallying cry was "Drain or Drown!" The resulting effort created a 150-mile corridor of newly constructed irrigation ditches, levees, drains, laterals, and canals to drain the swamps and reclaim lost land. The transformation created a riparian forest or "bosque" of cottonwoods and willows still unsurpassed in the United States.

The lands within and near Huning Castle's borders benefited tremendously from the project. Not only could reclaimed land be farmed, but it also opened the way for eventual development of homes, a golf course, a park, and zoo.

The newly created basin between levees on the east side of the river along the Huning property became the city's unlikely bathing beach. The mile-long beach, utilizing Civil Works Administration funding, went through several name changes before settling on "Tingley Beach." It was large enough for 7,000 swimmers when it opened as Albuquerque's favorite recreational site in 1931.

Note: Many photographs in this chapter are courtesy of the Middle Rio Grande Conservancy District, hereafter listed as MRGCD.

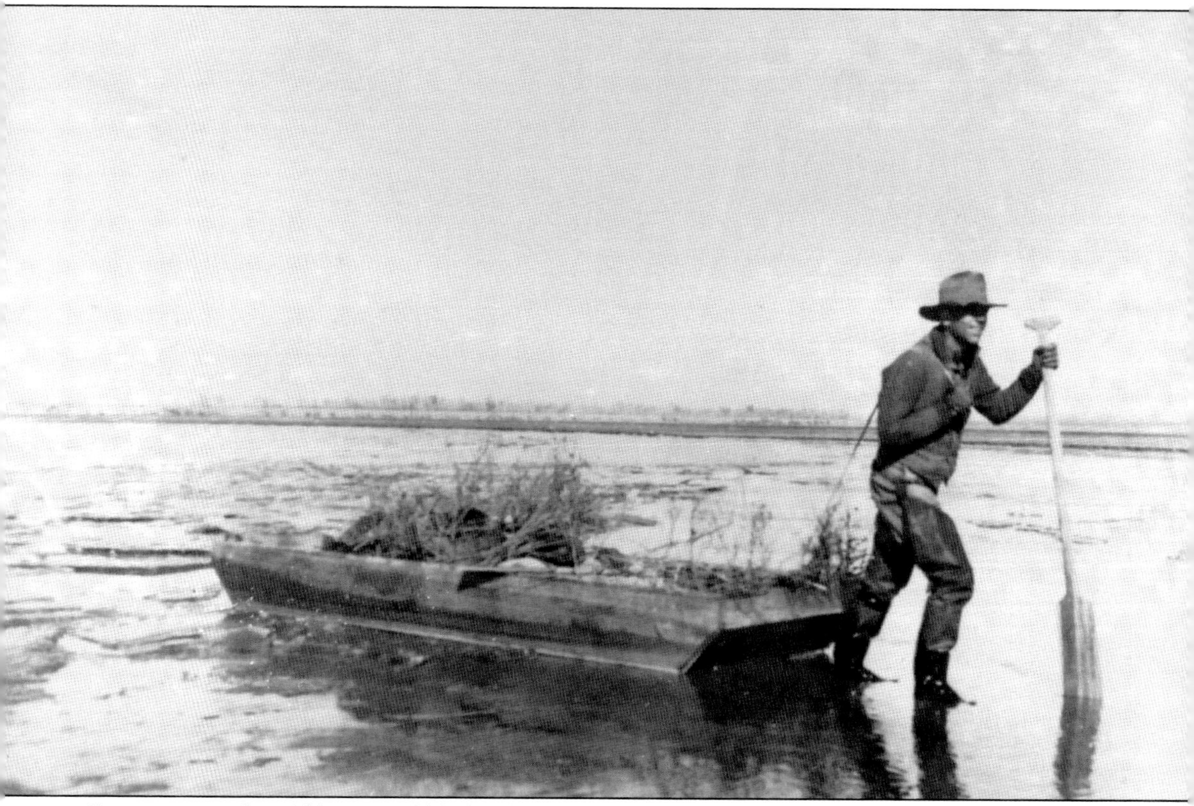

Environmentalist Aldo Leopold helped shape wilderness conservation throughout the United States. His early career with the US Forest Service (and later, the chamber of commerce) was in Albuquerque. Leopold and his family lived close to the Rio Grande on a stretch of Fourteenth Street, one of the first parcels of land sold by Arno Huning after his father's death. Platted as Huning Place in 1913, the addition was three blocks long and offered easy access to the river loved by Leopold's entire family. The photograph shows Leopold pulling his float, the *Binnacle Bat II*, along mud flats in the Rio Grande in 1918. Leopold was an eloquent advocate for the river's preservation, as well as the establishment of a park and zoo. His home, along with several others on the west side of Fourteenth Street south of Central Avenue, is now part of the Aldo Leopold Neighborhood Historic District. (Courtesy of Aldo Leopold Foundation.)

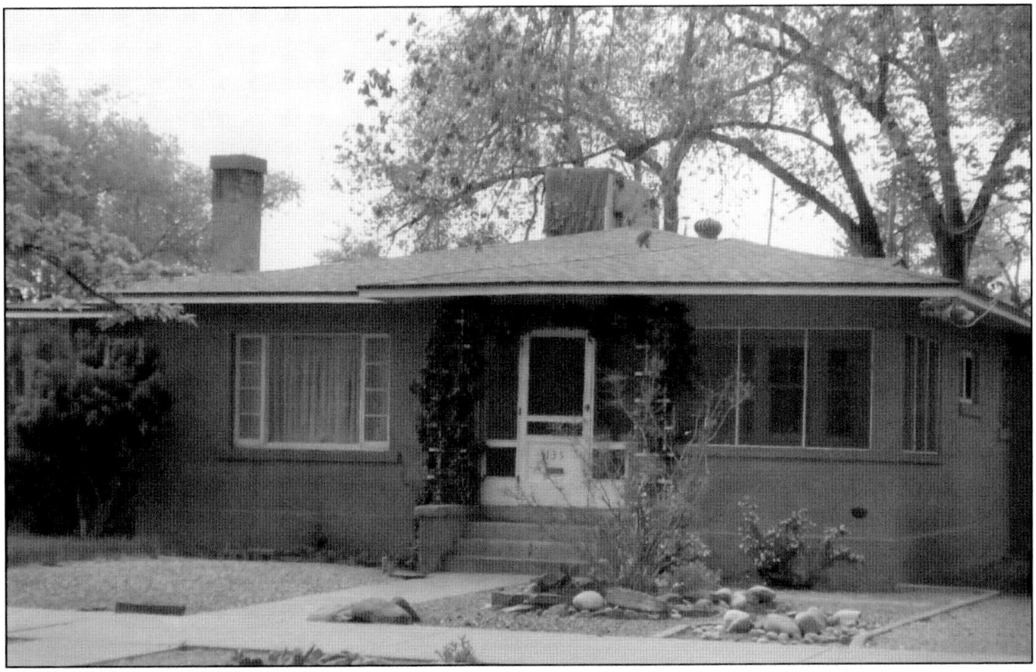

Aldo Leopold, his wife, Estella, and family resided at this adobe home at 135 Fourteenth Street SW from about 1916 to 1924. Later, rancher Bernard A. Trudelle moved his family into the former Leopold home. Mary Trudelle set up a kindergarten for neighborhood children. Later, she taught school in the old Huning Castle from about 1944 to 1954. (Courtesy of Judy Cook.)

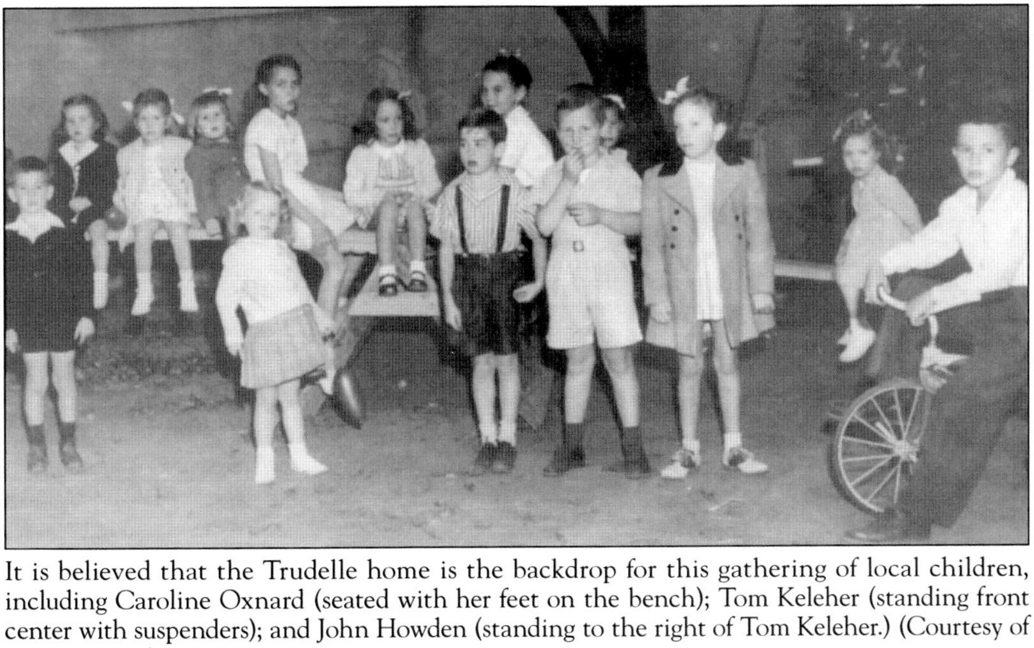

It is believed that the Trudelle home is the backdrop for this gathering of local children, including Caroline Oxnard (seated with her feet on the bench); Tom Keleher (standing front center with suspenders); and John Howden (standing to the right of Tom Keleher.) (Courtesy of Kylene Wing.)

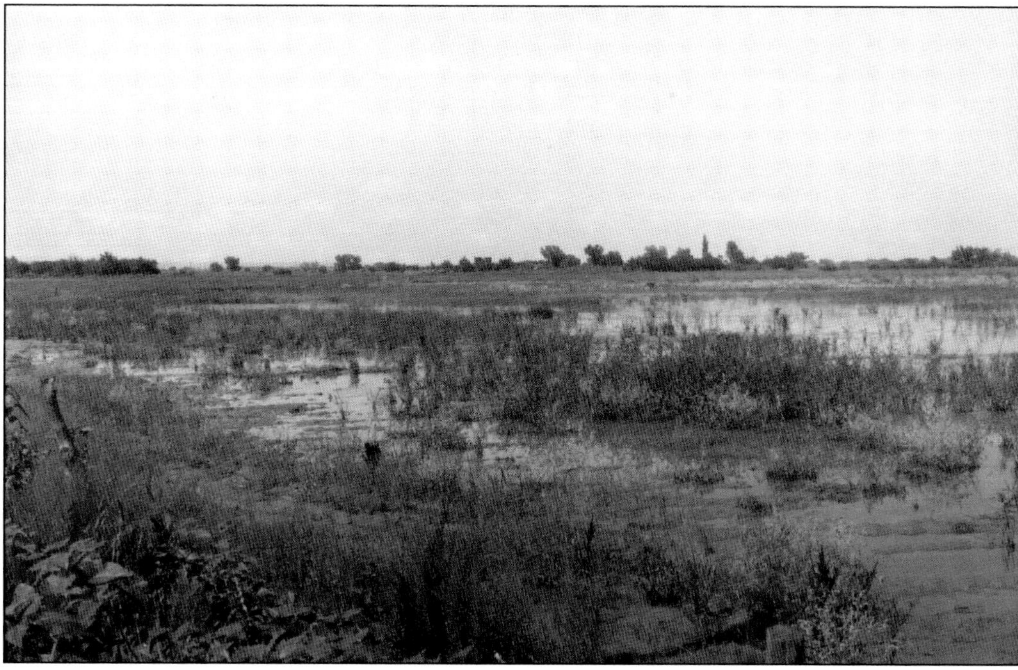

Increased agricultural use brought drainage and flooding woes to the once-fertile banks of the Rio Grande. Seepage of water into the fields turned farmland into salt marsh and swamp. Thousands of acres were in alkali and swampy salt grass, and there was the ever-present menace of flood. A 1909 photograph shows a waterlogged tract near present-day Central Avenue. Floods wiped out the Barelas Bridge across the Rio Grande, leading to increased support for a conservation program and the creation of an effective drainage system. (Above, courtesy of MRGCD; below, courtesy of UNM CSWR, Cobb Memorial Collection, 000-119-0624.)

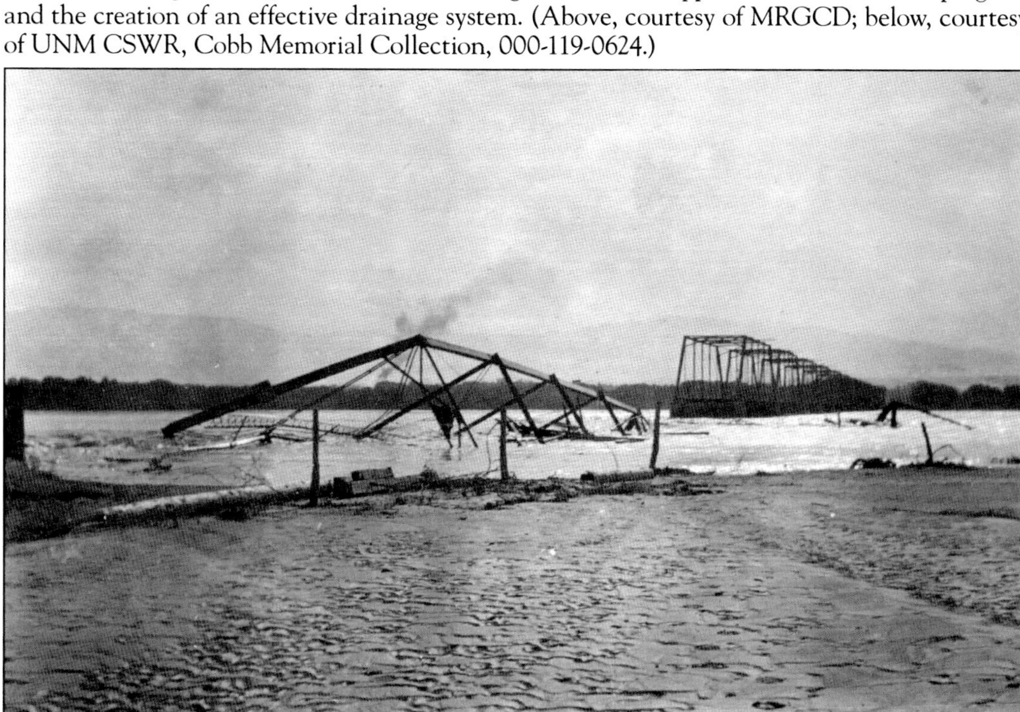

In 1923, about 140 concerned property owners met with Mayor Clyde Tingley and the chamber of commerce to discuss the formation of the Middle Rio Grande Conservancy District. Over the next few years, there was a push to formalize efforts and develop a master plan to improve flooding and drainage problems along the Rio Grande. The Middle Rio Grande Conservancy District was approved by 1928, outlining a plan to link acequias and build a network of drains, laterals and canals, and levees. Newspaper ads in the November 30, 1929, *New Mexico State Tribune* supported the issuance of $8.7 million in construction bonds to begin the improvements that today keep a 150-mile stretch of the river valley open through four counties and six Indian pueblos. (Both advertisements courtesy of *New Mexico State Tribune* archives.)

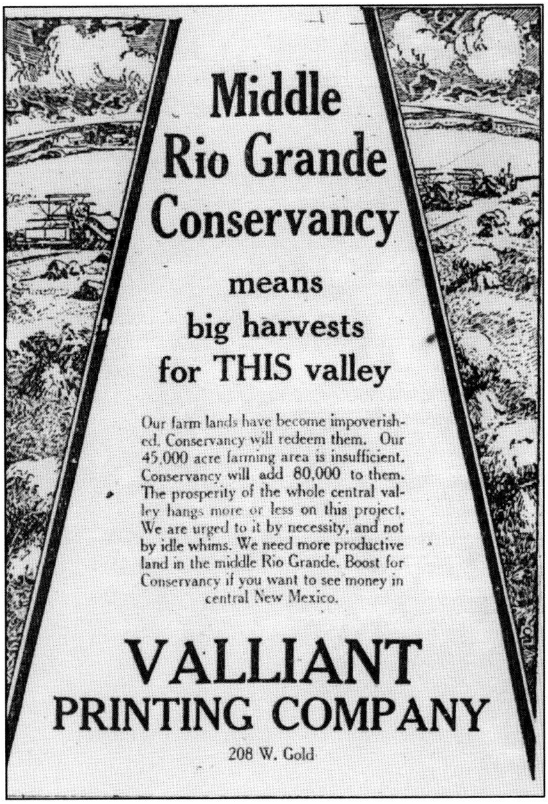

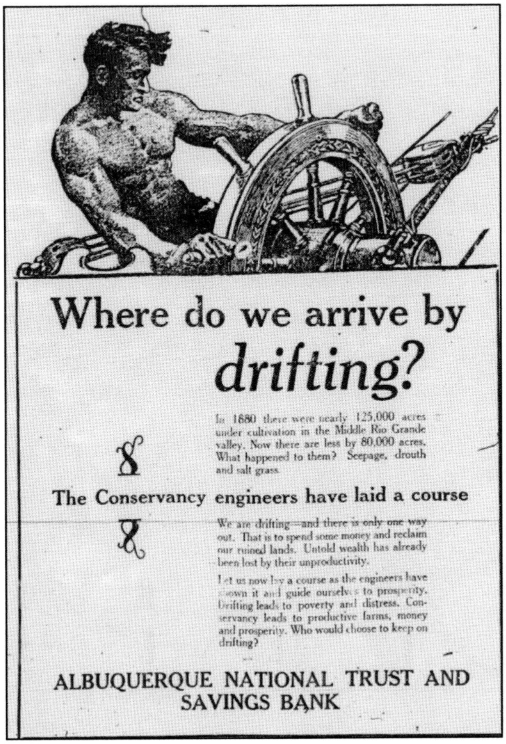

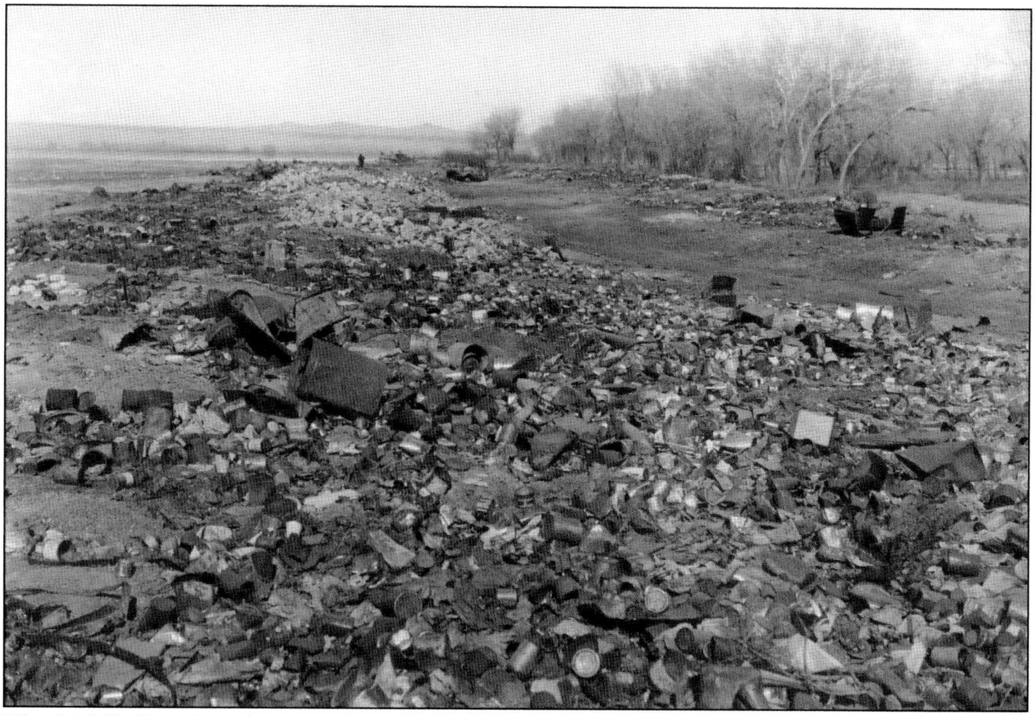

The Middle Rio Grande Conservancy District, under chief engineer Joseph Burkholder and at the urging of Mayor Clyde Tingley, turned the riverside levee into a roadway by cleaning up a city dump at the site of the present-day Tingley Beach Drive. It took three months to clear the city dump to begin its conversion into a scenic riverside drive. (Both, courtesy of MRGCD.)

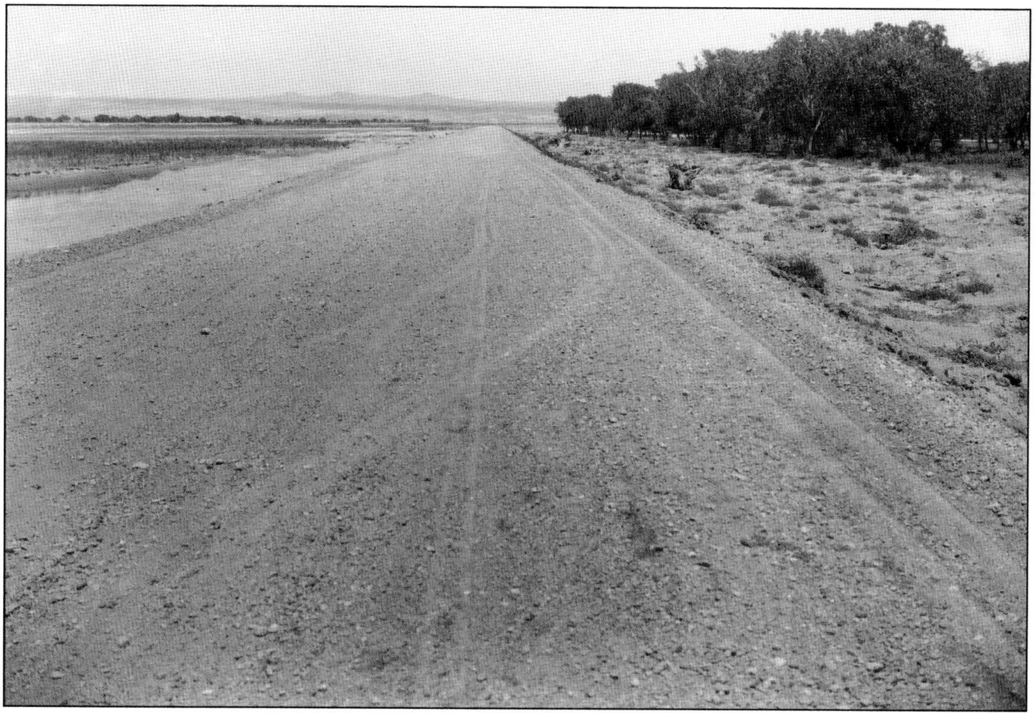

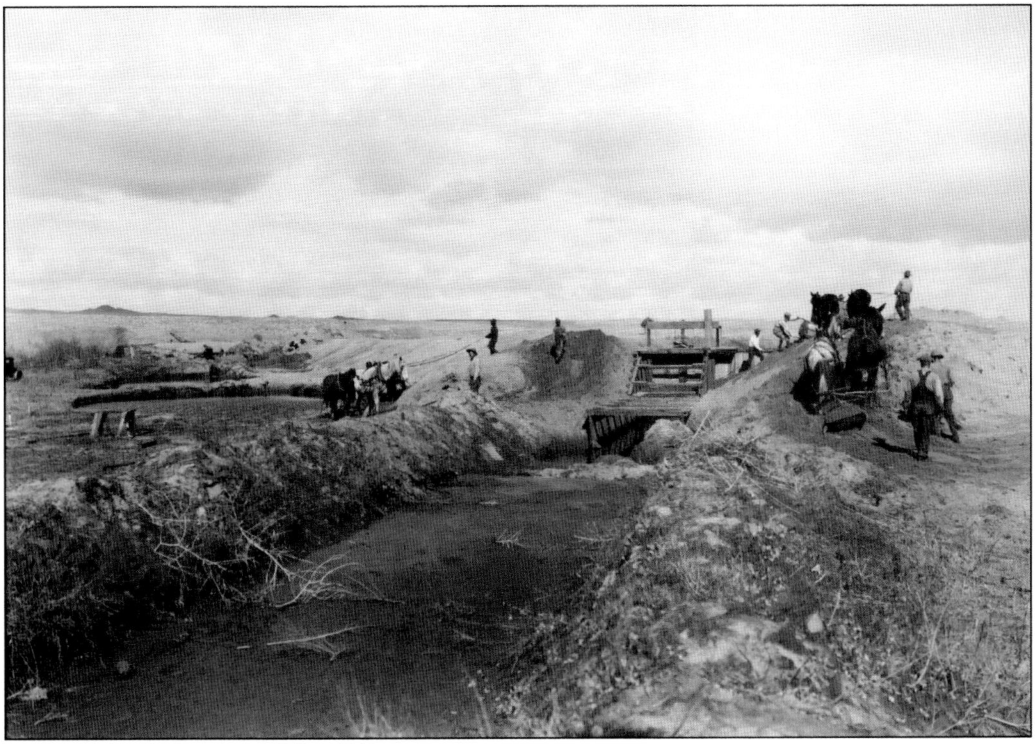

By 1931, work financed with federal funding was underway to create a drain and levee at the Atrisco Riverside using manpower, horsepower, and machinery. The record haul for this trencher during the month of March 1931 was the moving of 53,984 cubic yards of dirt. (Both, courtesy of MRGCD.)

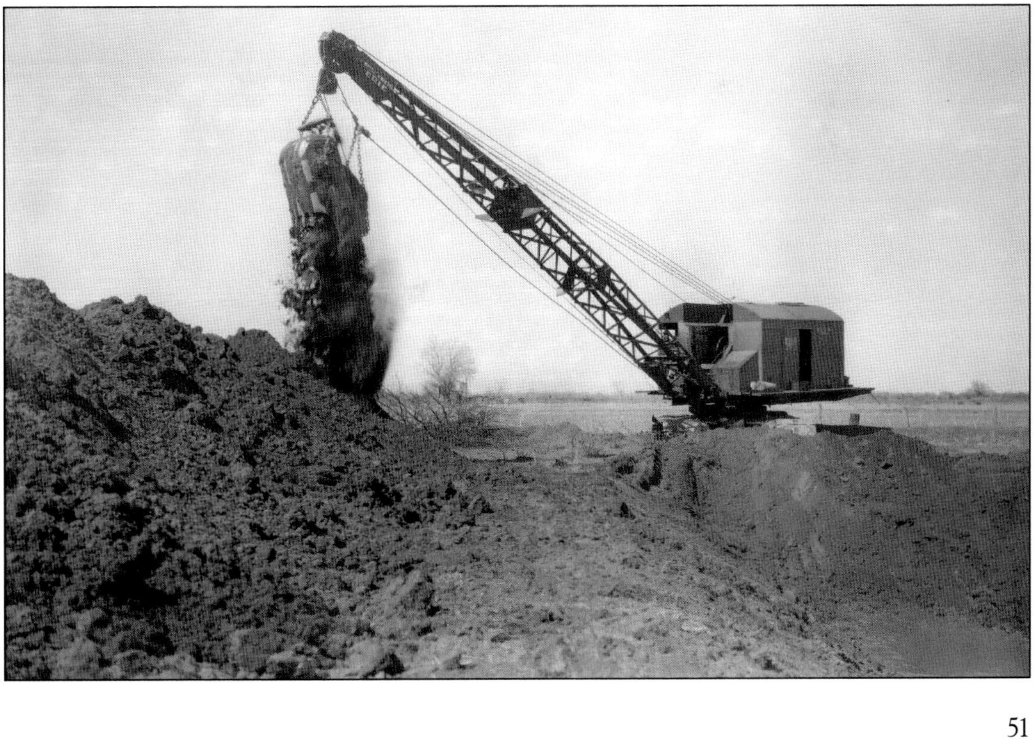

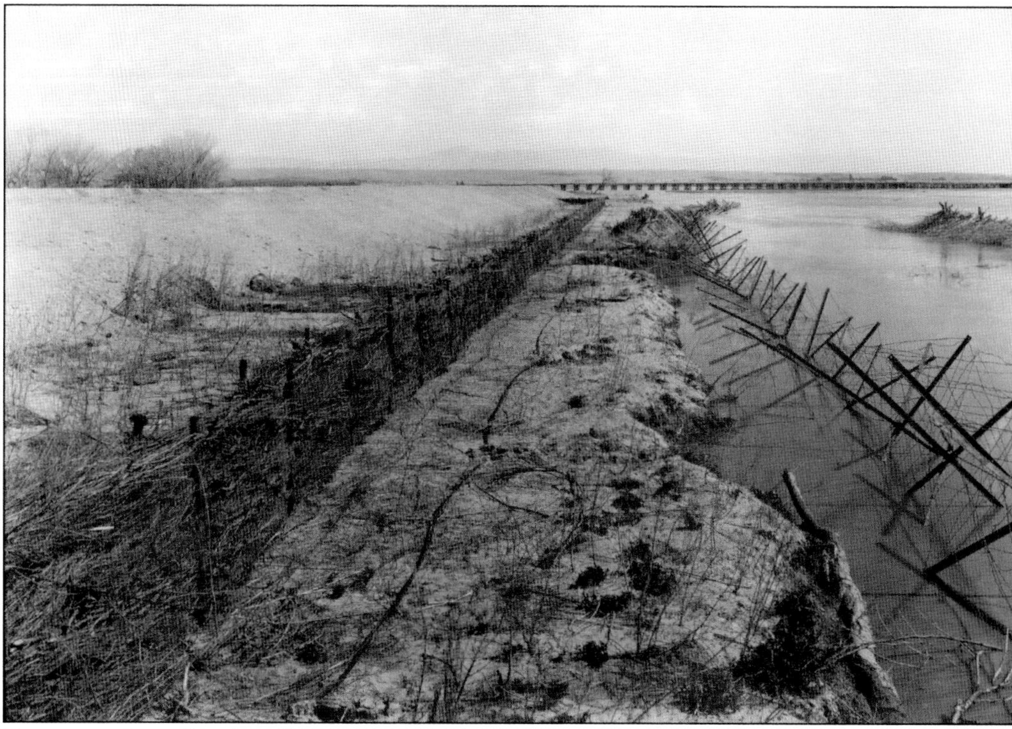

To protect the valley from floodwaters, the district erected 180 miles of riverside levees, ranging in height up to eight feet. Permeable jetties of brush and wire were placed at strategic points to force the river to deposit silt. Steel jetty-jacks still run through the bosque today. (Courtesy of MRGCD.)

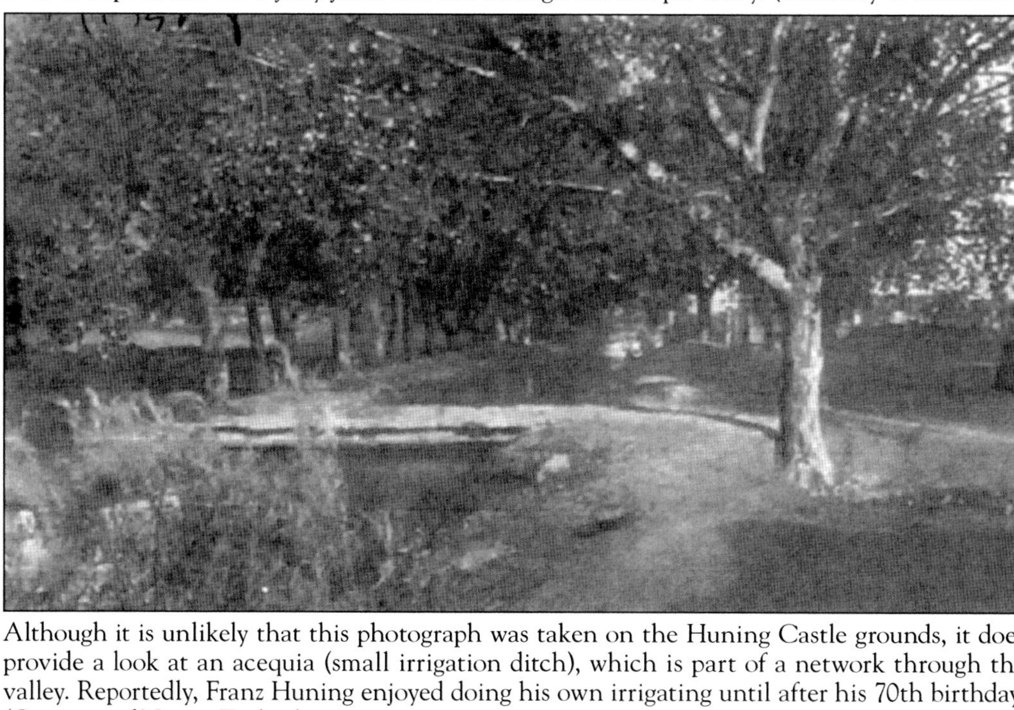

Although it is unlikely that this photograph was taken on the Huning Castle grounds, it does provide a look at an acequia (small irrigation ditch), which is part of a network through the valley. Reportedly, Franz Huning enjoyed doing his own irrigating until after his 70th birthday. (Courtesy of Nancy Tucker.)

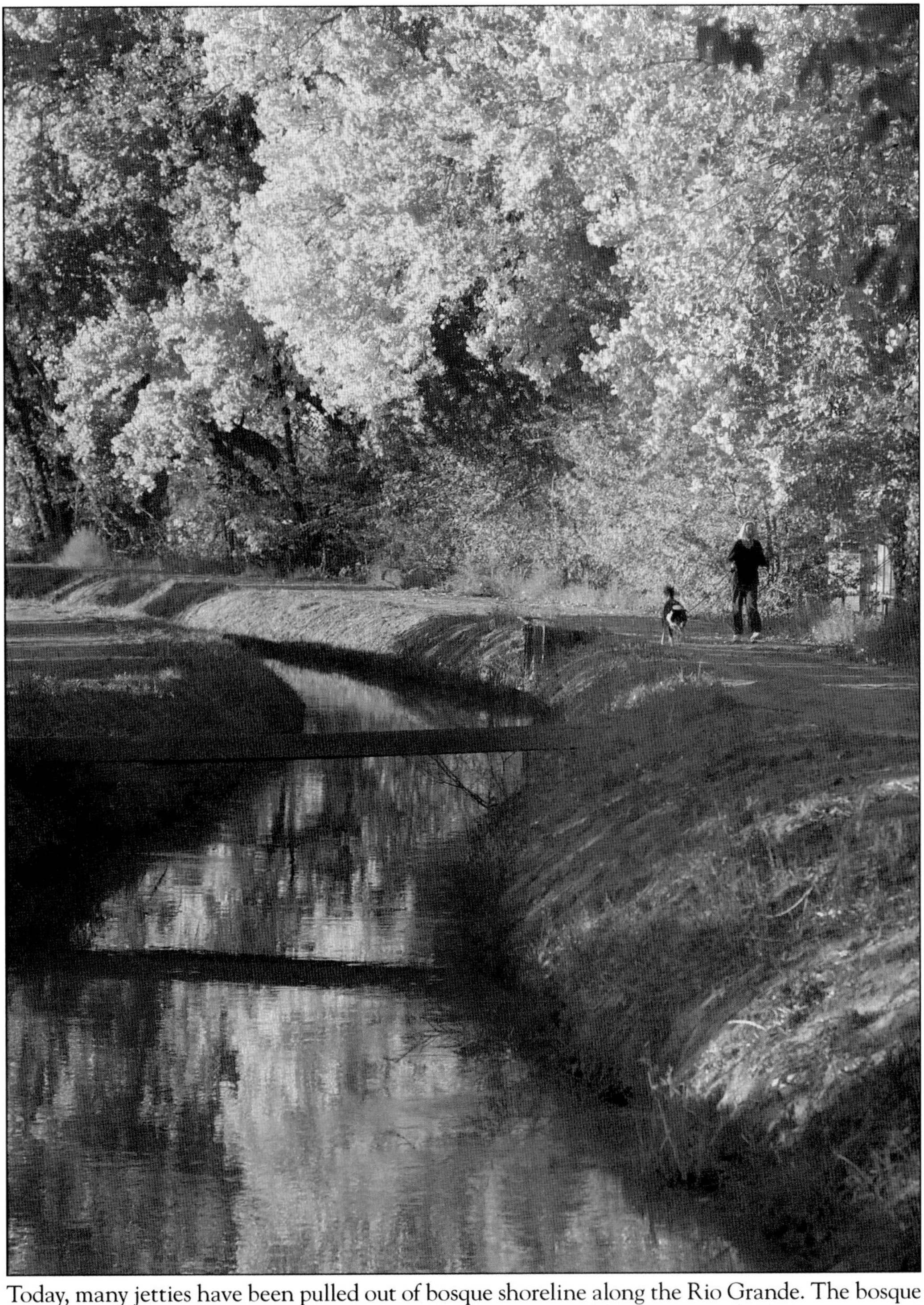

Today, many jetties have been pulled out of bosque shoreline along the Rio Grande. The bosque or woodlands along the Rio Grande is now regarded as one of the greatest unbroken cottonwood and willow riparian forests in the United States. Recent efforts have concentrated on clearing nonnative vegetation to reduce the wildfire hazard. (Courtesy of MRGCD.)

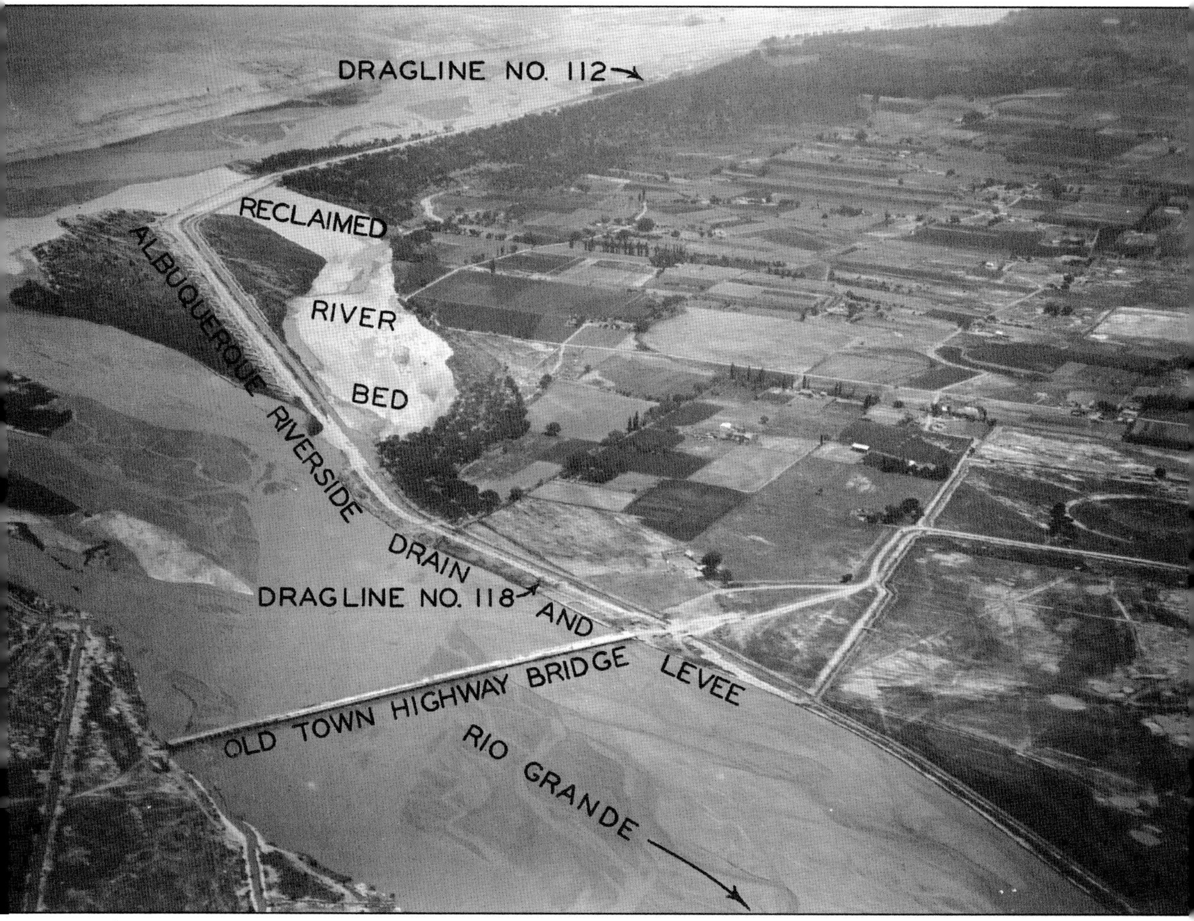

This 1931 aerial map of the improved riverside drain and levee shows 60 reclaimed acres near the site of the present-day Rio Grande Botanic Garden. The new fairways for the Albuquerque Country Club can be seen at the lower right. (Courtesy of MRGCD.)

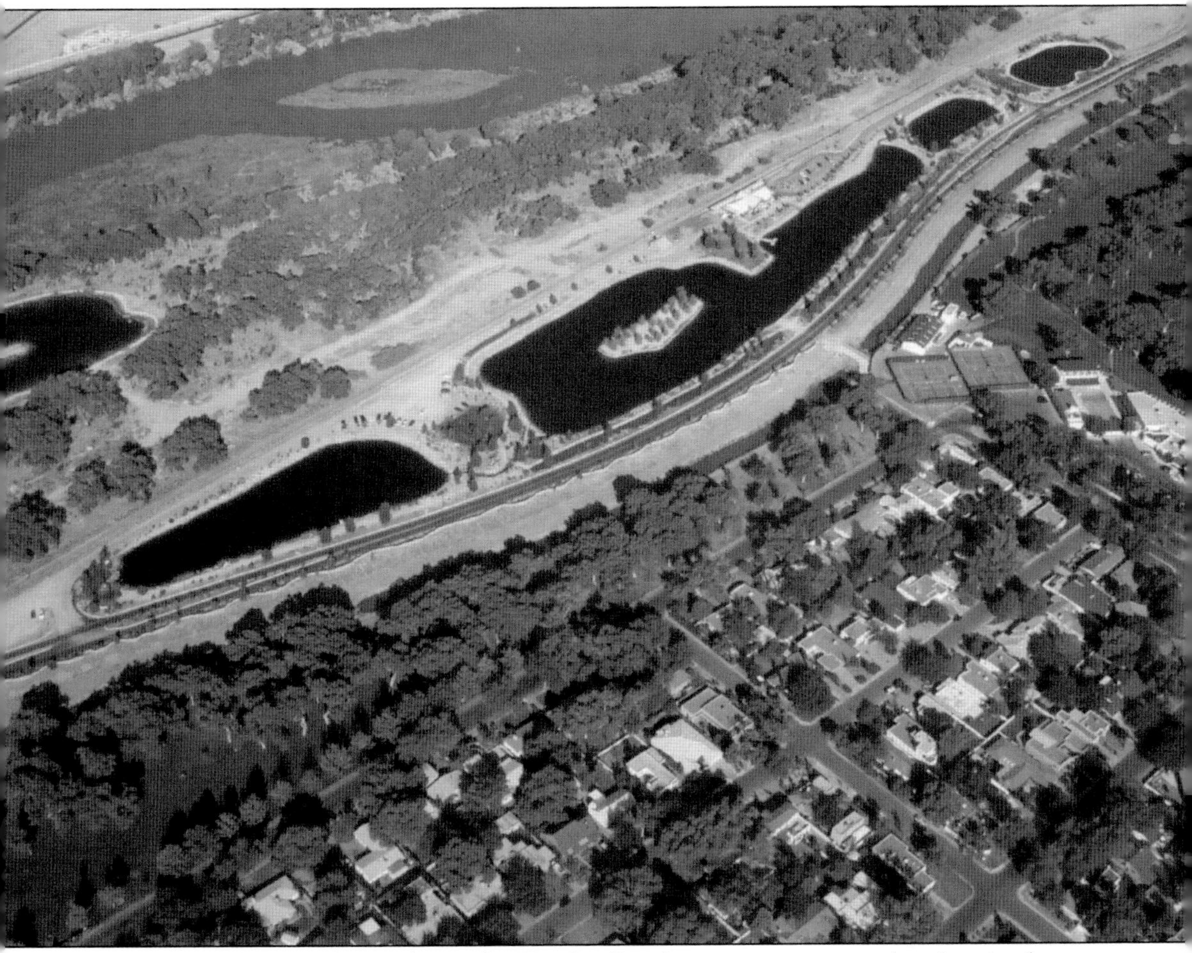

This modern-day aerial map shows the Tingley Beach reconstruction undertaken in the past decade, as well as portions of the cottonwood bosque, Albuquerque Country Club, and Rio Grande Zoo. The Huning Castle Addition and adjacent Raynolds and West Park residential neighborhoods remain desirable areas today. Many current owners are remodeling older homes in the area. (Courtesy of MRGCD.)

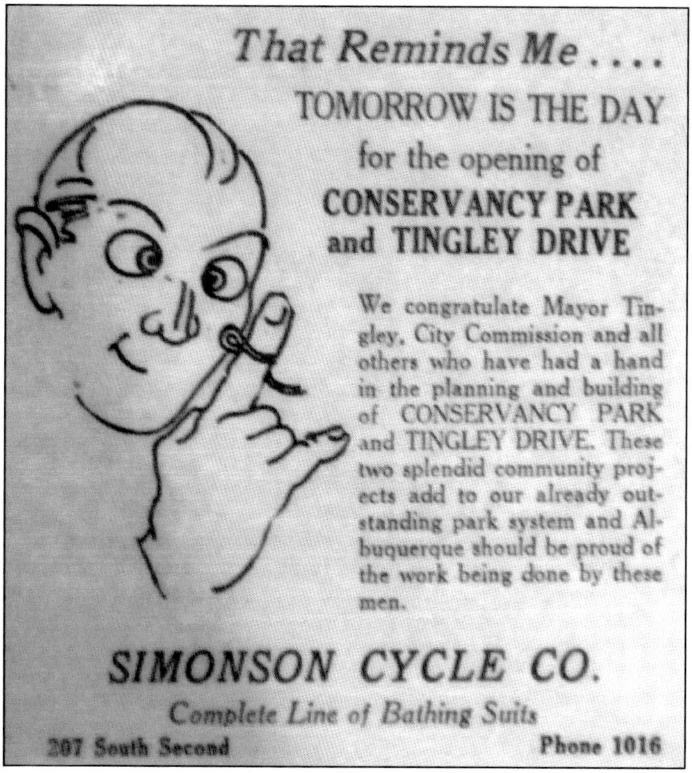

The City of Albuquerque and the Middle Rio Grande Conservancy District took advantage of the basin between the two new levees in the Huning Castle area to create what the newspapers touted as a mile-long swimming beach, which opened to the public in 1931. Local newspaper advertisements promoted the grand opening. (Both, courtesy of *New Mexico State Tribune* archives.)

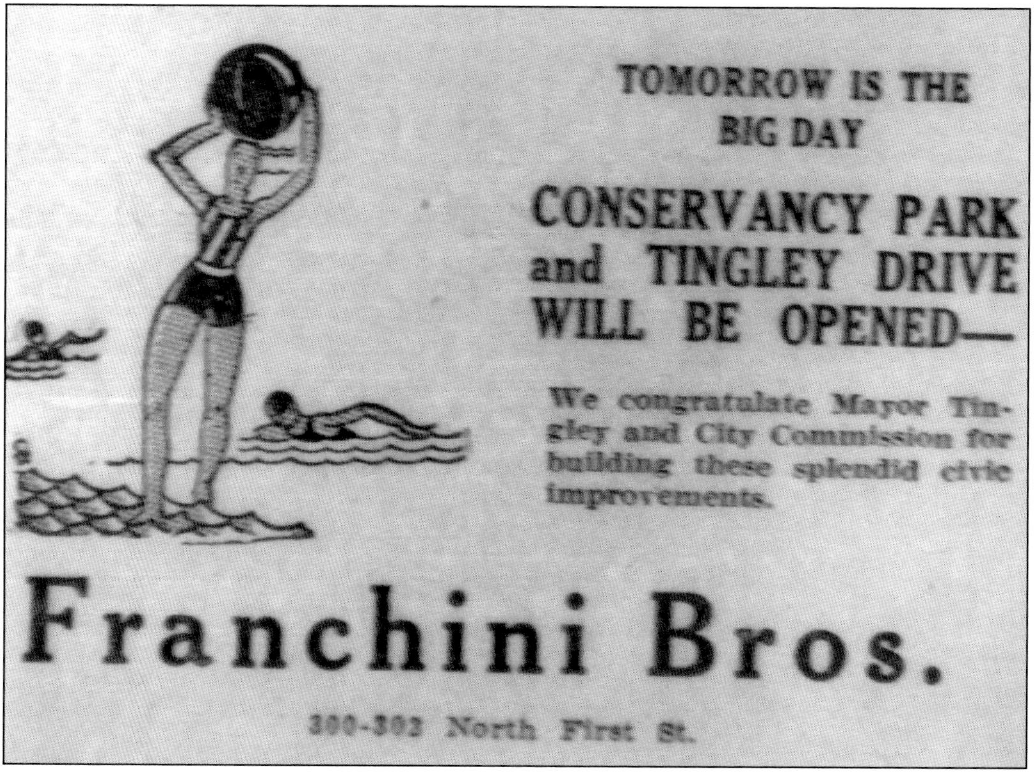

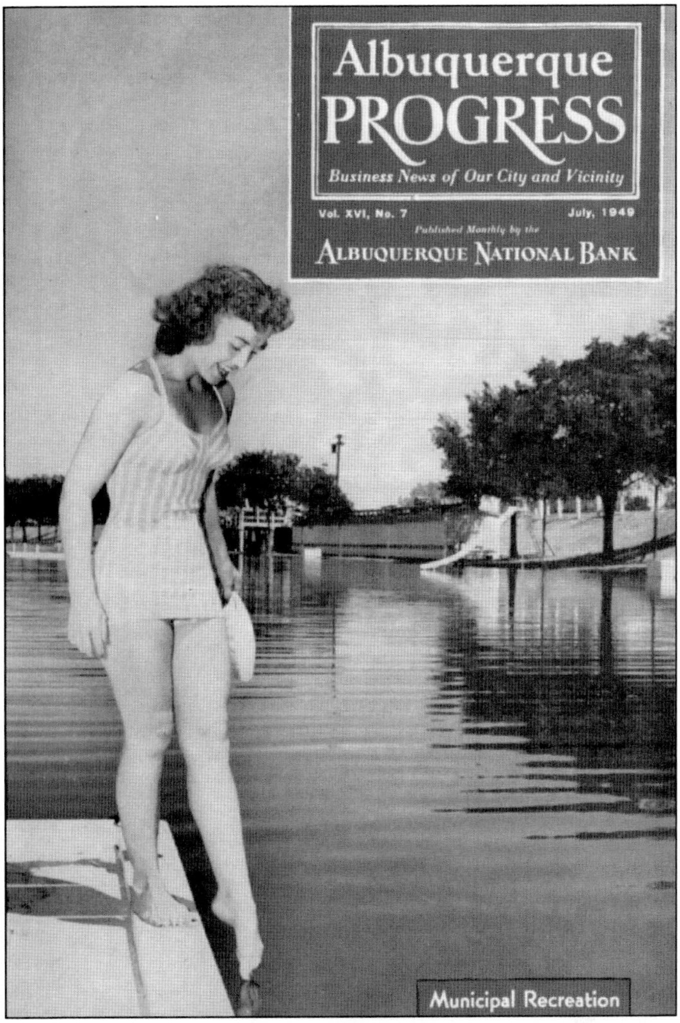

Originally called "Conservancy Beach," then "Municipal Beach," and occasionally "Ernie Pyle Beach," the swimming beach soon became better known as "Tingley Beach," honoring Mayor Clyde Tingley's role in the project. The *New Mexico State Tribune* reported the new swimming beach had a capacity for 7,000 swimmers. Beauty contests were part of the fun. (Both, courtesy of *Albuquerque Progress*.)

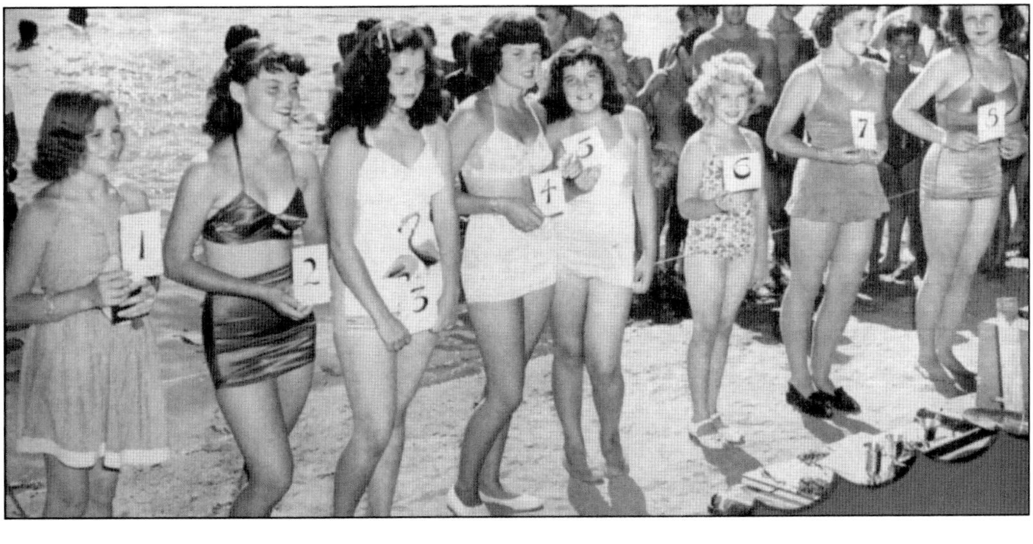

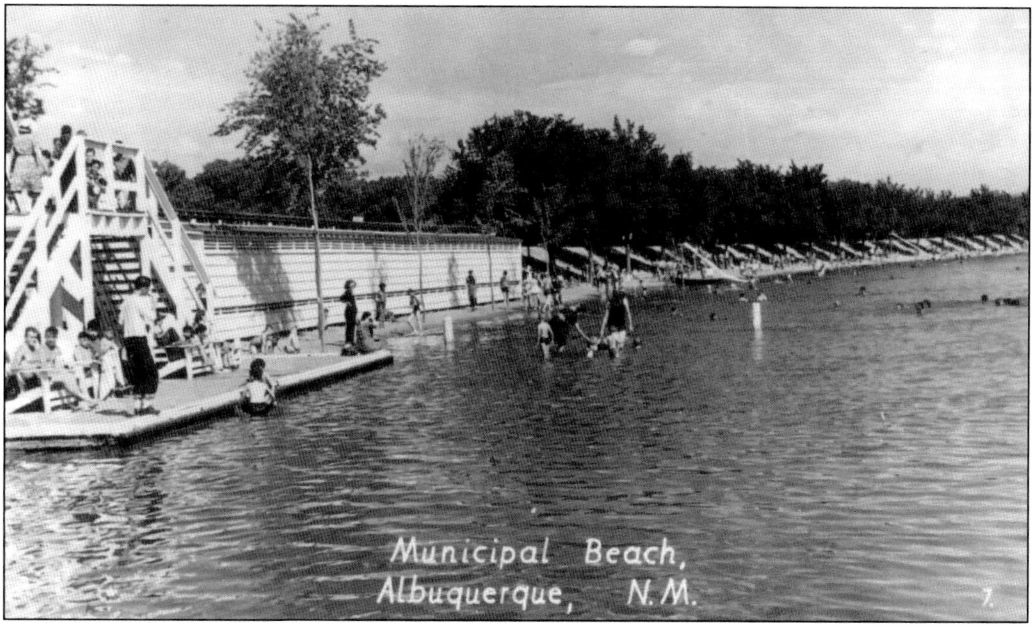

Sandy beaches attracted residents who enjoyed sunbathing as much as swimming. Water-skiing was not common, but it was possible at Tingley Beach. The swimming beach was 4,000 feet long and 400 feet wide with a maximum depth of 15 feet. (Both, courtesy Nancy Tucker.)

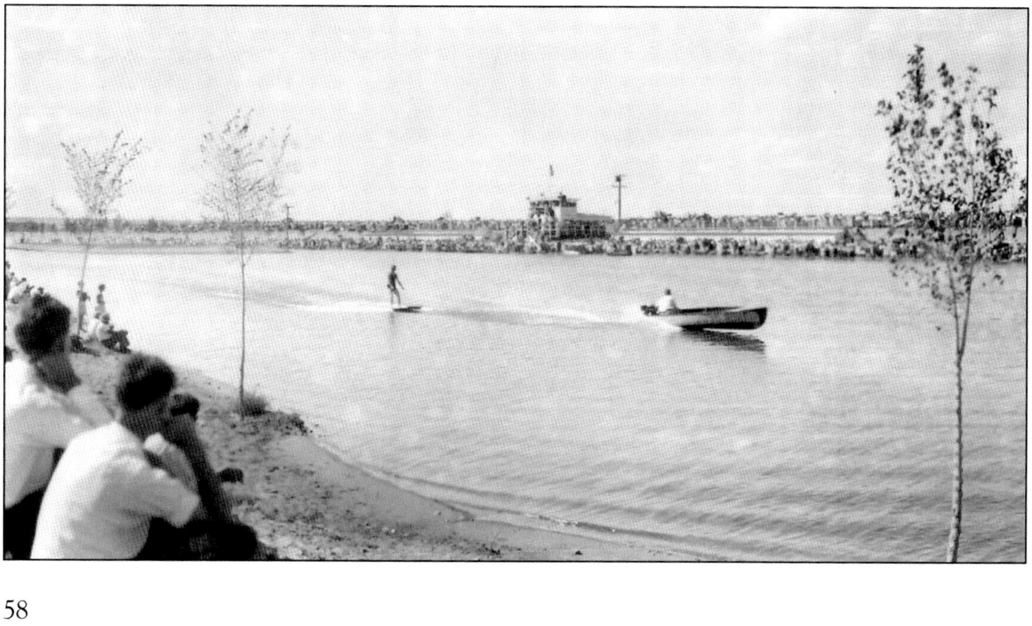

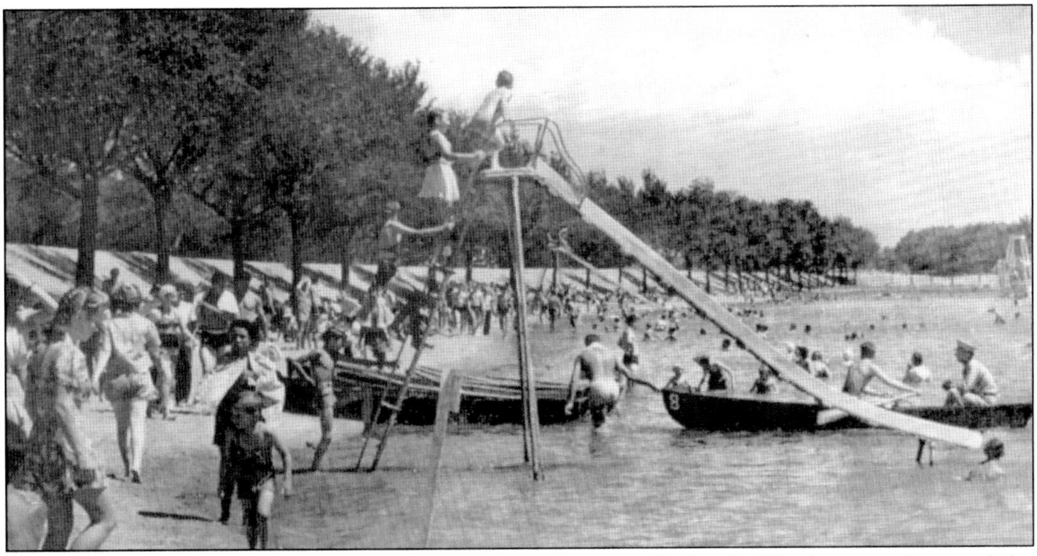

Tingley Beach featured a diving platform, slides, and two small islands. The levee road around the beach enabled viewers to watch swimmers from their automobiles. (Courtesy of Nancy Tucker.)

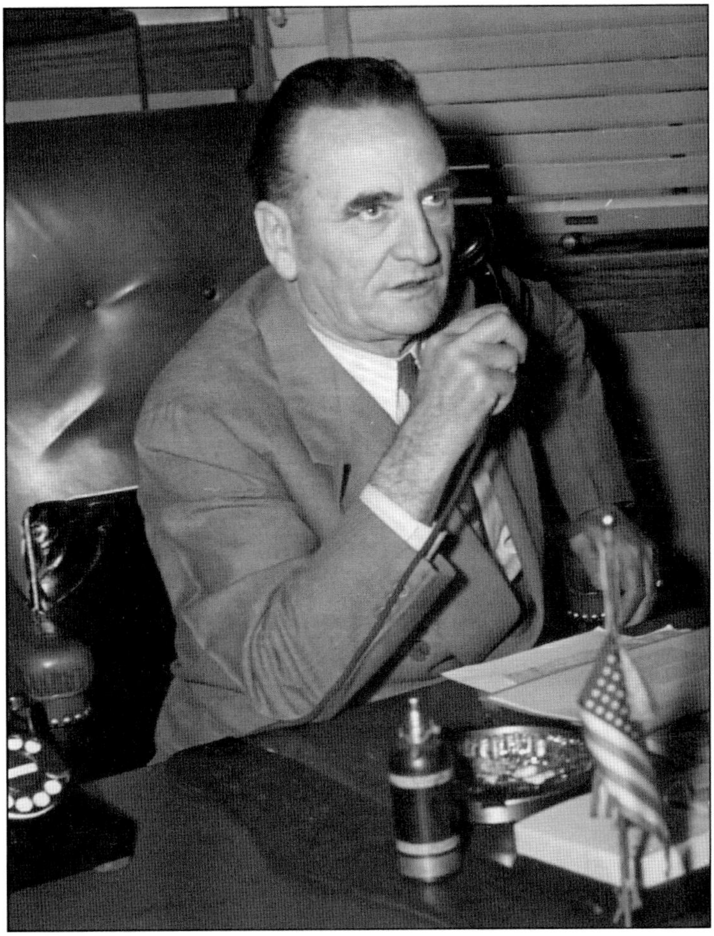

Mayor Clyde Tingley (1882–1960) christened the swimming beach in an elaborate ceremony in June 1931 by adding bottles of water from the Atlantic and Pacific Oceans sent by the mayors of Atlantic City and Los Angeles. (Courtesy of UNM CSWR, William A. Keleher collection, 000-742-0146.)

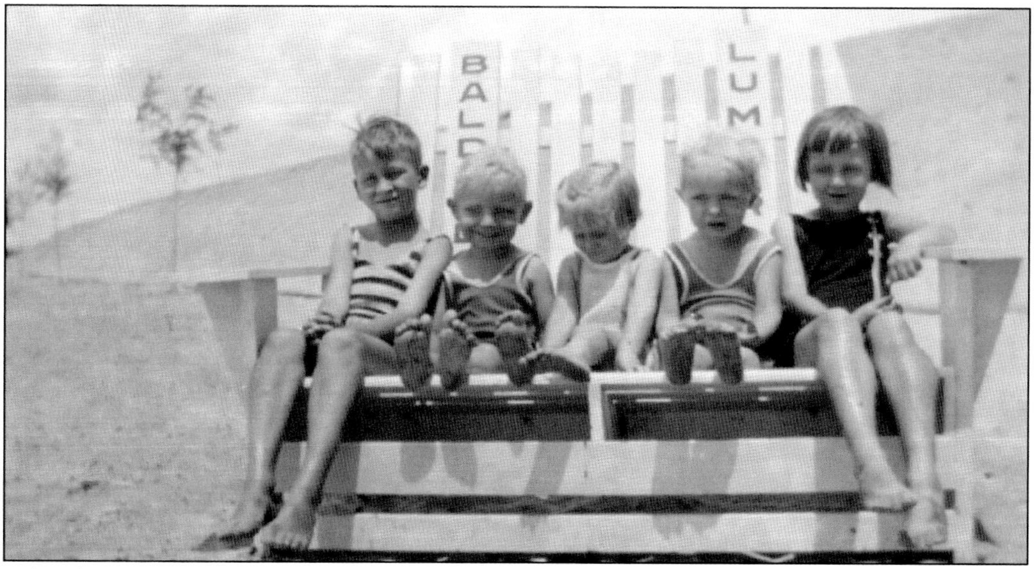

A beach of white sand 30 feet in width extended along the perimeter of Tingley Beach. It remained a favorite destination for several decades until 1951, when a polio scare closed the beach. The unidentified children enjoy a bench on the beach provided by Baldridge Lumber. (Courtesy of Historic Albuquerque, Inc., from the album of Marie Balling Milne.)

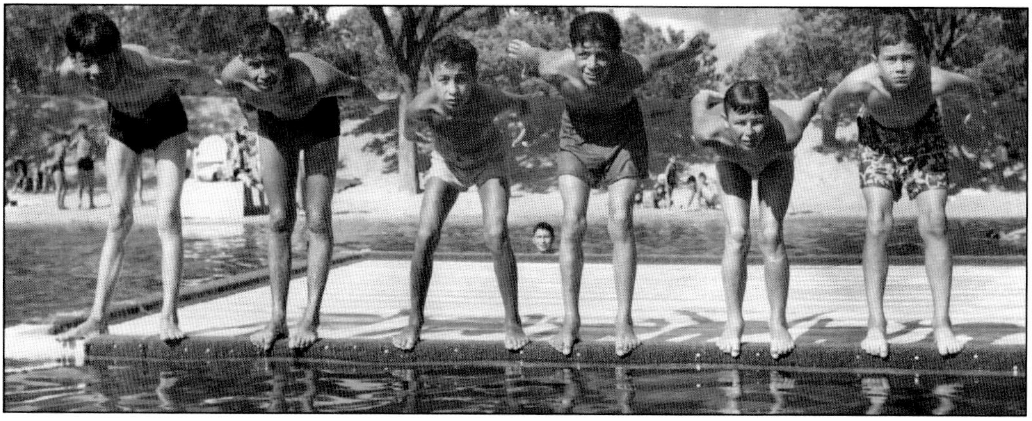

Young divers identified as lifeguards enjoyed the heyday of Tingley Beach in the 1930s and 1940s. By the 1950s, the grounds were in disrepair. Renovation came again in the early 2000s with fishing ponds, wetlands, a bike trail, and even a small train connecting the BioPark's zoo and aquarium via Tingley Beach. Today, however, swimming is not permitted, although paddleboats may be rented. (Courtesy of Albuquerque Museum Photograph Archives.)

Six

The Albuquerque Country Club

Gravel to Grass

Local boosters who felt a golf course was an amenity that would help attract new residents to Albuquerque founded the Albuquerque Country Club in 1914. They built what turned out to be an unsatisfactory nine-hole course and clubhouse on land near the University of New Mexico. Because of the lack of water, the course consisted of gravel fairways, sand greens, and the occasional rattlesnake.

By the mid-1920s, advocates for a golf course and clubhouse supported the relocation of the Albuquerque Country Club to the Huning Castle neighborhood, where developers A.R. Hebenstreit and William A. Keleher were platting an upscale residential neighborhood close to the Rio Grande on property purchased from the Franz Huning estate.

Developers from the Huning Castle Addition and the adjacent Raynolds Addition donated lots to the country club that were sold to finance the construction of a new clubhouse and golf course at 601 Laguna Boulevard. The land sales, in addition to the sale of the existing clubhouse, raised enough money for the country club to purchase 148 acres of property.

Construction on the club's first nine holes started in 1928 under the supervision of John Van Kleek of the then nationally prominent golf architectural firm of Styles & Van Kleek. Greenskeeper Tommy de Baca supervised construction with five teams of horses and 88 men. The first holes were opened that same summer. The second nine holes opened the next summer, making the Albuquerque Country Club one of the first 18-hole golf courses in New Mexico.

The California Mission–style clubhouse was designed by architect George Williamson and finished in time for New Year's Eve 1928. Subsequent renovations and additions to the clubhouse were designed by several prominent New Mexico architects, including John Gaw Meem and Louis Hessleden. The club's stylish tile roofs, towers, and arched windows were an inspiration to other architects and builders as they designed and built the residential neighborhoods nearby.

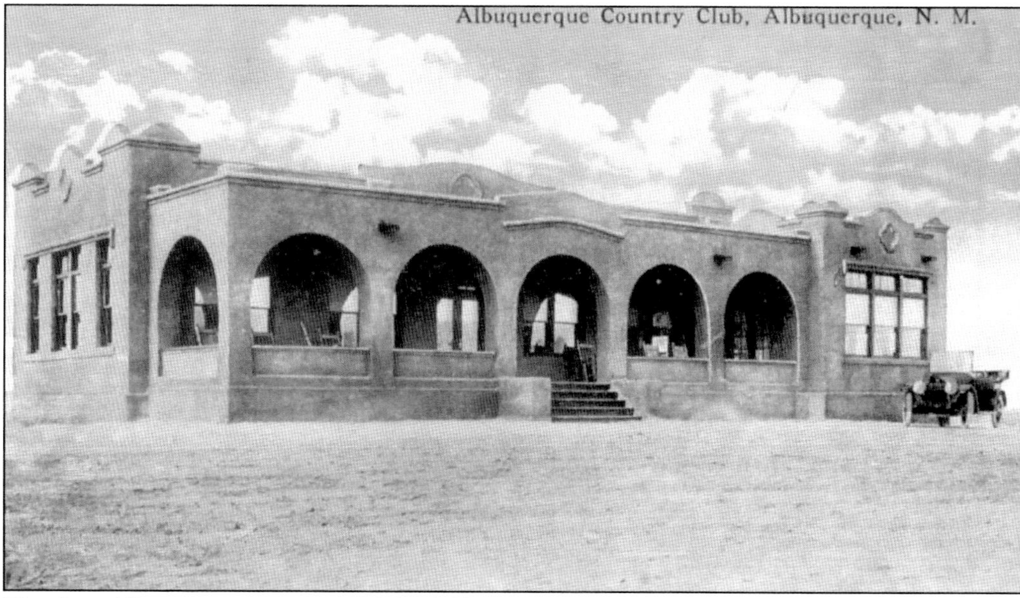

The first Albuquerque Country Club clubhouse, constructed in 1914 near University of New Mexico property, featured locker rooms, a living room, dining room, and café. The building was first sold to the Sigma Chi fraternity and eventually to the Aquinas Newman Center. (Courtesy of Nancy Tucker.)

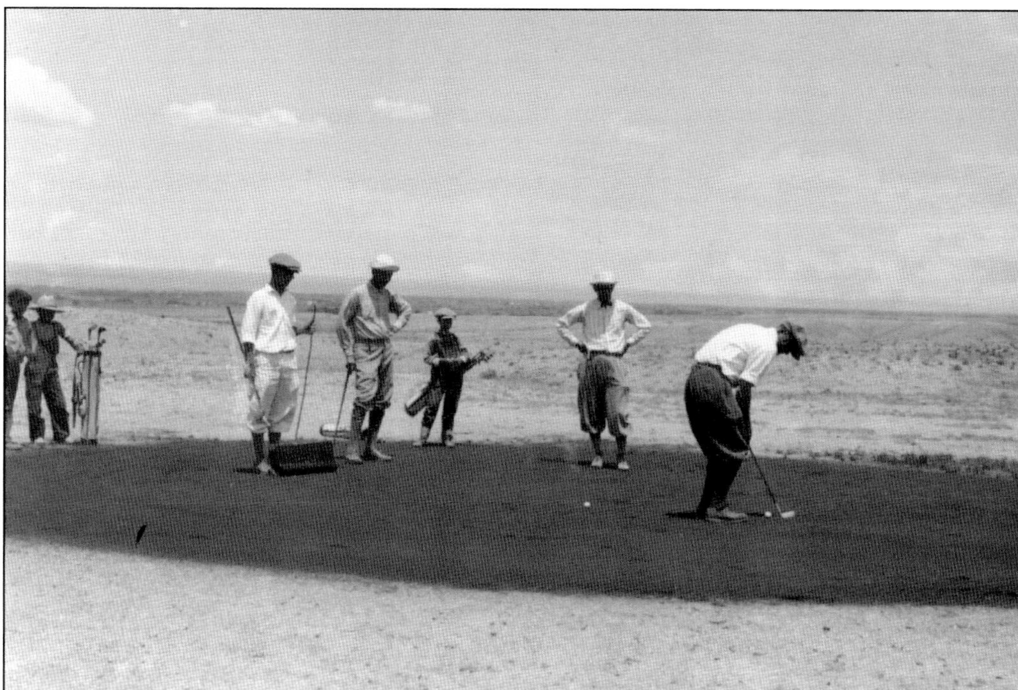

The original fairways and greens at the country club's University of New Mexico location were constructed of gravel and oiled sand. Even after the move to the new course on former Huning land, the greens were constructed of dirt from the traps, which were then covered with rolled cottonseed hulls. (Courtesy of the Albuquerque Country Club.)

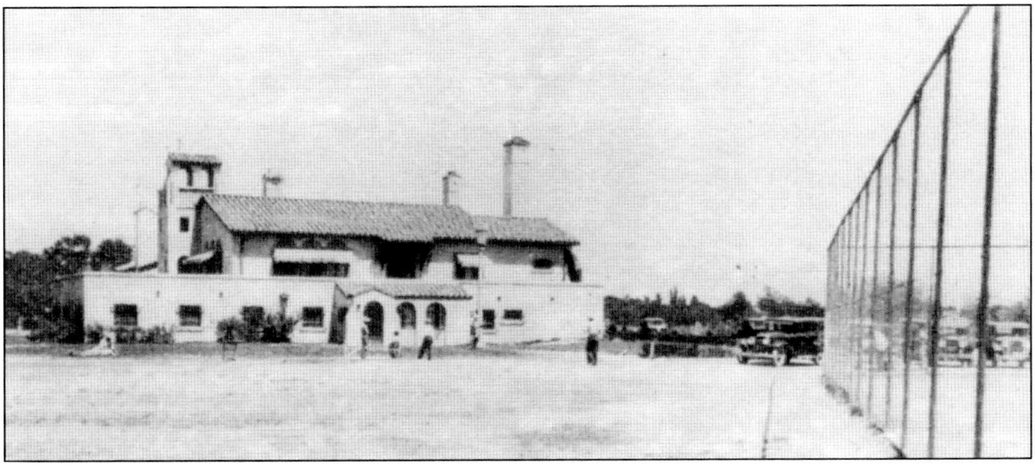

This photograph depicts the Albuquerque Country Club as it was completed in 1928. The clubhouse designed by George Williamson incorporated a California Mission style. The distinctive features were incorporated in homes throughout the neighborhood. The aerial shot from 1932 shows the clubhouse to the left of the divided-lane Laguna Boulevard. Tingley Beach is in the foreground. (Both, courtesy of the Albuquerque Country Club.)

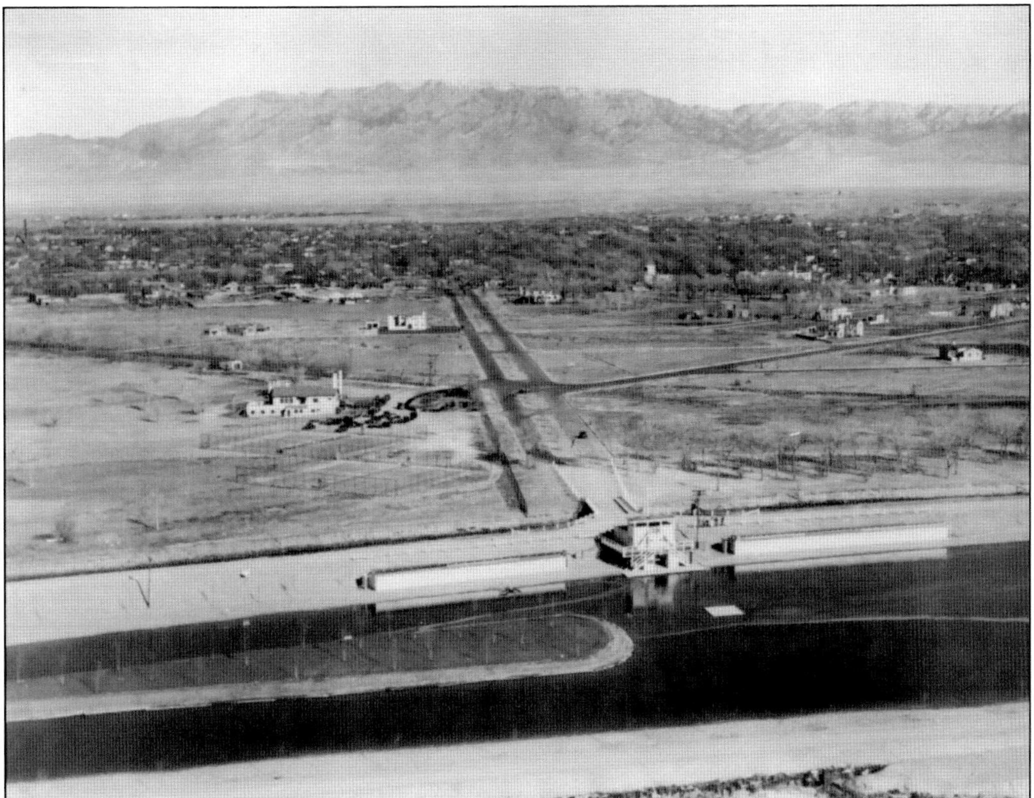

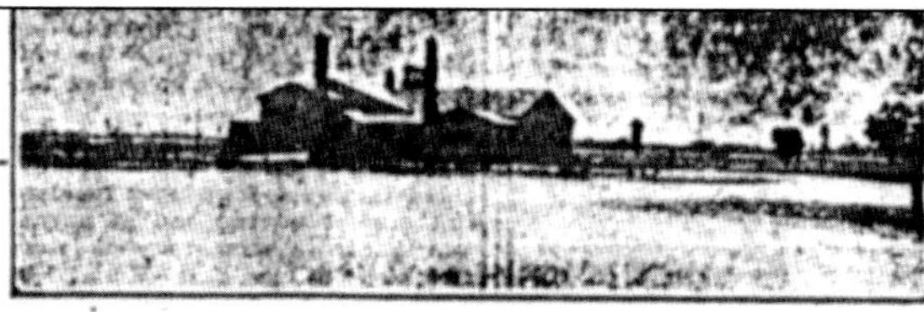

NEW COUNTRY CLUB

Specialists Who Created This Unique Structure

General Building Contract

Edward Lembke Co.

Vell known in Albuquerque as builders of arge and small buildings, whose experince covers all types of architecture, and vhose advice is worth while in all matters f construction.

Roofing by

Edward Sackett

Notice the pleasing effect of the modern ile roofing on the Country club building. This is a style handled exclusively by Sackett, and one that is becoming popular.

Electrical Wiring by

Huning Electric Company

he reason you see so many of the new uildings being wired by Huning is that we 're known to have all the necessary equipent and experience to do every job as it ould be done.

Heating Equipment by

Strumquist Engineering Company

A Country club must be comfortable—and this building is equipped with a Capitol Boiler that will furnish exactly the right temperature in all weather, and do it automatically.

Tile Work by

Albuquerque Tile Company

For cleanly attractiveness, what can equal tile? The examples shown at the Country club will give you an idea of what may be accomplished in your home.

Yale Locks and McKinney Forged Iron Hardware by

Raabe & Mauger Co.

The hinges, latches and locks add a characteristic touch to this Spanish type club house.

Lighting Fixtures by

Walter B. Gilbert

Created in old Spanish design, made by hand of wrought iron in our shops on West Gold avenue. The modern trend to Spanish and Indian pueblo types has created a need for original adaptations in lighting fixtures worked out by our expert wrought iron craftsmen.

Dining Service and China by

Korber's China & Gift Store

Whether it's a single piece of china or equipment for a public dining room, Korber's have the facilities to offer both quality and choice.

Grading by

Shufflebarger Transfer Company

Who are equipped to take care of grading, transportation and excavation on any size of job.

This advertisement for a country club open house ran in the June 29, 1929, *New Mexico State Tribune*. The ad recognized the specialists who created the unique clubhouse: general contractor Edward Lembke Company; roofing by Edward Sackett; electrical wiring by Huning Electric Company; heating by Strumquest Engineering Company; tile work by Albuquerque Tile Company; Yale Locks and McKinney Forged Iron Hardware by Raabe & Mauger Company; lighting fixtures by Walter B. Gilbert; dining service and china by Korber's China and Gift Store; and grading by Shuffelbarger Transfer Company. (Courtesy of *New Mexico State Tribune* archives.)

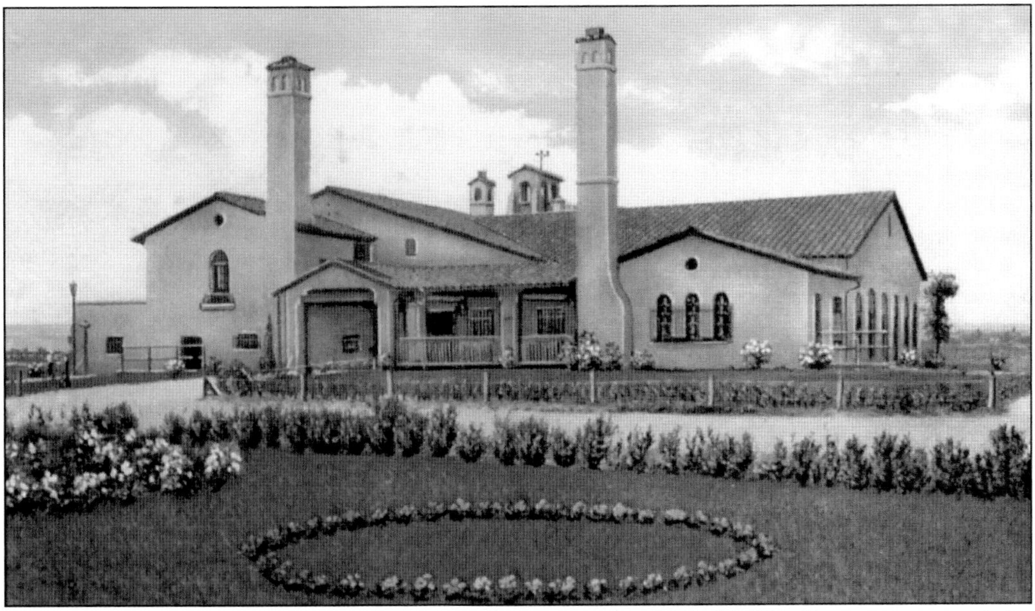

The stock market crash of 1929, the Great Depression, and World War II years impacted the country club, taking membership down to 205 members by the end of 1942. Only 176 members were paying dues; the rest were in military service. (Courtesy of Nancy Tucker.)

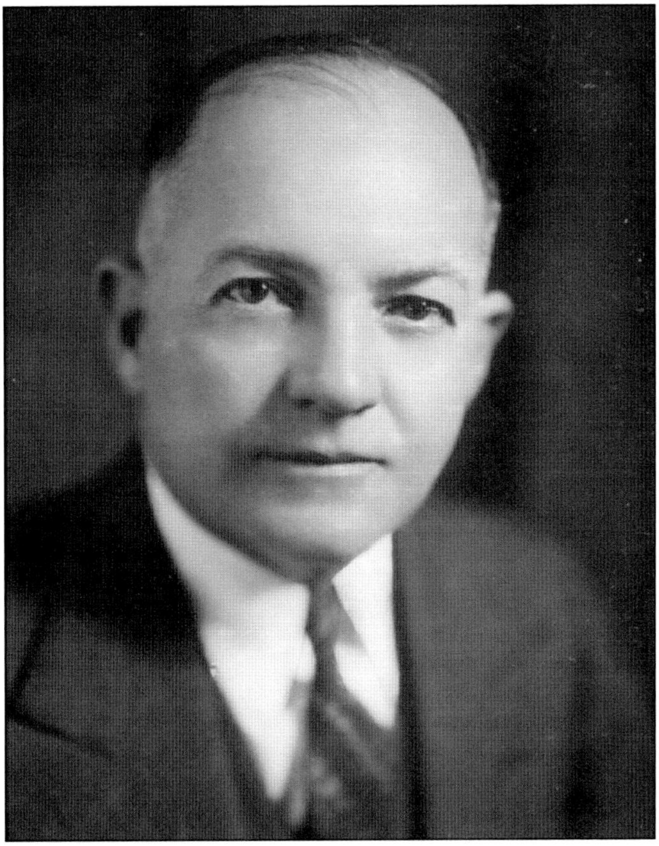

Charles Lembke was the general contractor for the country club. Lembke built many homes throughout the neighborhood and lived in one of them at 401 Laguna Boulevard until he died in 1989 at age 100. (Courtesy of Ellen Ann Lembke Ryan.)

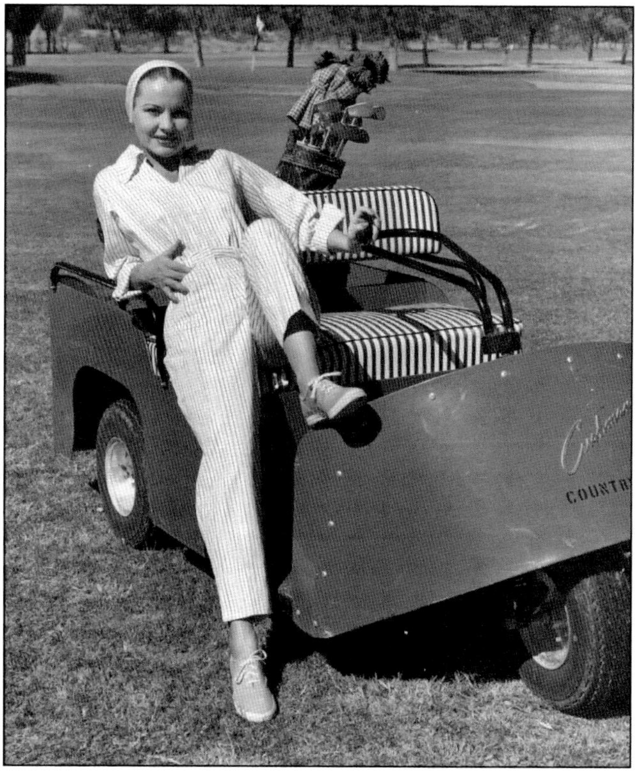

The beautiful greens of the Albuquerque Country Club were the backdrop for this photography shoot in the early 1940s featuring neighborhood resident Nancy Tonkin. (Courtesy of Albuquerque Museum Photograph Archives.)

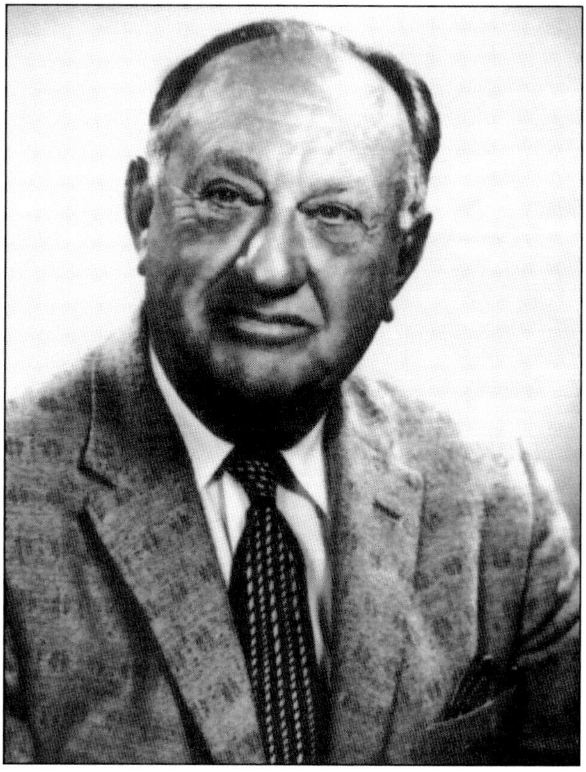

Despite the threat of war, 1941 was a time of celebration at the club. On the Fourth of July, the country club hosted a party that attracted 700 members and guests for fireworks and to watch club president Arthur Prager burn the mortgage. Prager (1890–1974) served on the club's board for many years and was president of the Southwestern Golf Association. He was the first president of Albuquerque Gas and Electric Company, later renamed the Public Service Company of New Mexico. He lived in the Huning Castle Addition at 1523 Park Avenue in the mid-1940s. (Courtesy of Public Service Company of New Mexico.)

Seven

The Huning Castle Addition

Noteworthy Homes and Citizens

Several of Albuquerque's most recent downtown area neighborhoods, including the Huning Castle Addition, took root in the sprawling acreage that once comprised the gardens, orchards, and gristmill of Huning Castle built by German immigrant Franz Huning in 1883. The mansion fronted present-day Central Avenue at Fifteenth Street SW until it was demolished in 1955. Huning's heirs began selling portions of the estate after their father's death in 1905.

Attorney William A. Keleher and former city manager A.R. Hebenstreit purchased the bulk of the property for development. The pair proved to be an effective development team and platted the new Huning Castle Addition in 1928. By the time the stock market crashed in October 1929, builder Charles Lembke had already completed the new California Mission–style clubhouse for the Albuquerque Country Club.

Hebenstreit's own home at 200 Laguna Boulevard was the first in the new development. Both the country club's new clubhouse and the neighboring homes set a precedent for an exclusive enclave that would attract some of Albuquerque's most influential businessmen and professionals. Wide boulevards and tree-filled medians became the hallmark of this neighborhood. Although the Great Depression and World War II slowed development, it soon became known as the Albuquerque Country Club area and was a notable neighborhood from its inception. The *Albuquerque Tribune* reported that the average building permit in the housing addition was more than $10,500—or twice that of permits issued in the city's other new suburbs.

Certainly, the amenities of the Huning Castle Addition were numerous. City residents were encouraged to enjoy Sunday drives to see the broad, gracefully built, paved roads with shade trees in the parkways. Promotional materials promised wide and deep building lots, adequate sanitary and storm sewers, gas mains laid to the lot lines, unlimited fresh water from new cast-iron pipelines, electric lights, telephone, and ample parks, playgrounds, and access to churches and schools.

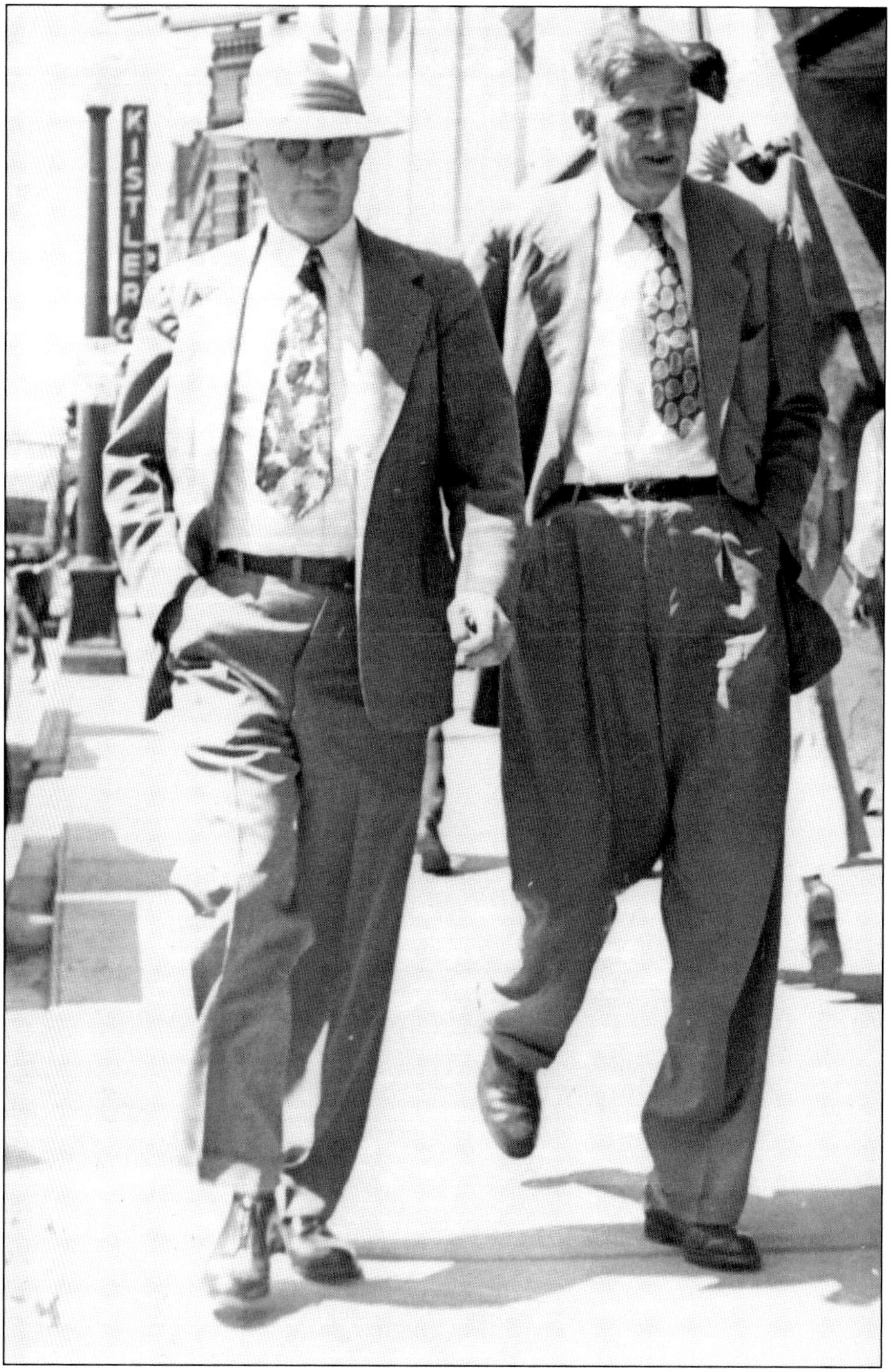

The developers of the Huning Castle Addition were, from left to right, A.R. Hebenstreit (1889–1969) and William A. Keleher (1886–1972). Hebenstreit was Albuquerque's city manager from 1918 to 1920. Keleher worked as a city editor at the *Albuquerque Journal* and, after attending law school at Washington and Lee University in Virginia, became one of the most successful practicing attorneys in New Mexico. (Courtesy of UNM CSWR, William A. Keleher collection, 000-742-0977.)

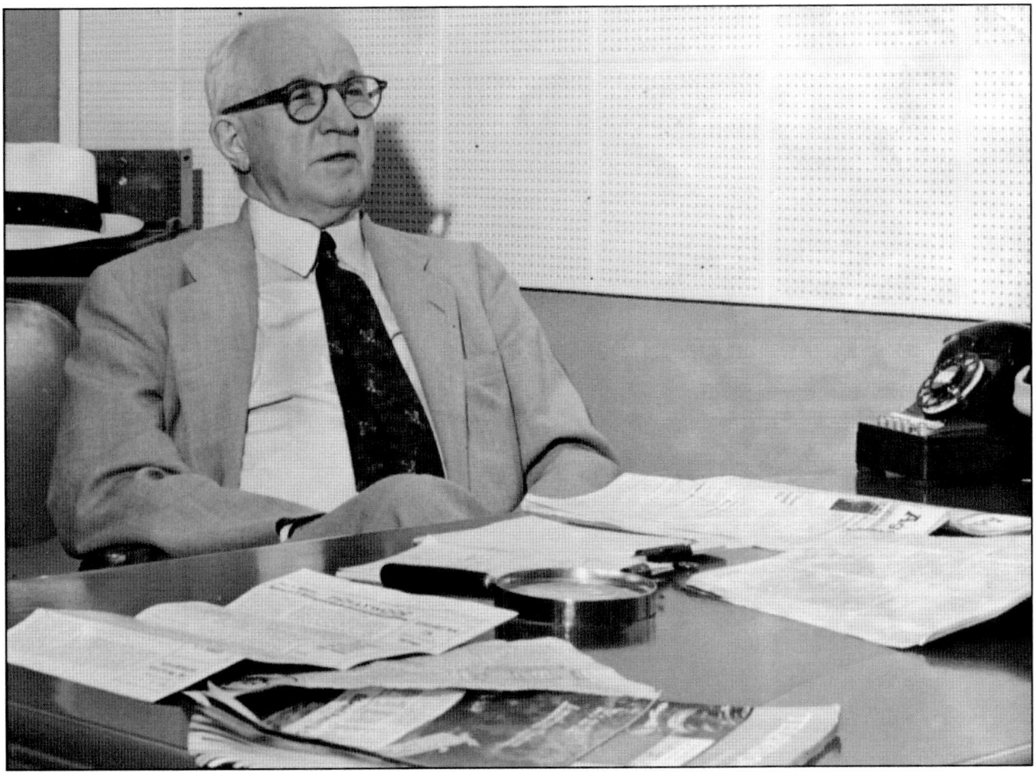

A.R. Hebenstreit moved his wife, Goldie, and young family to Albuquerque in 1918 and helped develop the city's budget system under the direction of city council president Clyde Tingley. (Courtesy of the Hebenstreit family.)

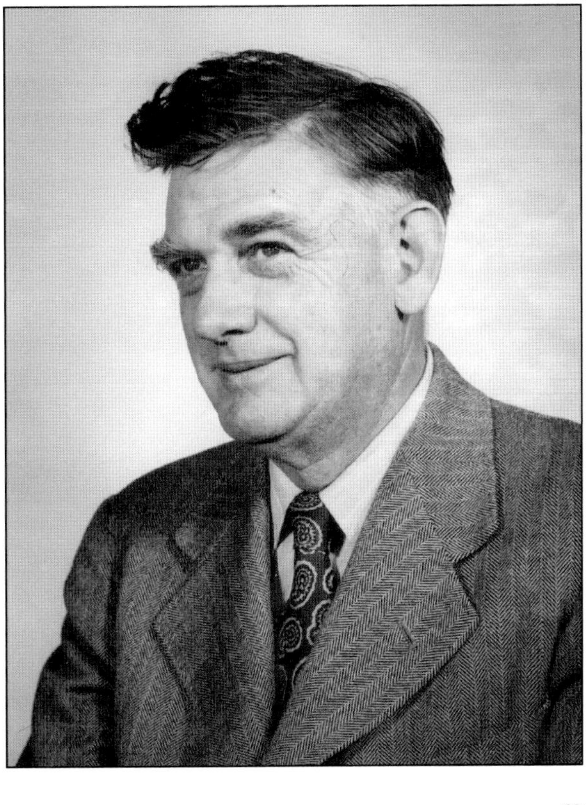

William A. Keleher not only was an attorney and developer but was also a well-recognized author with a love of historical research. Among his five books about New Mexico are *Maxwell Land Grant*; *Fabulous Frontier: Twelve New Mexico Items*; *Violence in Lincoln County, 1869–1881*; *Turmoil in New Mexico*; and *New Mexicans I Knew: Memoirs, 1892–1969*. Sunstone Press in Santa Fe has republished the books recently. (Courtesy of the Keleher family.)

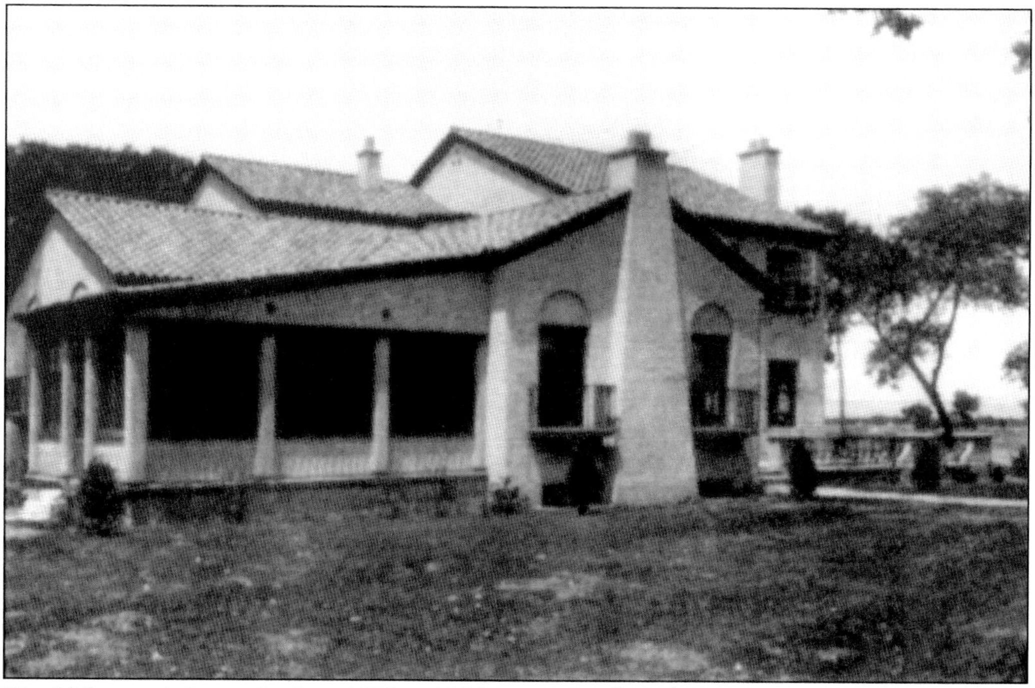

The Hebenstreit home, built in 1929 at 200 Laguna Boulevard, was 2.5 stories of stuccoed clay brick topped by a red tile roof. It was designed by the architectural firm of Gaastra and Gladding in a Spanish Baroque Revival style and constructed at a cost of about $30,000. (Courtesy of Huning Castle Neighborhood Association.)

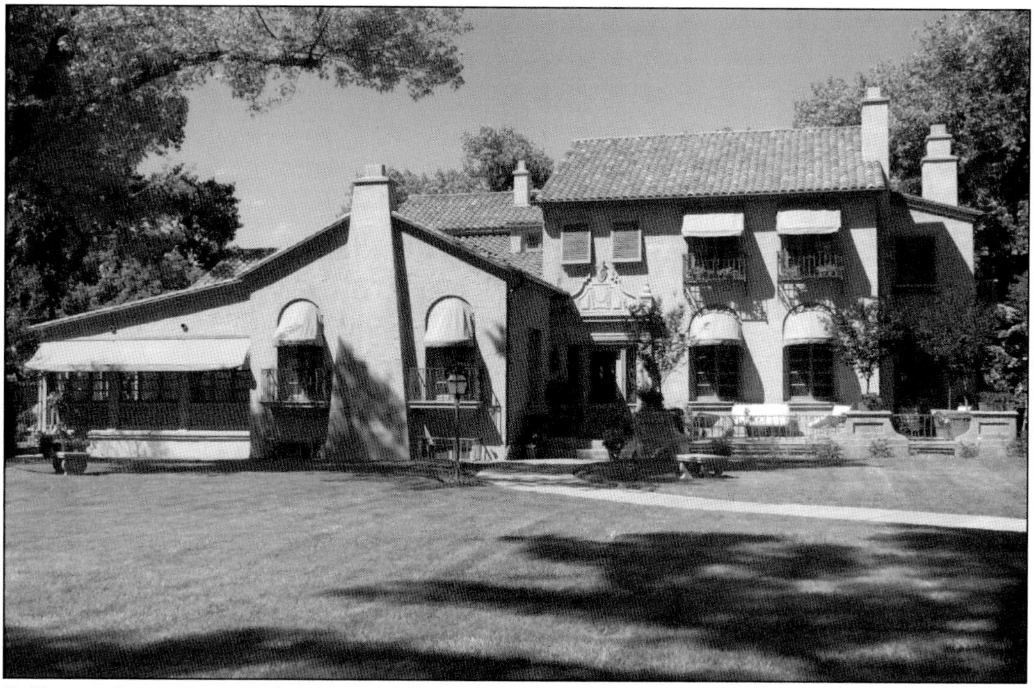

Still considered a landmark home of the Huning Castle neighborhood, the Hebenstreit house has been under the stewardship of Sheilah Garcia since 1982. (Courtesy of Judy Cook.)

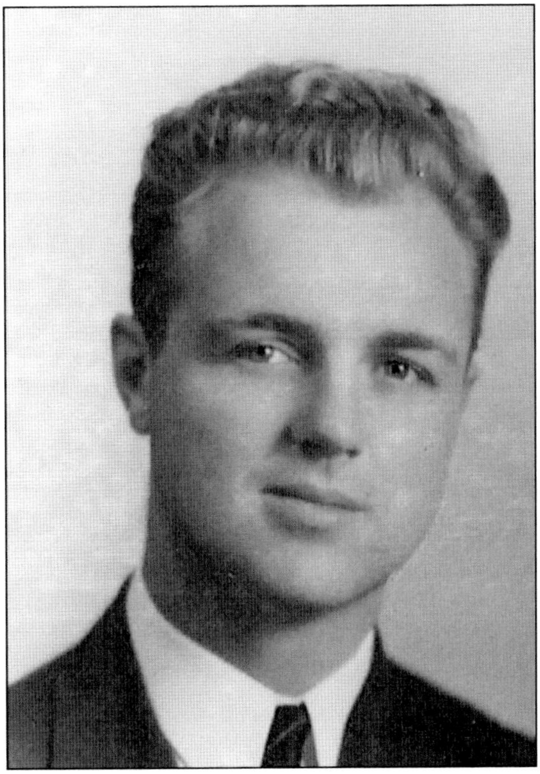

A.R. Hebenstreit's son Bruce Hebenstreit and his wife, Ann (Smith), joined forces to become a creative team of home designers and builders in the 1950s. Ann Hebenstreit was a graduate of the American Academy of Art in Chicago and brought her talents to the couple's home design and building business in the Huning Castle Addition with her use of color, interior arrangement, and selection of building materials. (Both, courtesy of the Hebenstreit family.)

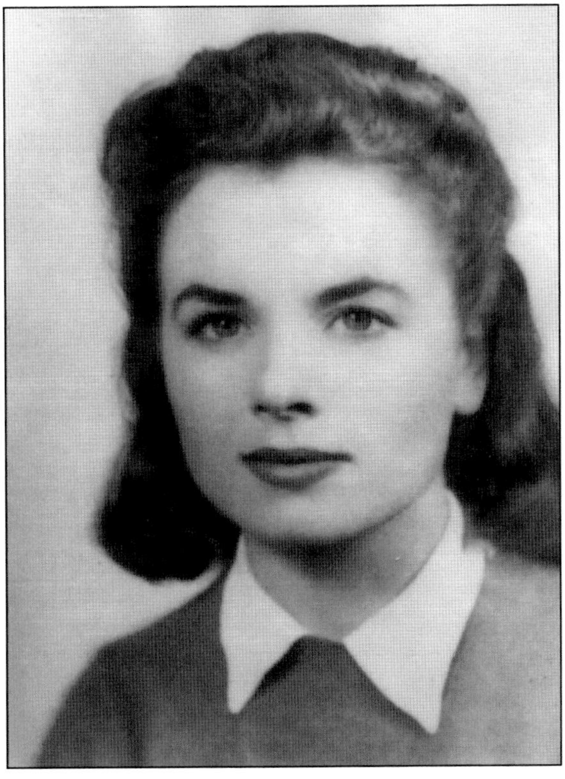

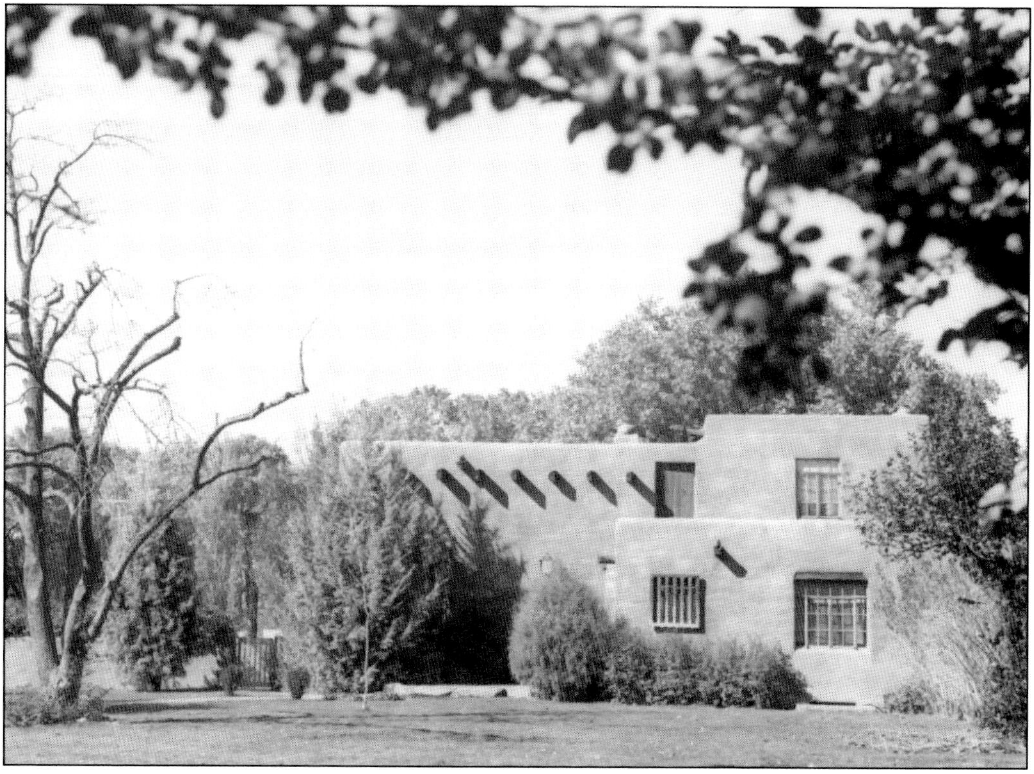

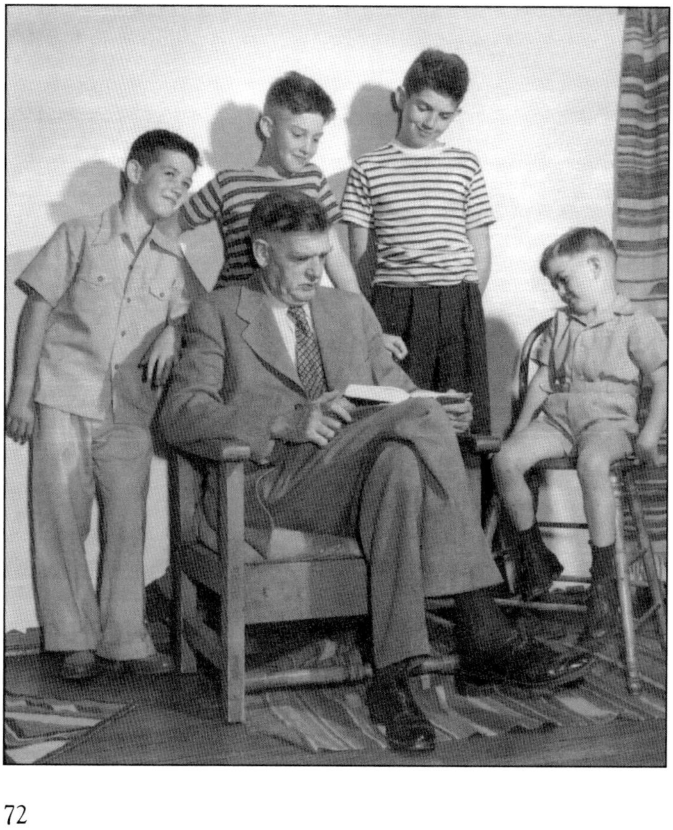

The William A. and Loretta Keleher home at 123 Fifteenth Street was featured on a family Christmas card in the mid-1930s. The home, built in 1931 by Leon Watson for $8,000, was first purchased by the With family, owners of a grocery on Mountain Road. The Kelehers purchased the home two years later. It is a fine example of Spanish Pueblo Revival style. William A. Keleher is shown reading to his sons, from left to right, John, Michael, William, and Tom. (Both, courtesy of the Keleher family.)

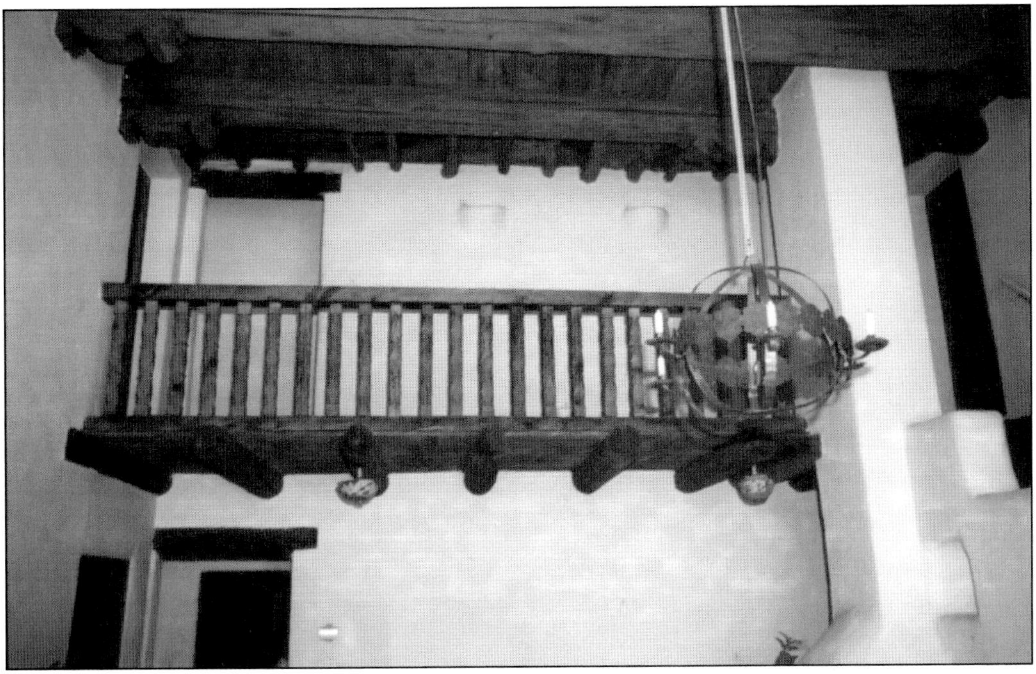

The Keleher home featured beautiful interior hand-carved woodwork, including old corbels copied from the church at Taos, pottery lamps, and (to the right) a candelabra that could be lowered by a pulley to light the candles. To accommodate his growing family, Keleher had this addition to the family home built in 1940. (Both, courtesy of the Keleher family.)

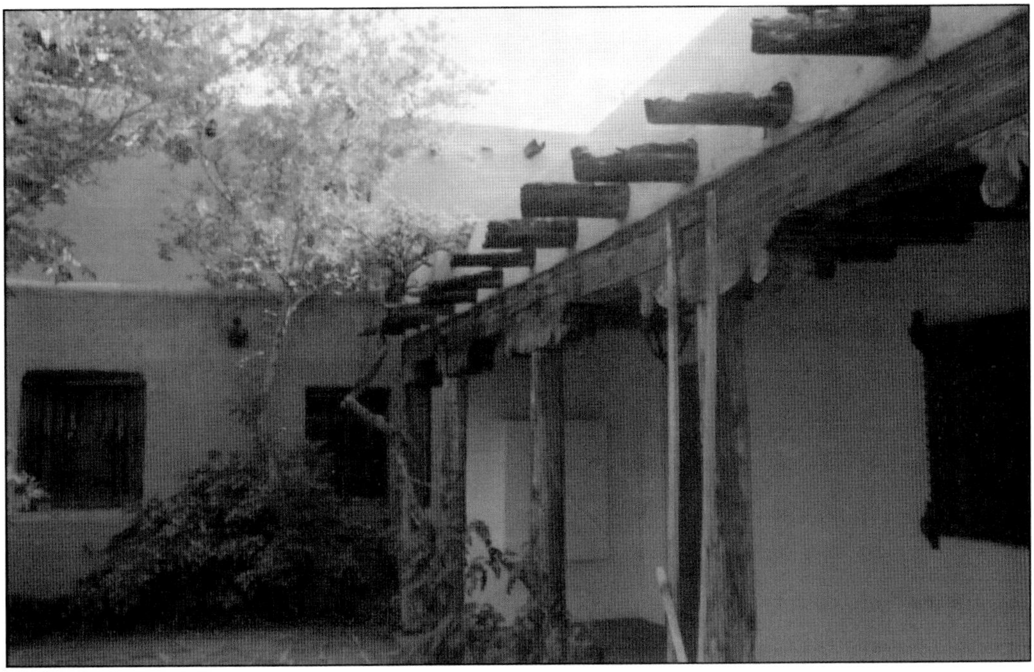

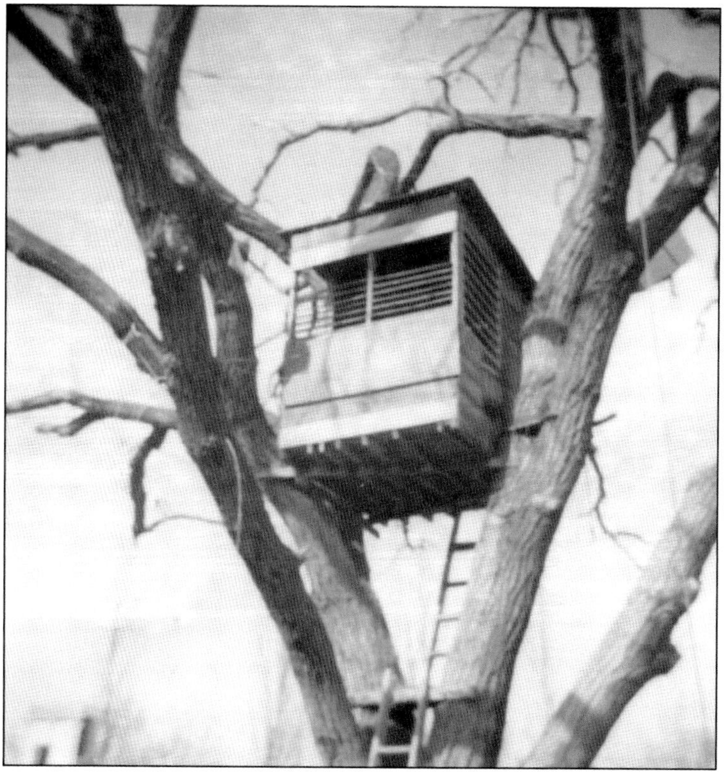

This image of a tree house, built by the Keleher brothers in their childhood, is part of the family's personal photograph album. (Courtesy of the Keleher family.)

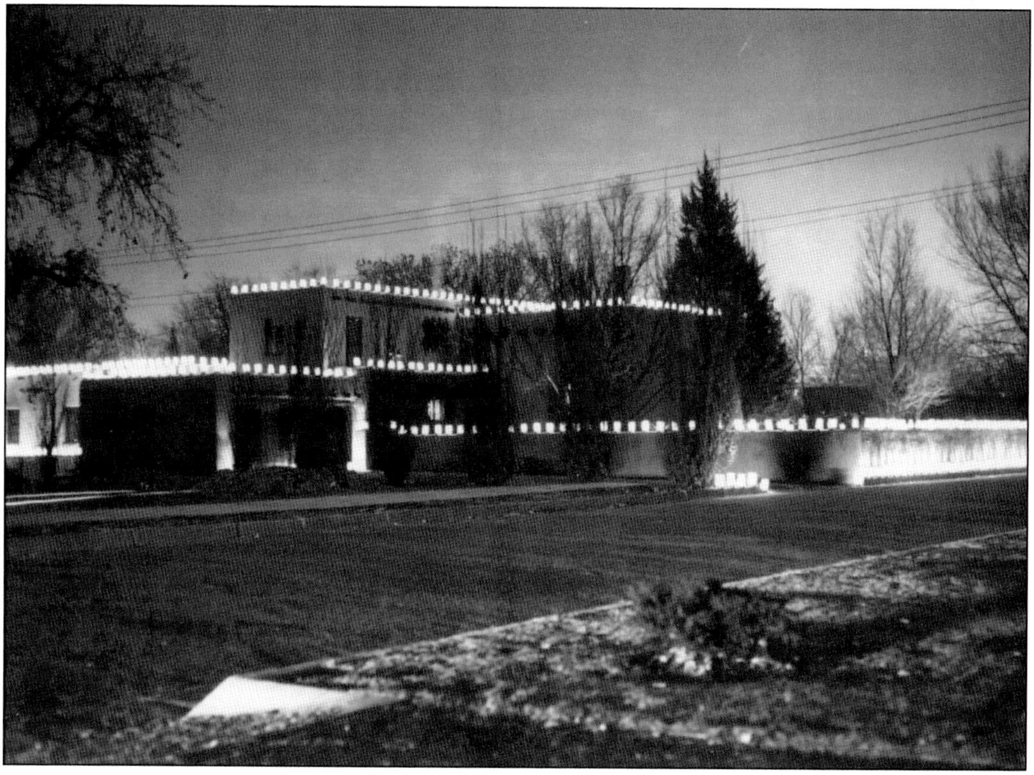

Like other homes in the Huning Castle Addition, the Keleher residence displayed luminarias on Christmas Eve, except during the war years. William A. Keleher's wife, Loretta, lived in the family home until she passed away in 2000, just a few weeks shy of her 103rd birthday. (Courtesy of the Keleher family.)

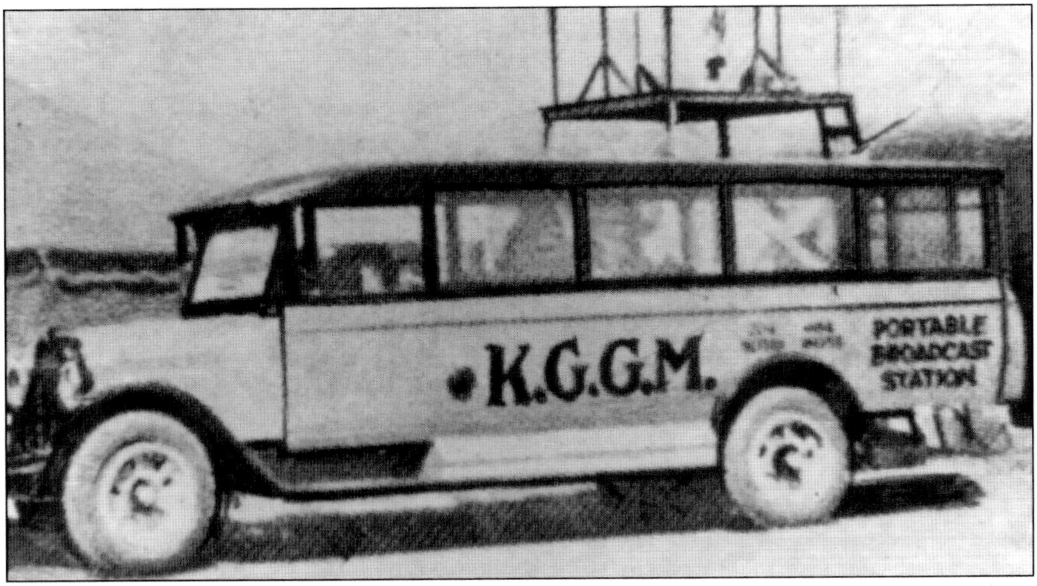

A.R. Hebenstreit founded Albuquerque's first radio station, KGGM, in 1928 after buying a broken-down radio truck that was following a cross-country footrace passing through Albuquerque. He used the new station as a means to dispel frequent criticism in the *Albuquerque Journal* about his municipal contracts for road paving and construction. (Courtesy of the Hebenstreit family.)

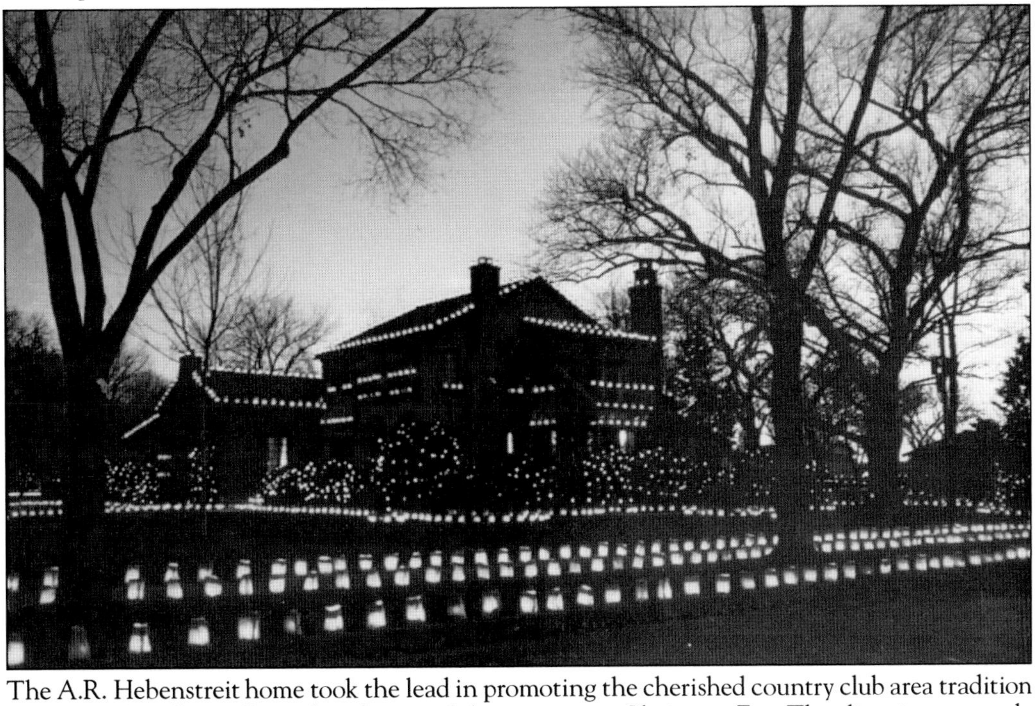

The A.R. Hebenstreit home took the lead in promoting the cherished country club area tradition of lining sidewalks, walls, and rooftops with luminarias on Christmas Eve. The glittering spectacle of twinkling votive candles secured and weighted down in small paper bags filled with sand still brings thousands of visitors to the country club area and Old Town. At times, the Hebenstreit house displayed more than 6,000 luminarias and thousands of tiny electric blue lights. (Courtesy of the Hebenstreit family.)

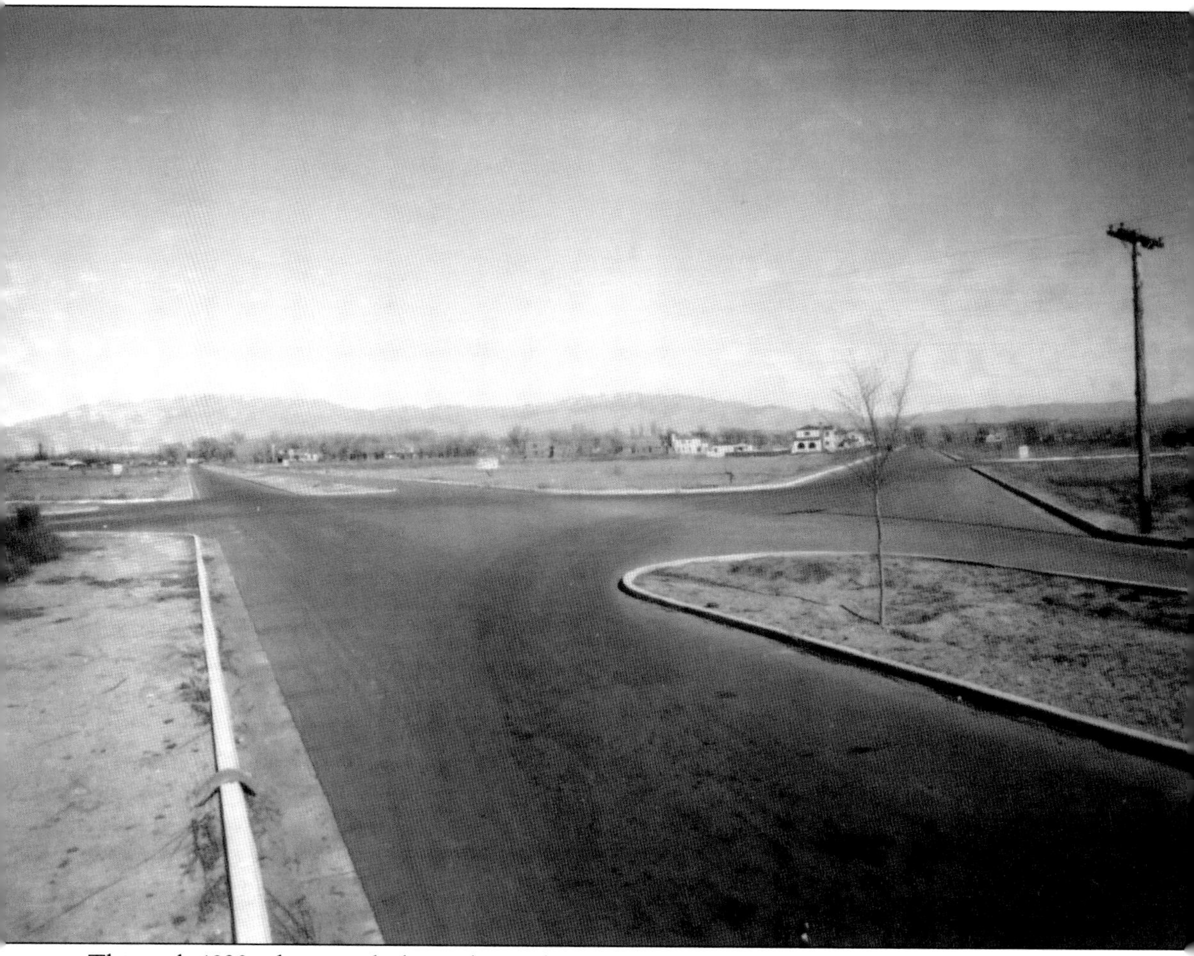

This early 1930s photograph shows the road construction to accommodate the new Albuquerque Country Club. The same general view can be seen today by standing in Laguna Boulevard directly south of the present-day clubhouse entry. A divided Laguna Boulevard runs toward Sandia Crest, and Park Avenue angles to the right. The light-colored homes in the background are believed to be the Robert Katson and Steve Dikitolia residences. Making a sharp left turn on the left side of the photograph is San Pasquale Avenue. From the addition's beginnings, the developers created large home lots and wide streets—some with medians. For some years, the Albuquerque Garden Club maintained flowers and trees in the Laguna Boulevard median. (Courtesy of Kylene Wing.)

Opposite Page: The late 1920s promised to be banner years for the Huning Castle Addition Company. Advertisements such as "It is Lilac Time in the Huning Castle Addition" touted the new neighborhood's paved streets, landscaped medians, and lush yards. "Every effort has been made to make Huning Castle Addition something entirely new in subdivisions in Albuquerque," promised this advertisement in the *Albuquerque Journal* on April 25, 1929. The stock market crash in October, followed by the war years, slowed the development. (Courtesy of *Albuquerque Journal* archives.)

IT IS LILAC TIME

In the Huning Castle Addition

Please be patient a bit longer and—

Then you will find an entirely new part of Albuquerque at your disposal. South of Central avenue and west of Fourteenth street, you will soon find that the Huning Castle Addition will be ready to welcome you. Paved streets and all other improvements that go to make up a most modern, most desirable residential district.

More than a half century ago, Franz Huning, one of Albuquerque's first settlers, selected for his home a large tract of land on what is now West Central avenue, west of Fourteenth. Here he built the Huning Castle, one of the show places of the city. Here he planted trees and shrubs and grew flowers, demonstrating the fertility of the soil and the agricultural and horticultural possibilities of the grounds.

Huning Castle Addition is carved out of the original Huning Castle grounds. City planners have laid out the streets and avenues according to 1929 ideas. There are no alleys in the addition, but each lot is wide enough to permit a driveway from the front for the accommodation of motor cars. The lots are so platted that each owner will receive and enjoy a maximum of freedom and comfort.

Streets are wide and have good lines. Every effort has been made by the designers to get away from cut and dried ideas in subdividing, to offer home builders something in the way of a lot that will afford them joy and happiness for years to come. The predominating thought has been to make available for home builders a district in which residences may be constructed not only for use and enjoyment for a year, or a few years, but for many, many years. To that end engineering problems have been most intelligently handled. Because of that, most stringent restrictions have been inserted in deeds of conveyance, affording to purchasers a positive, absolute declaration and covenant that no one can build, or will be permitted to build a structure that is not in harmony with the district.

People are to be asked and invited to buy lots and build homes in the Huning Castle Addition with the express understanding that commercial ventures are prohibited and will not be tolerated. People are to be invited to make their homes in the Huning Castle district with assurance that they may plant trees and put in lawns and beautify their premises as a permanent proposition.

Every effort has been made to make Huning Castle Addition something entirely new in subdivisions in Albuquerque. The owners of the addition reached the conclusion that Albuquerque was ready now to get into the big city class in the way of subdivisions, and the Huning Castle Addition is the result.

Within the next two or three weeks you will be able to drive west from Tenth street on Park avenue straight through the Huning Castle Addition to Albuquerque's new and beautiful Country Club. Central avenue is being paved west from Fifteenth street to a point where it intersects with Laguna Boulevard, and within a short time you may drive through Huning Castle Addition to the new Country Club and pick up a new road, taking you two miles south to Rio Grande Park.

Atmosphere for a home place means something. Environment means something. Atmosphere plus environment mean almost everything. Huning Castle Addition will offer everything worth while to a person thinking of a new home. Think it over. You wish to live in a place where you will be happy. You will be happy in the Huning Castle Addition.

Huning Castle Addition Co.

A New Mexico Corporation

Owners and Developers of the Huning Castle Addition, Albuquerque's Newest, Most Desirable Subdivision

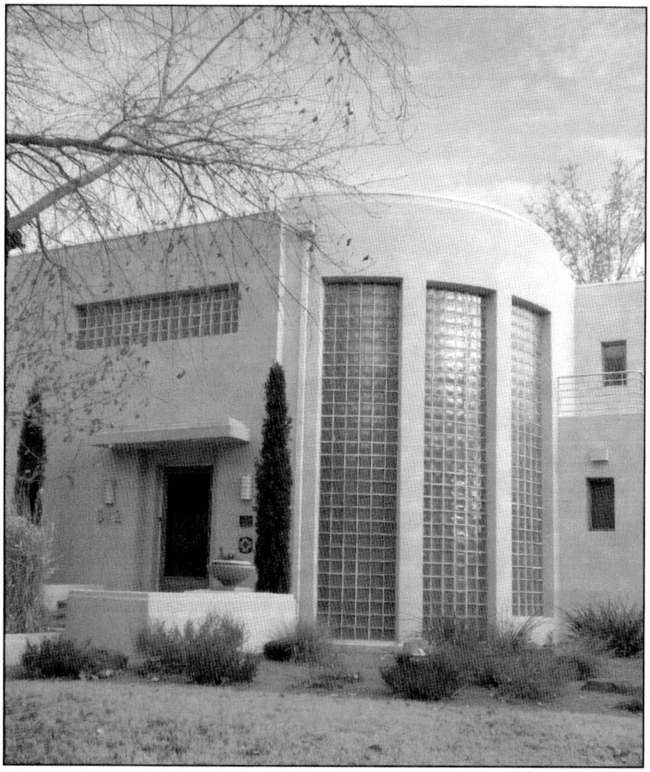

Built for $15,000 by contractor Charles Lembke, also its first occupant along with wife "Bunnie" and family, the Lembke home at 312 Laguna is notable for its Moderne International style that features a bank of glass brick windows to illuminate the staircase. It was designed by Townes and Funk of Amarillo, Texas. Later owners included Dr. and Mrs. Harrison Brehmer and then the Franklin Bond family. (Photograph by the author.)

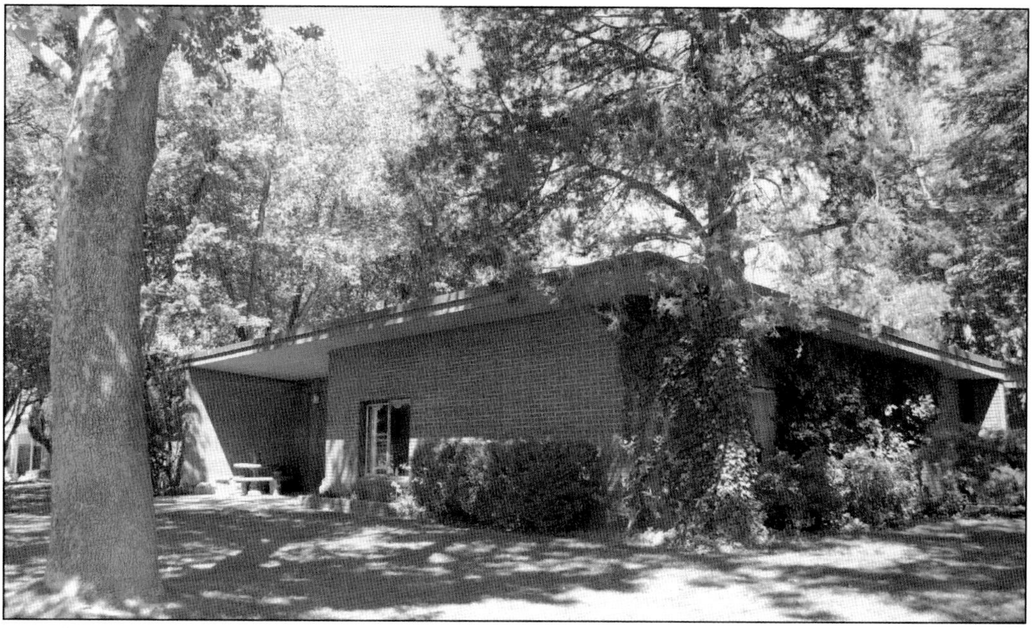

Charles Lembke got his start in the construction business with his father, Edward. He built dozens of homes in the neighborhoods around the country club. The brick home with a sloping, butterfly-like roof at 401 Laguna Boulevard was his personal home when he died in 1989 at age 100. The home was designed by Jason P. Moore of the Max Flatow office in 1954. (Courtesy of Judy Cook.)

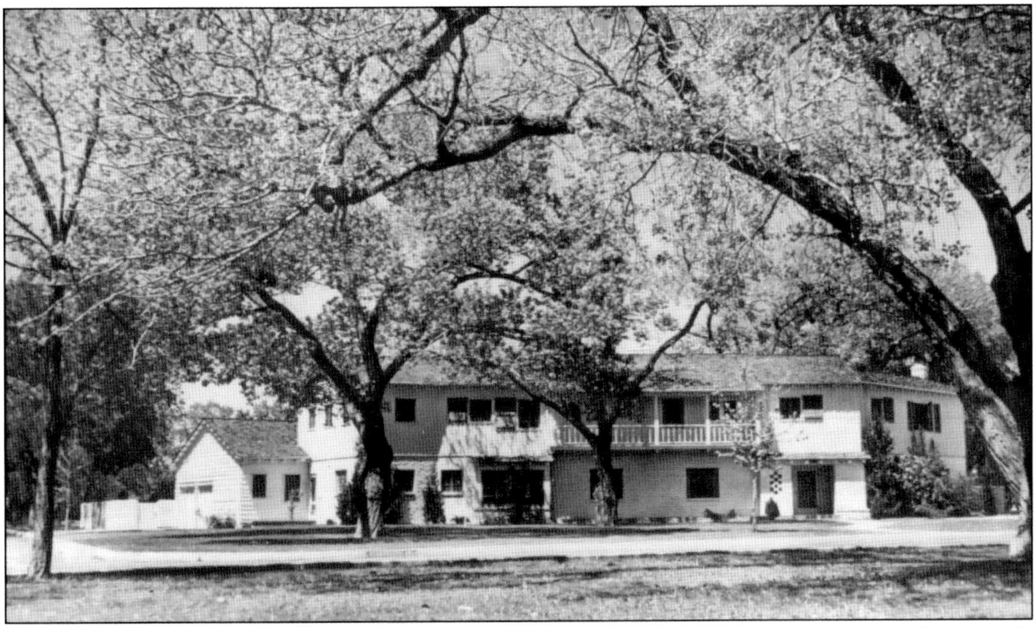

James Oxnard and his wife, Edna, were moving into their large 14-room home at 215 South Sixteenth Street in July 1941 on the very day their daughter Caroline was born. Like many fine, older homes in the neighborhood, it was designed by architect Tom Danahy. Oxnard was president of Aircraft Holdings, Inc., and a primary investor and builder of the Albuquerque Airport, later known as Oxnard Field and now a part of Kirtland Air Force Base. The home has remained in the Oxnard family. The family photograph was taken on the front porch about 1943 and shows James and Edna Oxnard with Caroline. (Both, courtesy of Caroline Oxnard Meade.)

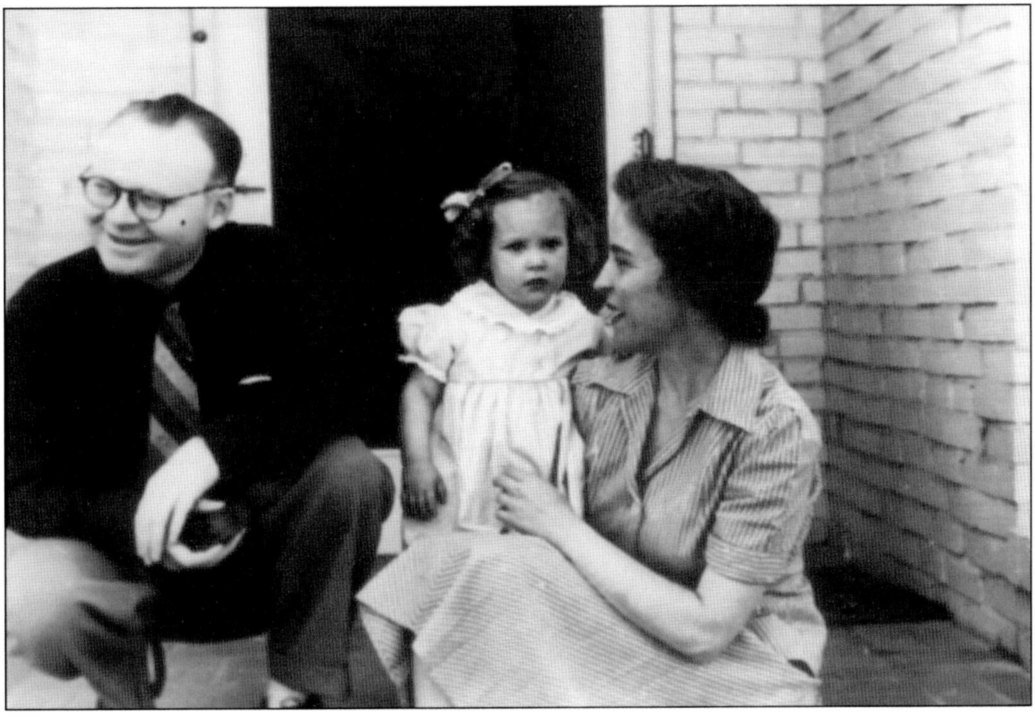

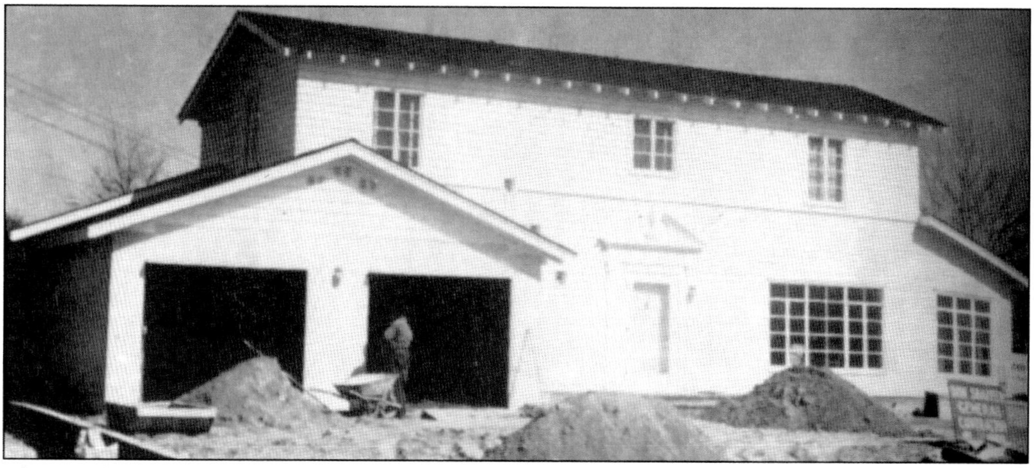

This new home at 1709 Park Avenue was being built in 1942 for Lenhart G. and Mildred Engelhart, of the Engelhart Baking Company at 115 West Gold. Architect Tom Danahy and builder Don Shaffer often worked as a team, as they did on this home. (Courtesy of *Albuquerque Progress.*)

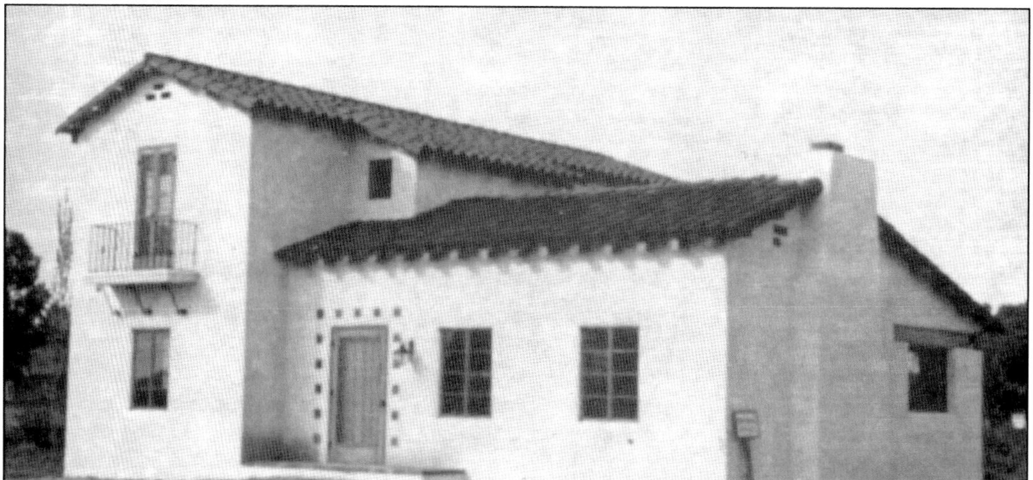

This home at 1503 Silver Street was built in 1939 for Robert and Louise Wigeley. Many neighborhood homes have had remodeling work, but most are easily recognizable and try to adhere to the original style. Wigeley was a branch manager for the fire department's adjustment bureau. (Courtesy of *Albuquerque Progress.)*

The Dr. J.J. Garduno home at 1608 Los Alamos Avenue SW is a Spanish Moorish style typical of the homes that builder Leon Watson had been building in Miami, Florida, prior to moving to Albuquerque. The home was built for $4,200 in 1930 and is decorated each year for Christmas Eve. Extensive ironwork and a spiral design create a memorable staircase. By the early 1940s, Leon Watson advertised as a designer and builder of air-conditioned, low-cost adobe homes with monthly payments as low as $25. (Both photographs by Barry Kirk, courtesy of owners Barry Kirk and Kylene Wing.)

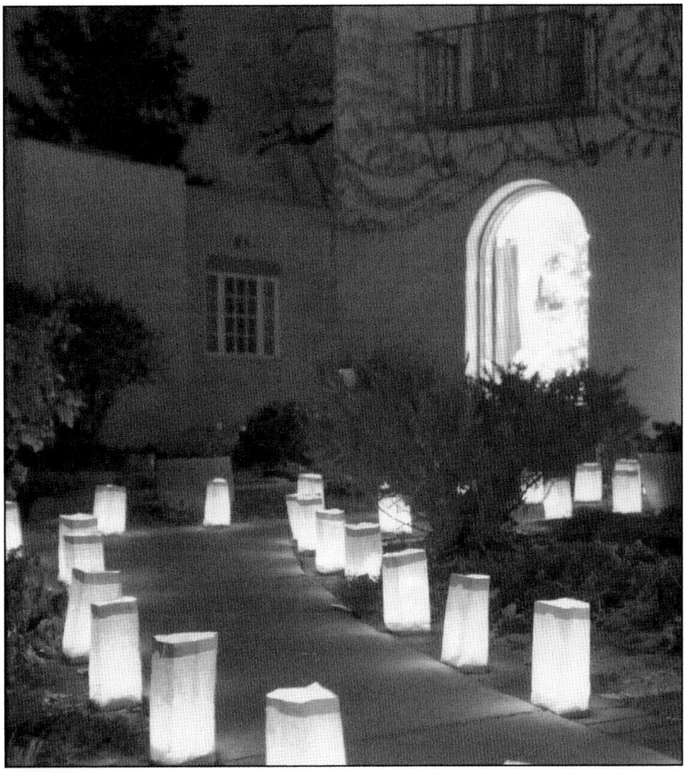

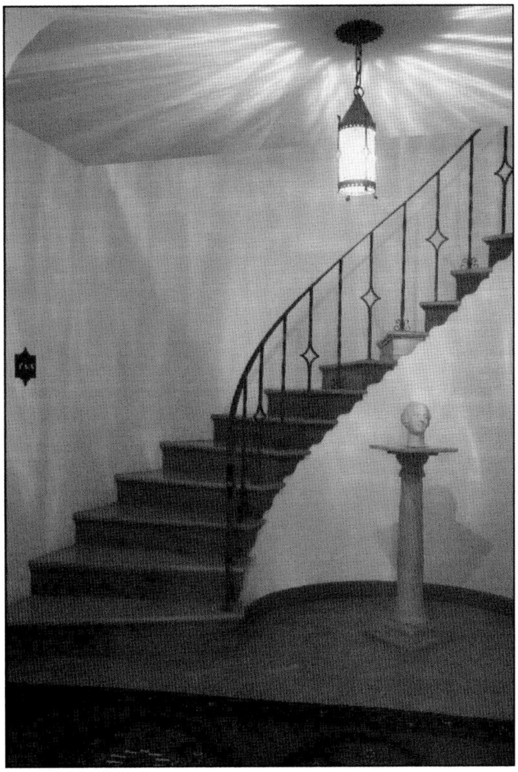

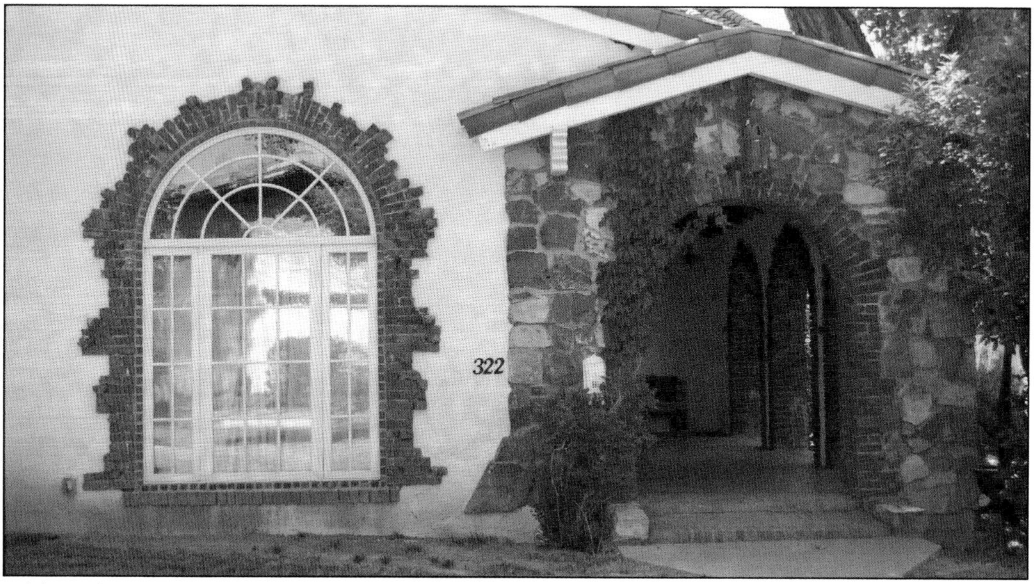

Although Leon Watson would later become known for building adobe houses in the nearby Chacon Addition, his first homes in Albuquerque were constructed of hollow clay tile, sometimes called penitentiary tile. Stonework around the doors, windows, chimneys, and fireplaces became his trademark. There are at least five Watson homes in the Huning Castle Addition. This home at 322 Sixteenth Street was built in 1931 for Ernest Everly. It is better known today as the television home of Jesse Pinkman, a character in television's *Breaking Bad* series. (Both, courtesy of Judy Cook.)

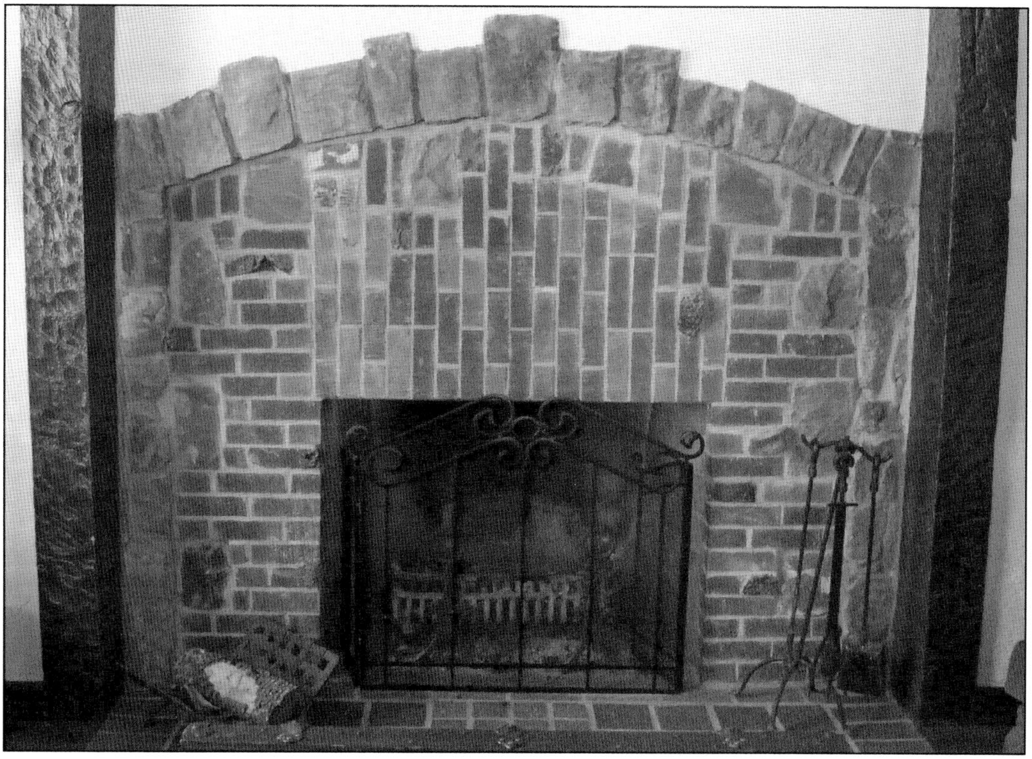

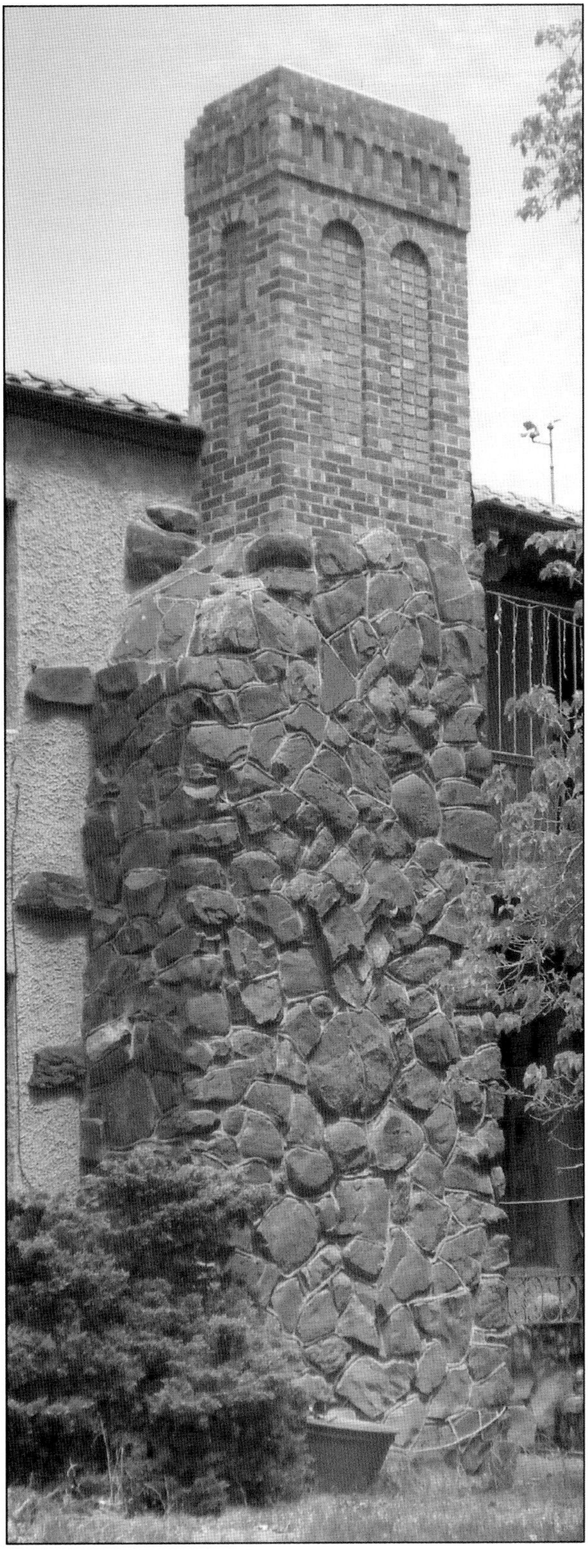

Stonework and brickwork stand out on this chimney at the Robert and Penelope Katson home at 1621 Park Avenue. The building permit for the 1931 home was issued to Harry Keyser. The Katsons operated the Court Café at 107 North Fourth Street. This home was later purchased by the George P. and Dorothy (Keleher) Valliant family, former owners of Valliant Printing. Today, it is home to Dennis and Margery Valliant. (Photograph by the author.)

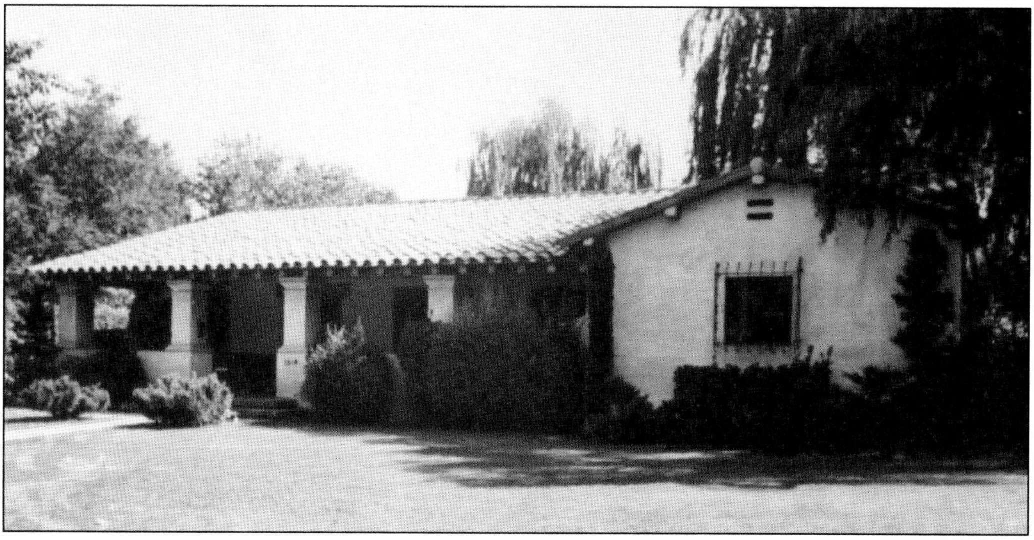

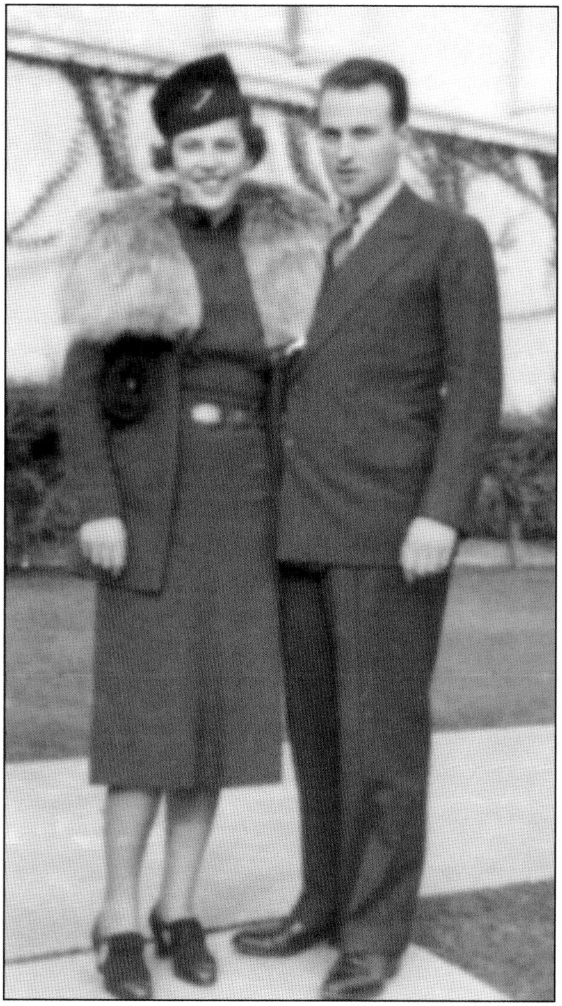

In 1938, Rudolf and Clare Dreyer moved into this $10,000 home, which was designed by Tom Danahy and built by Joe Gagner at 1514 Park Avenue SW, after returning from their honeymoon in San Francisco. The slope of the roof is unusually long, a unique combination of Mediterranean and Bungalow styles. Wooden columns support the front porch roof. Dreyer owned Zork Hardware on Fourth Street. (Both, courtesy of Clare Dreyer.)

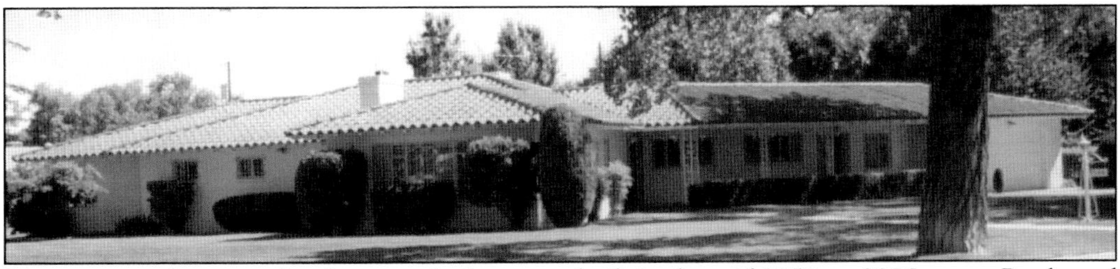

The one-story home in the photograph above was built in the mid-1950s at 300 Laguna Boulevard SW and combined a Mediterranean red tile roof with ranch home styling of white painted bricks. The home (originally owned for two years by Elmer and Rosalee Elliott) was purchased in 1956 by the Frank and Mickey Peloso family, New Yorkers who had moved to Albuquerque in the early 1940s. Peloso, an attorney and businessman, managed and owned several movie theaters in the city, including the Sunshine Theater and the Hiland Theater, which eventually was donated to an arts group and is now home to the National Dance Institute. Daughter Antoinette Peloso and her husband still reside at the Laguna home. (Courtesy of the Peloso family.)

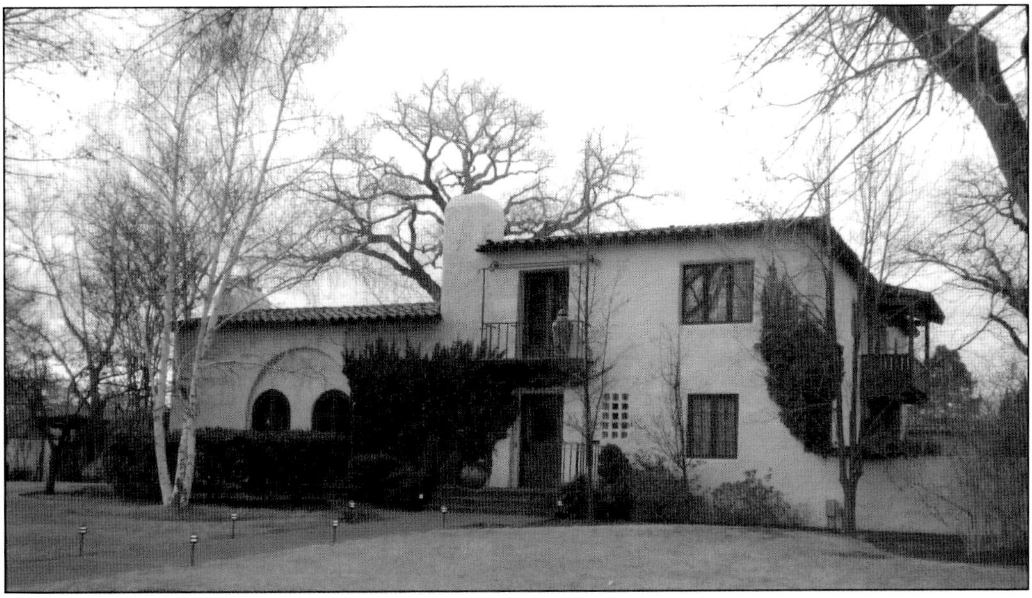

One of the older and larger homes in the Huning Castle Addition, the Mediterranean-style residence of Frank and Gertrude Shufflebarger at 311 Laguna Boulevard was built by the owner for an economical $12,000 in 1932. It featured an original wrought-iron balcony over an arched front door. Shufflebarger owned the Shufflebarger Transfer Company. (Photograph by the author.)

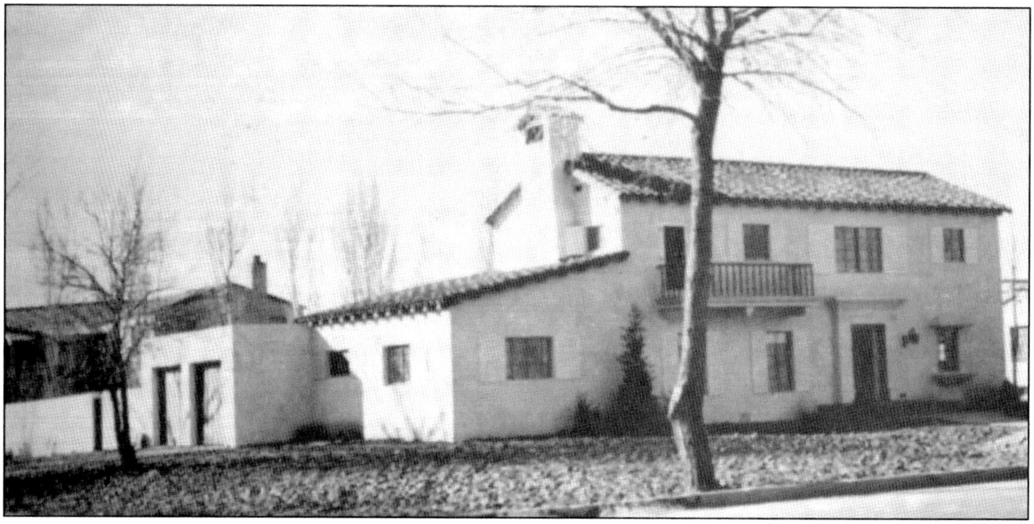

Sen. Dennis Chavez and his wife, Imelda, had their home built at 1600 Los Alamos Avenue in 1938, using plans by architect Tom Danahy and contractor Robert Gardner. A Democrat, Chavez served in both the House of Representatives (elected 1952) and then became the first person of Hispanic descent to be elected (1940) to an entire six-year term in the Senate. Other notable Albuquerqueans later owned the house, including Louise and Earl Moulton, president of the Charles Ilfeld Company, and then Harvey and Jan Yates. (Above, courtesy of Albuquerque Progress; below, courtesy of UNM CSWR, Dennis Chavez Collection, 000-394-0012.)

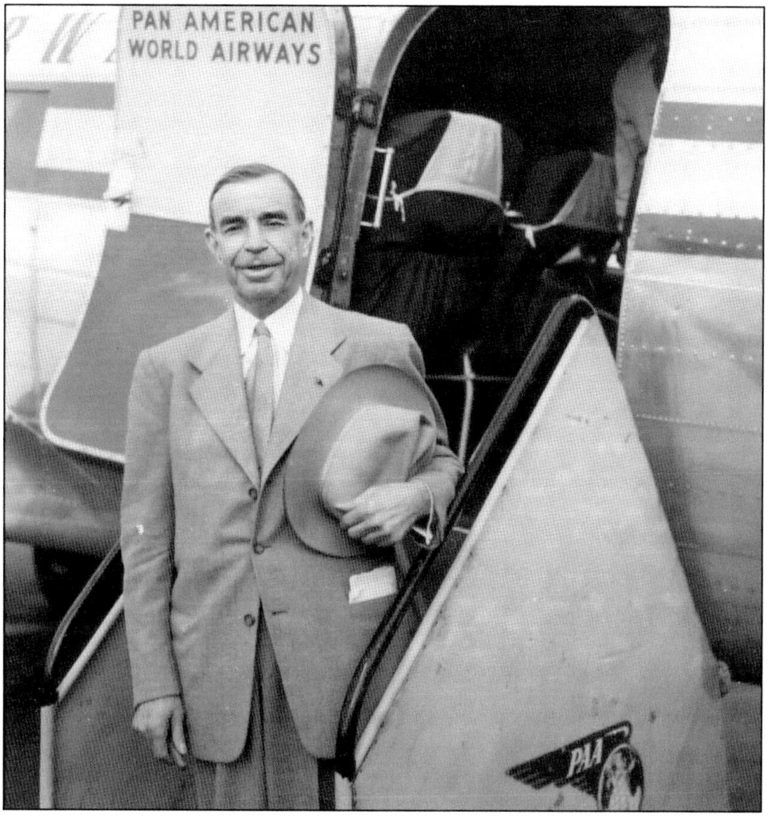

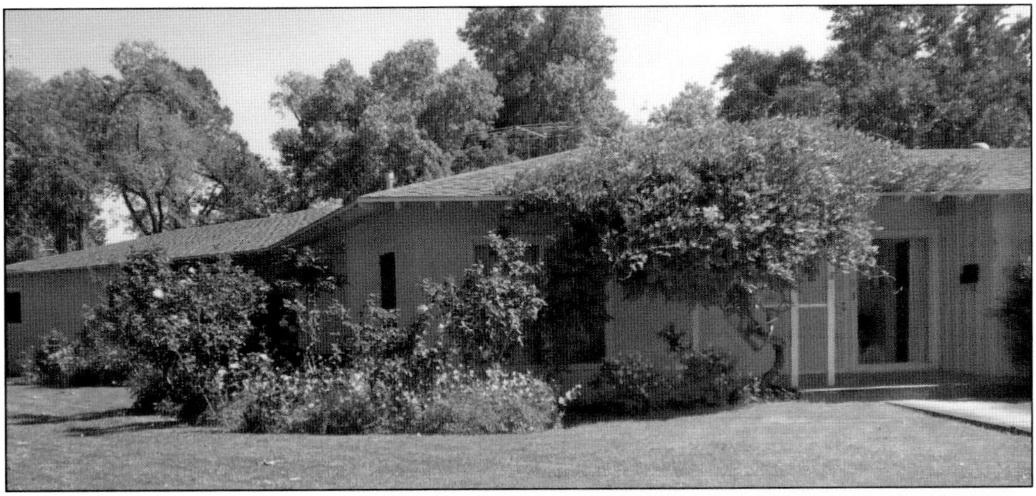

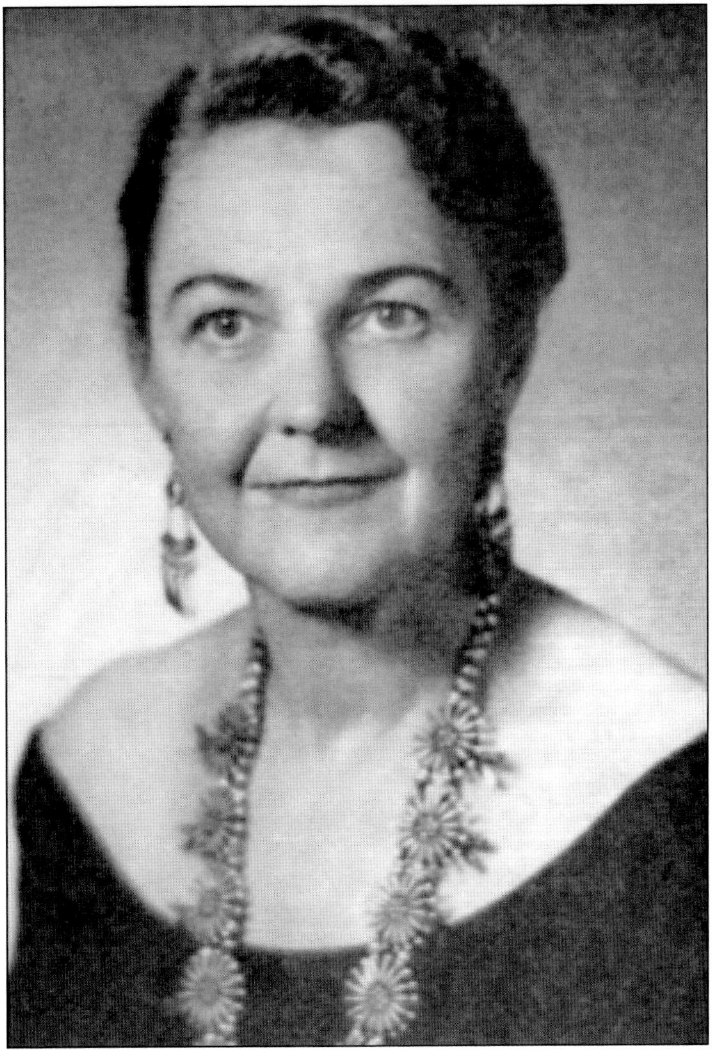

George and Rosalie Doolittle moved into a one-story Ranch-style home at 1500 San Cristobal about 1950, and garden expert Rosalie turned the yard into an oasis of flowers. Rosalie Doolittle is best remembered for her book *Southwest Gardening*, considered a local classic. She served as president of the Pacific Southwest District of the American Rose Society. George Doolittle was president and general manager of the Albuquerque Lumber Company. (Above, courtesy of Judy Cook; right, courtesy of Phoenix Rose Society.)

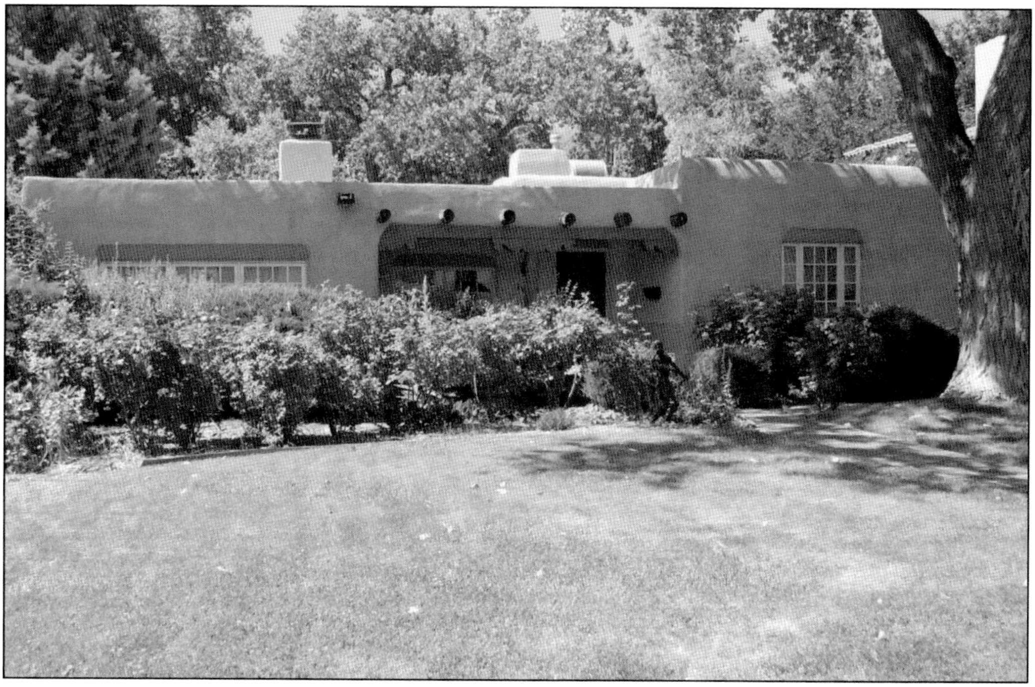

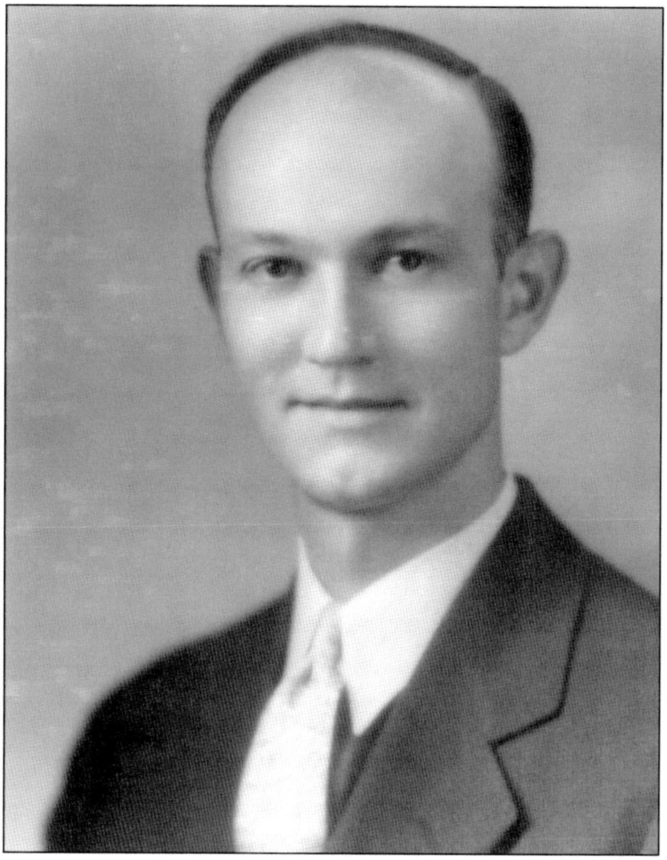

Jack and Jeannette Stromberg were the first owners of this Pueblo Revival one-story home at 1606 Los Alamos Avenue. The family moved to Albuquerque from Trinidad, Colorado, to open Stromberg's Quality Mens Wear on Central Avenue downtown. Later, additional stores were built at Nob Hill and Winrock shopping districts. Jeannette Stromberg was the first woman elected to the school board and served three terms. (Above, photograph by the author; left, courtesy of the Stromberg family.)

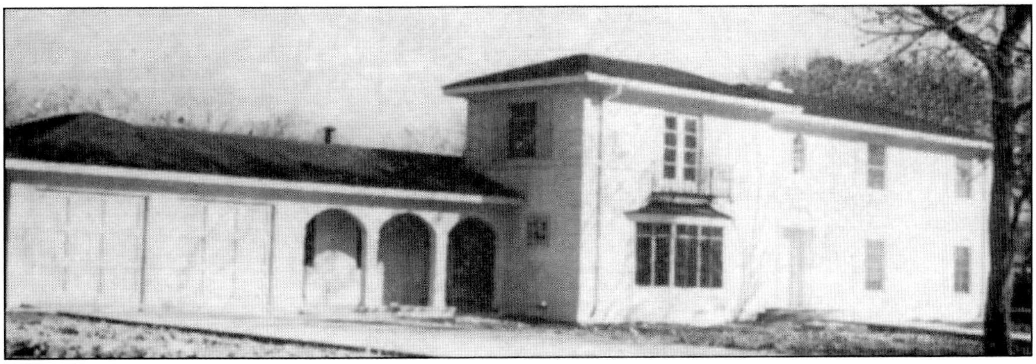

One of the largest homes in the Huning Castle Addition was built in the 1940s for the Cale and Alice Carson family at 1601 Los Alamos Avenue. He was the president of the First National Bank in Albuquerque. The family of Bill and Pat Bates has occupied the home for many decades. (Courtesy of *Albuquerque Progress*.)

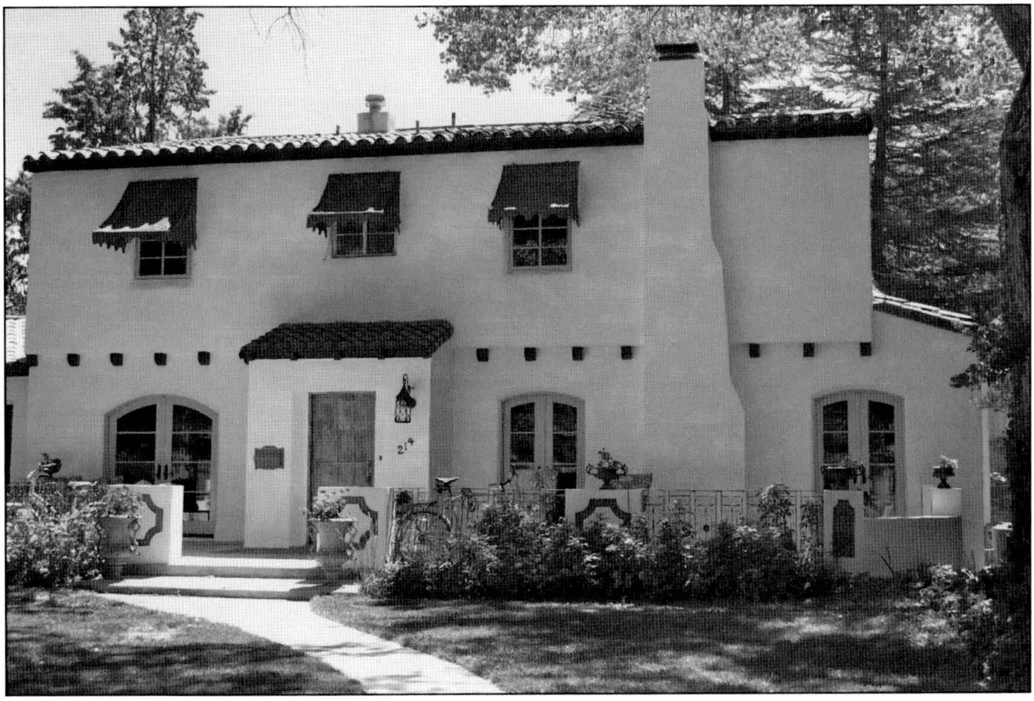

Built as a spec home in 1938 by contractor K.L. House, George and Helen Savage purchased this residence at 214 Sixteenth Street SW, just one of several houses the Savage family would eventually own in the neighborhood. George was a partner with William Sganzini in a real estate and insurance firm. (Courtesy of Judy Cook.)

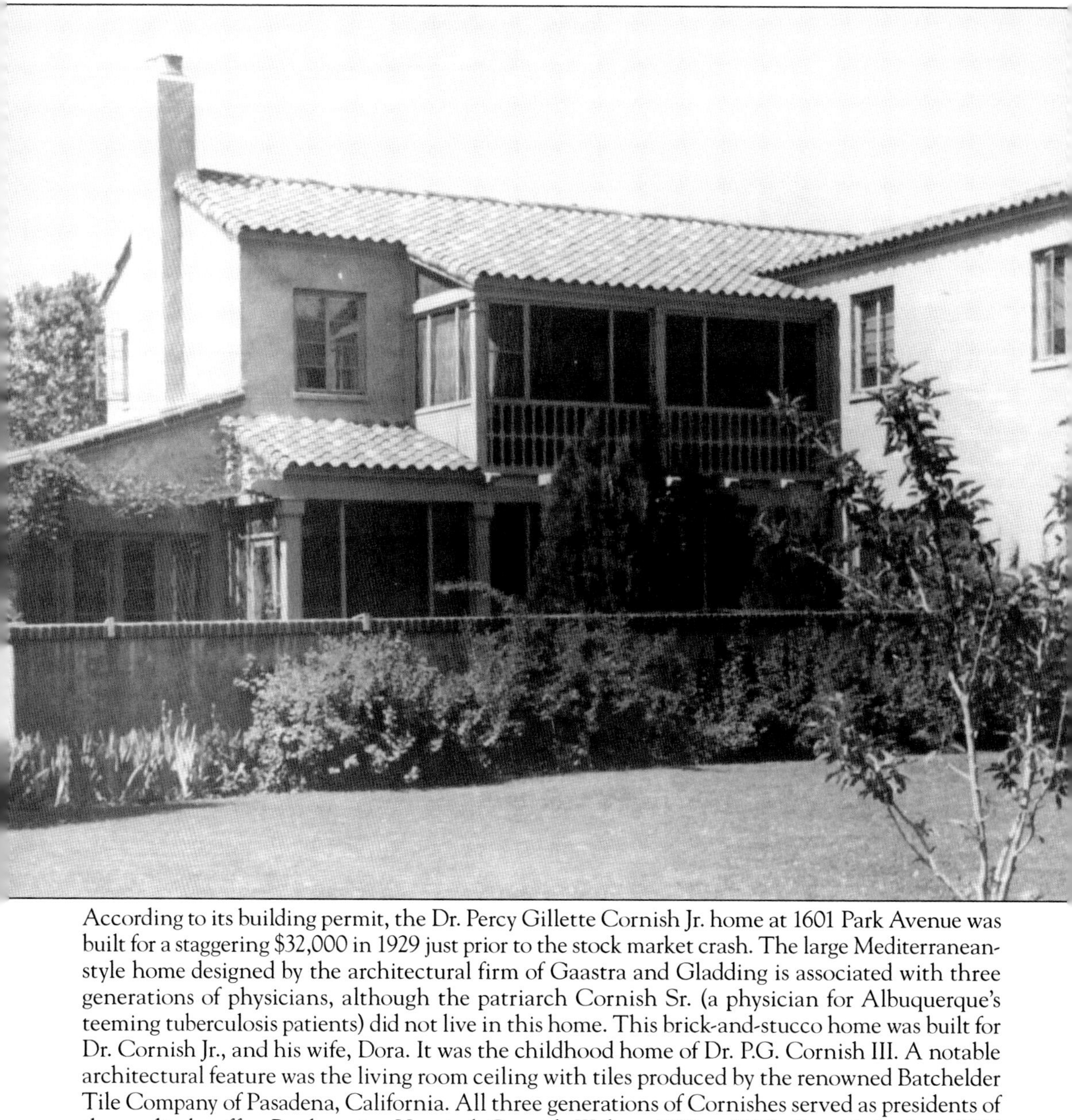

According to its building permit, the Dr. Percy Gillette Cornish Jr. home at 1601 Park Avenue was built for a staggering $32,000 in 1929 just prior to the stock market crash. The large Mediterranean-style home designed by the architectural firm of Gaastra and Gladding is associated with three generations of physicians, although the patriarch Cornish Sr. (a physician for Albuquerque's teeming tuberculosis patients) did not live in this home. This brick-and-stucco home was built for Dr. Cornish Jr., and his wife, Dora. It was the childhood home of Dr. P.G. Cornish III. A notable architectural feature was the living room ceiling with tiles produced by the renowned Batchelder Tile Company of Pasadena, California. All three generations of Cornishes served as presidents of the medical staff at Presbyterian Hospital: Cornish III from 1973 to 1975; Cornish Jr., from 1938 to 1939; and Cornish Sr.; date unknown. In 2011, the Cornish home reportedly was advertised for $1 million in the *Wall Street Journal's* real estate section. Another longtime resident of the home was Dr. Monroe Thompson and family. (Courtesy of Charlotte Cornish Edmonds.)

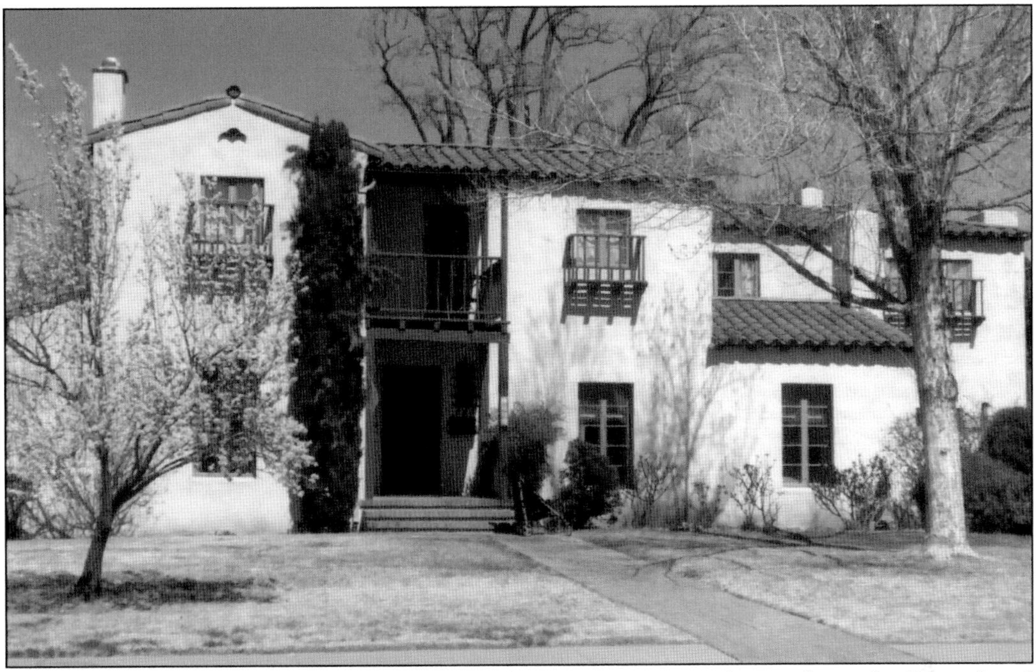

The Mediterranean-style home at 1521 Los Alamos Avenue was the residence for Samuel and Elizabeth (Nordhaus) Minces. Joe Gagner built the home in 1935. Samuel Minces was owner of the Nehi–Royal Crown Cola Bottling Company. (Courtesy of Judy Cook.)

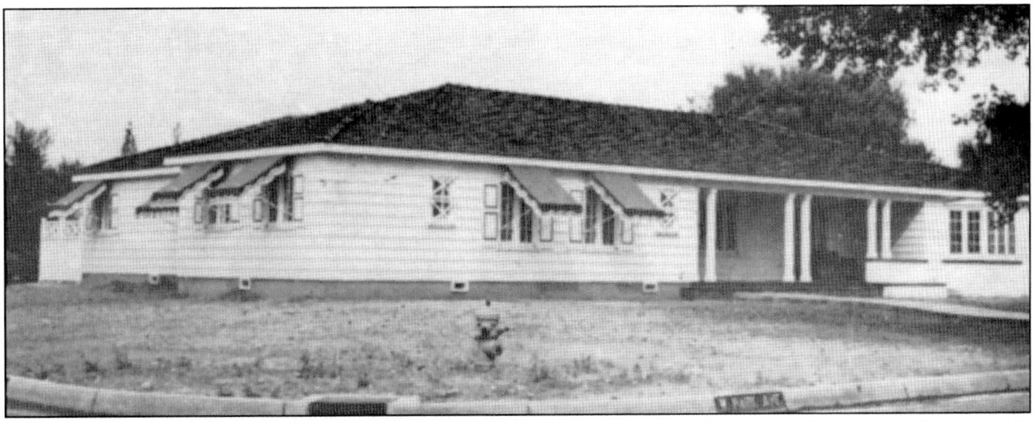

The importance of the Ranch-style home can be seen in the neighborhood starting about 1940. The unusual wood home with its original wood shingles at 1415 Park Avenue was built for $9,000 for Caroline and Thomas P. Gallagher. He was the managing partner of the Bernalillo Lumber Company. This home was designed by Tom Danahy and built by Don Shaffer in 1941. (Courtesy of *Albuquerque Progress.*)

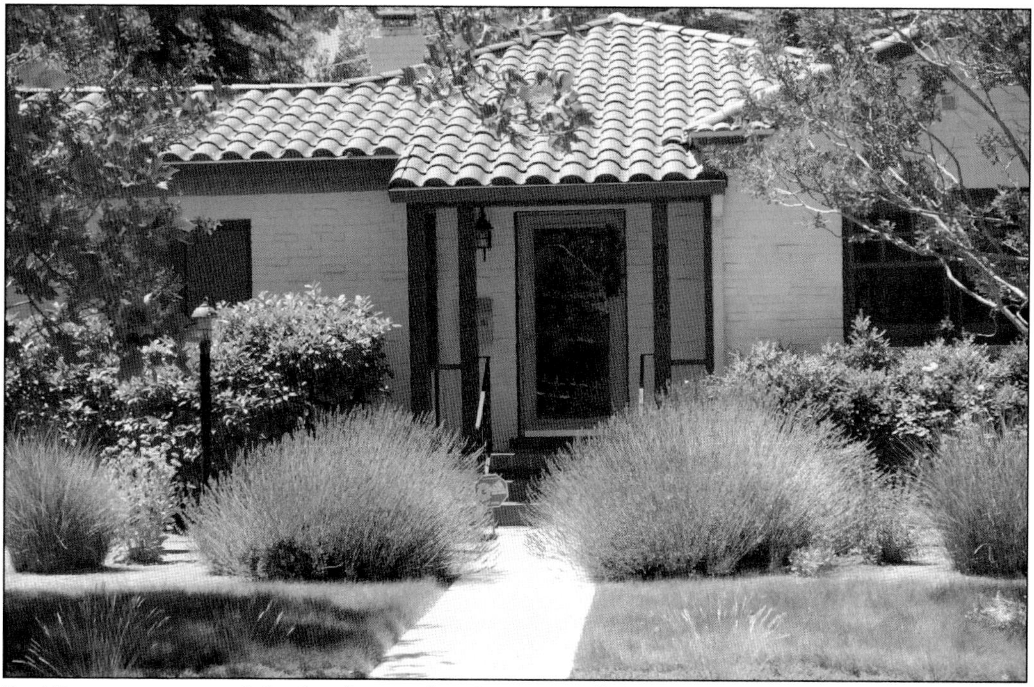

Paul Butt, a partner with his brothers in four Butt's Rexall drugstores, owned this charming home at 1510 Park Avenue with his wife, Kittie. (Courtesy of Judy Cook.)

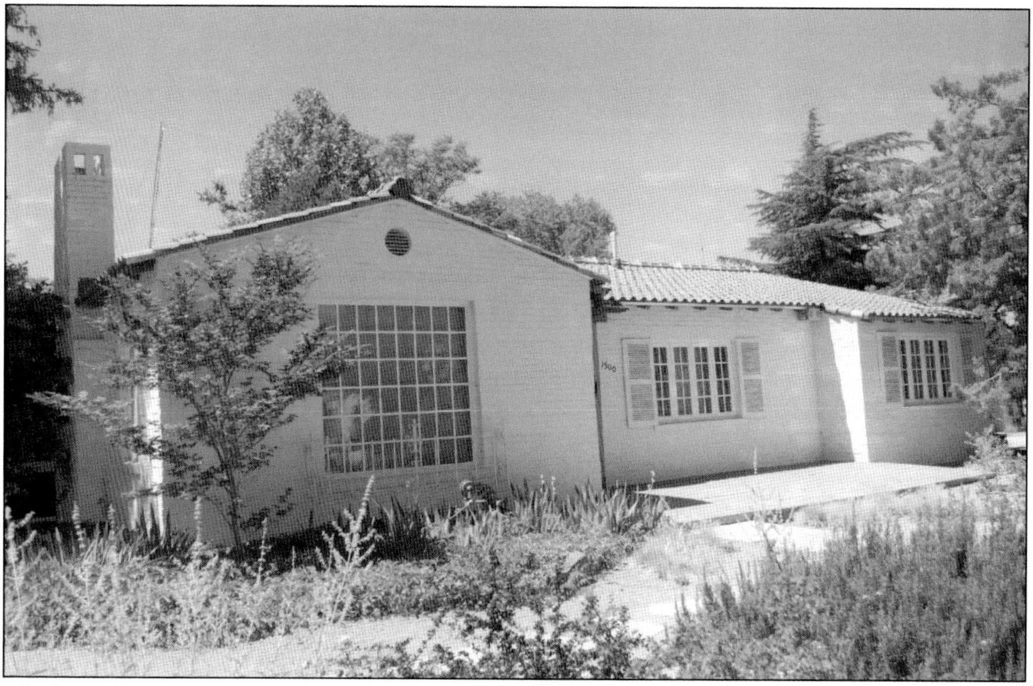

The home for Dr. Emmett and Phoebe Royer is another Lembke-built house with a generous bank of windows. It was built for $11,000 in 1936 at 1500 Park Avenue. (Courtesy of Judy Cook.)

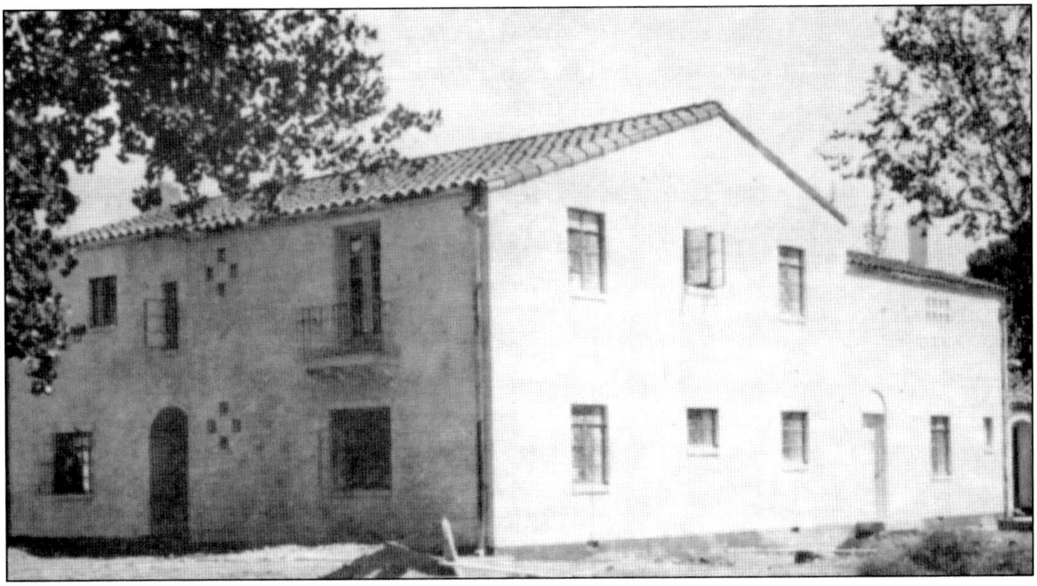

Contractor J.E. Box built this home for attorney Allen Tonkin and his wife, Nancy, at 1524 Park Avenue in 1939. The two-story home was—and still is—white painted brick. The photograph above shows the home before it acquired its distinctive ivy layer that wraps around the front windows, shown in the image below. The home is still owned by a daughter from the original family. (Above, courtesy of *Albuquerque Progress*; below, courtesy of Judy Cook.)

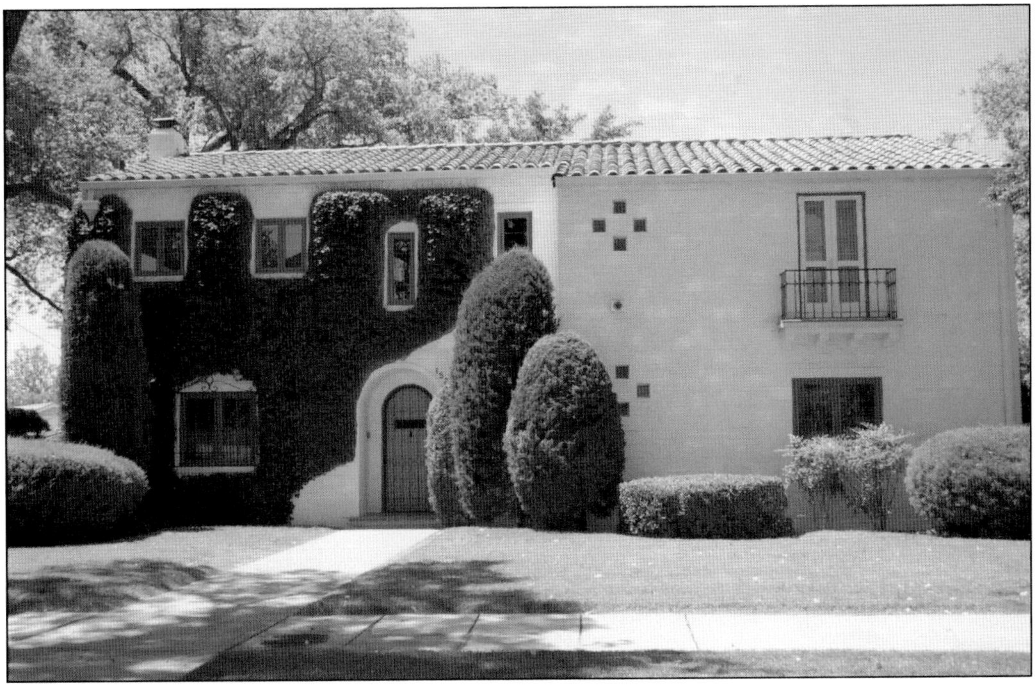

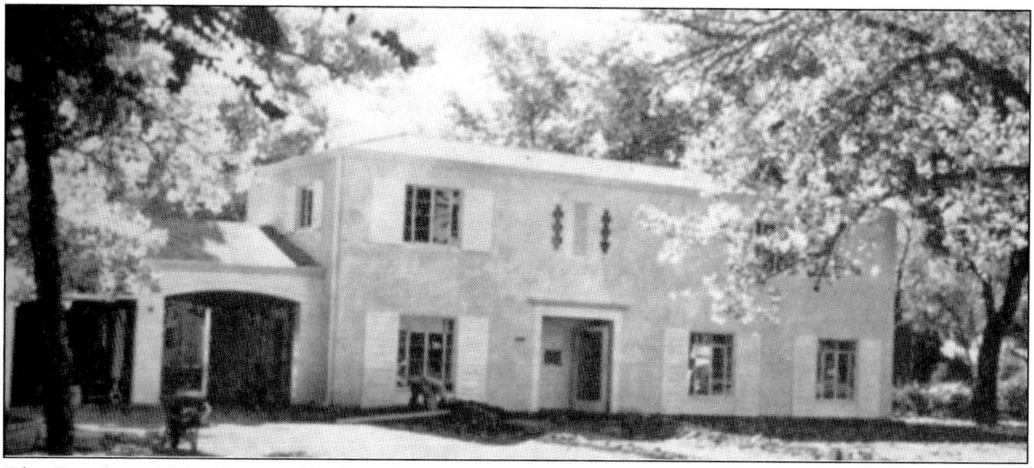

The Frank and Maude Mindlin home at 314 Sixteenth Street was built in 1939. Mindlin was the owner of Mindlin Jewelers, a local store carrying diamonds, watches, silverware, and china. The architect was Tom Danahy and the contractor was Ivan Rose of Building Service, Inc. (Courtesy of *Albuquerque Progress*.)

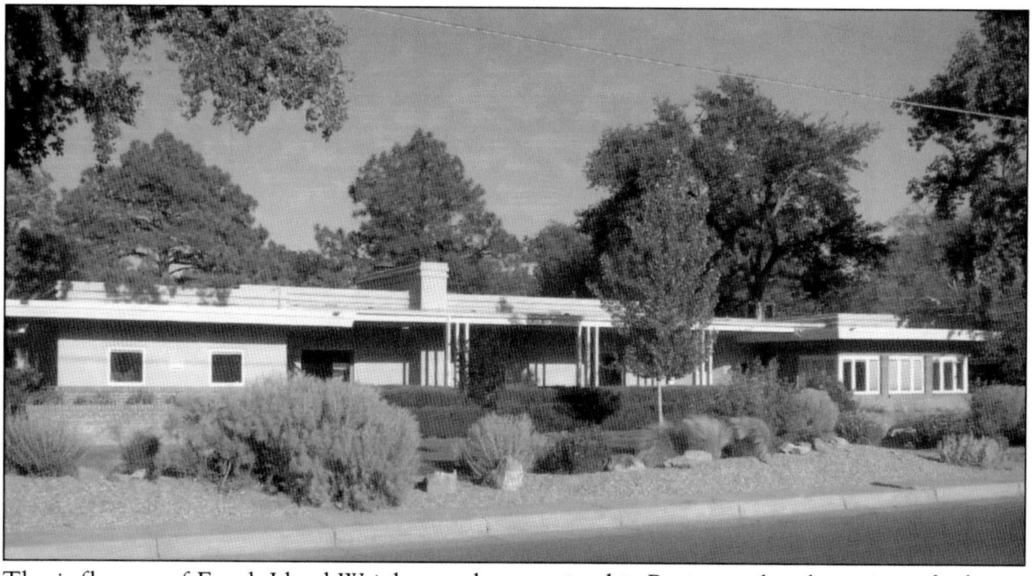

The influence of Frank Lloyd Wright can be seen in this Prairie-style adaptation of a home built for a member of Chicago's Spiegel Catalog family in 1950. Arthur H. Spiegel and his wife, Eleanor Friedman Spiegel, built the home with its unique horizontal lines and overhangs at 400 San Pasquale Avenue SW. (Photograph by the author.)

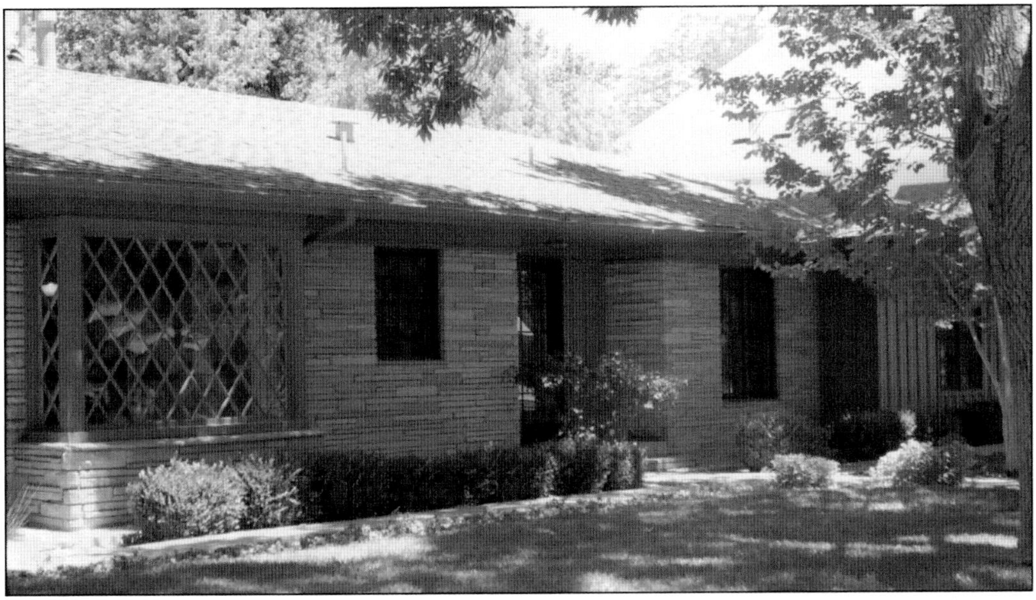

By the 1950s, Ranch-style homes were popular within the Huning Castle Addition, in part because the lot sizes accommodated large one-story homes. An excellent example is the 5,000-square-foot Maurice and Margarite Liberman home at 1701 Chacoma Place SW. Liberman and his brother owned Duke City Lumber, but the home was built of flagstone from Arizona. (Courtesy of Judy Cook.)

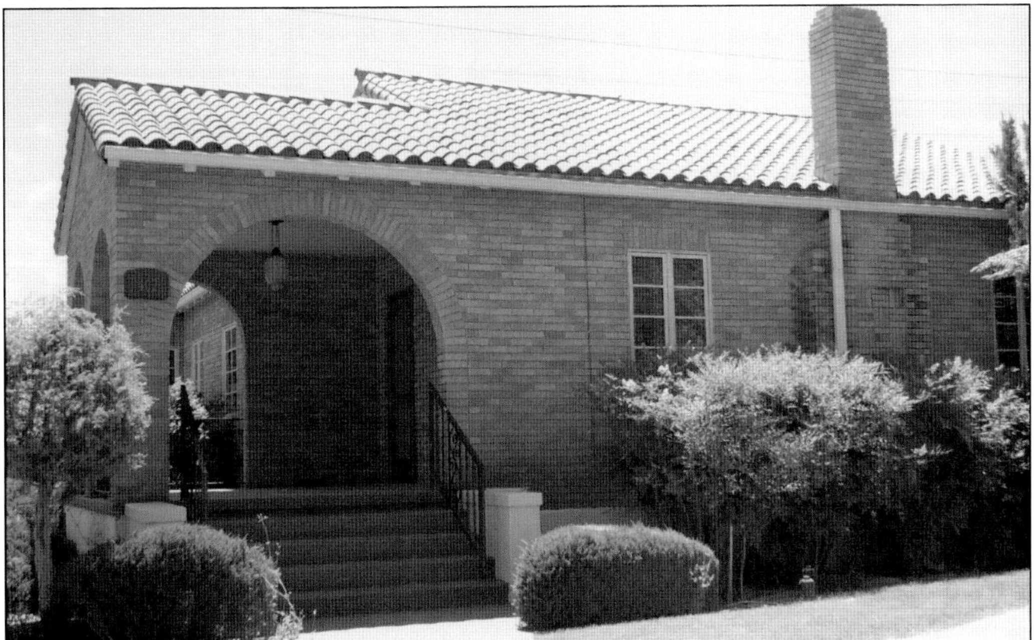

Sen. Pete V. Domenici lived in this home at 402 Fifteenth Street as a boy, making him the second senator to come from the Huning Castle area. (The first was Dennis Chavez.) Retired senator Domenici's parents were grocers. They bought this brick home about five years after it was built by K.L. House. Pete Domenici, the future politician, was about 11 years old at the time. (Courtesy of Judy Cook.)

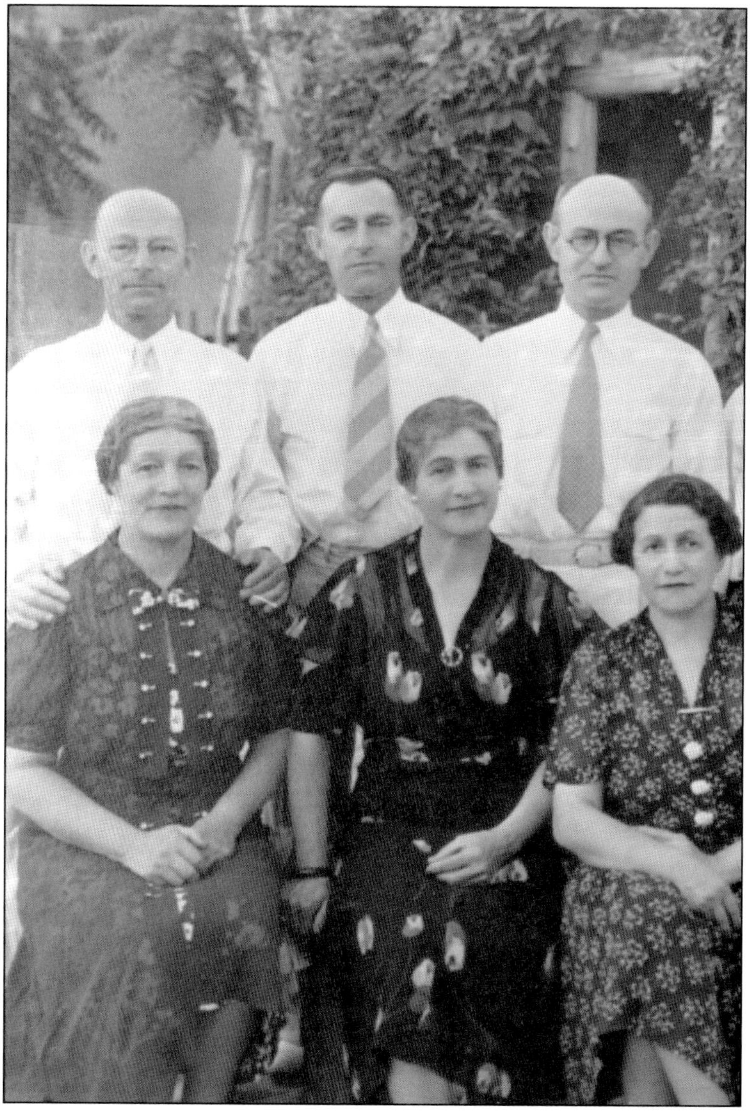

The extended Seligman family and their descendants have owned up to six homes in the Huning Castle Addition, many at the same time. Three Seligman brothers married three Block sisters, and they all built their homes in the area. In this 1937 photograph, the married couples are, from left to right, Julius and Blanche Seligman, Siegfried and Meta Seligman, and Carl and Lucille Seligman. (Courtesy of Susan Seligman Kennedy.)

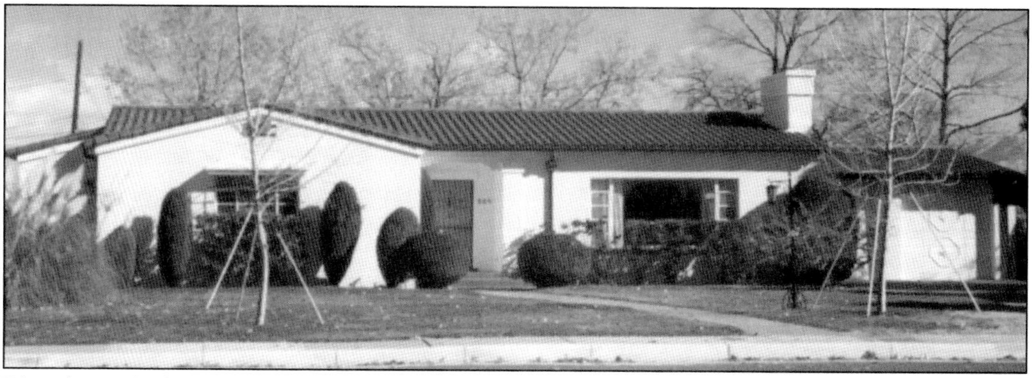

Blanche and Julius Seligman built their home at 204 Sixteenth Street and lived there from 1946 to 1962. (Courtesy of Susan Seligman Kennedy.)

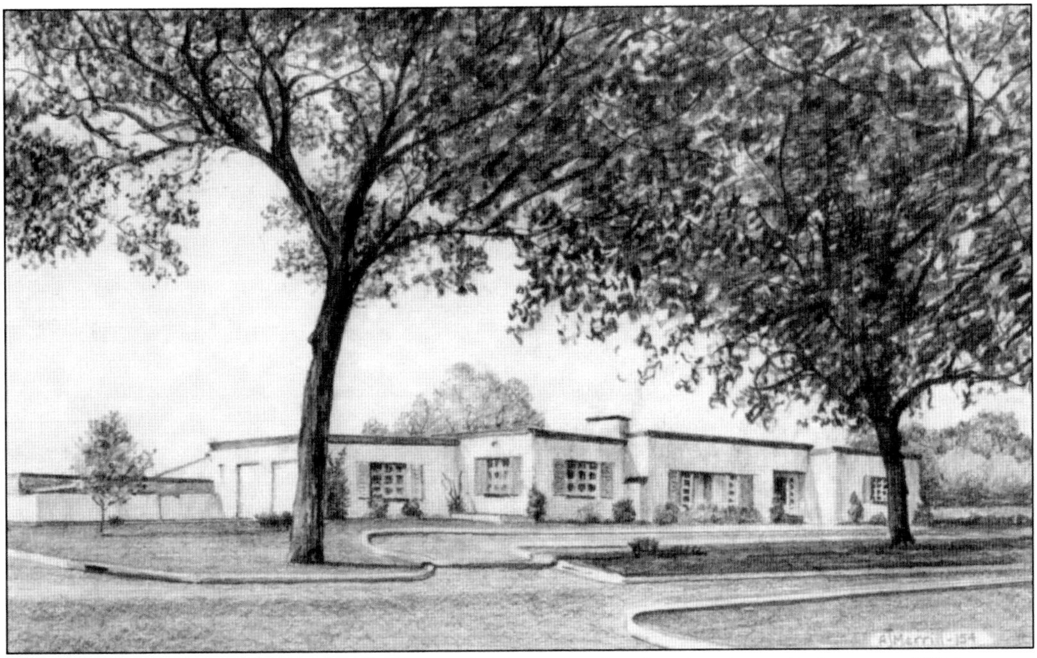

Julius Seligman's son Thornton and his wife, Doris, built a Territorial-style home at 207 Laguna Boulevard in 1947 and 1948. The architect was Robert C. Munro Jr., and the builder was George Rutherford. (Sketch by A. Merrill, courtesy of Susan Seligman Kennedy.)

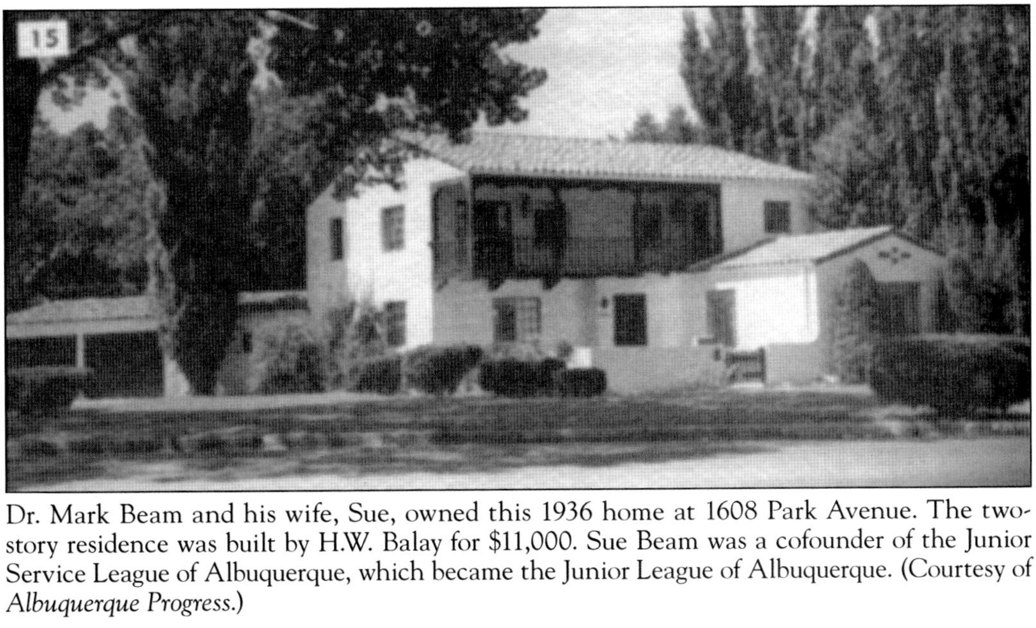

Dr. Mark Beam and his wife, Sue, owned this 1936 home at 1608 Park Avenue. The two-story residence was built by H.W. Balay for $11,000. Sue Beam was a cofounder of the Junior Service League of Albuquerque, which became the Junior League of Albuquerque. (Courtesy of *Albuquerque Progress*.)

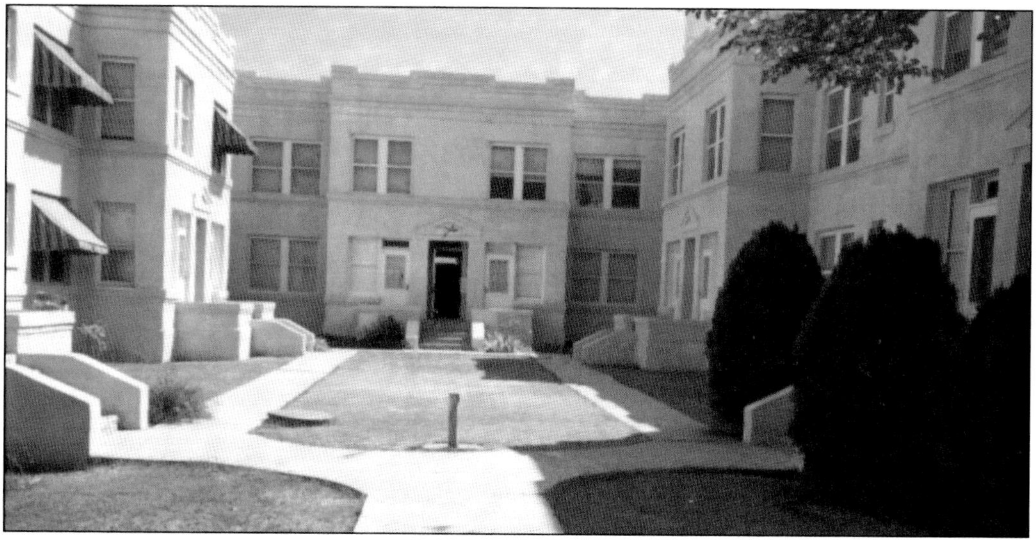

Hearts broke throughout Albuquerque when the elegant Castle Apartments burned in August 2009. The apartments (front and side views shown here) were designed by Franz Huning's son, Arno, in 1922 and named after the sprawling Huning Castle next door. The 20 apartments at 1410 Central Avenue SW were large for their time—600 to 750 square feet each. The complex was listed in the National Register of Historic Places. (Both, courtesy of the William Snead family.)

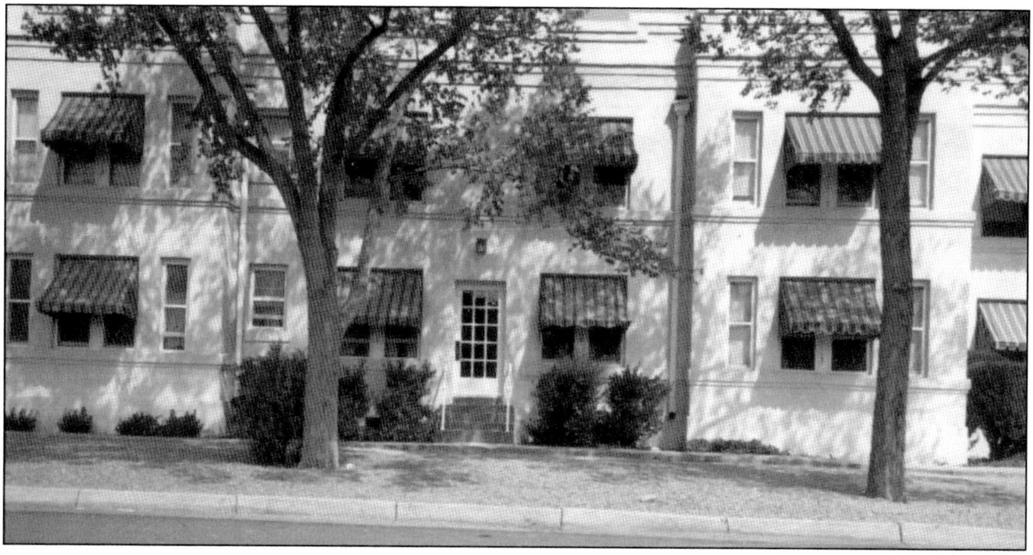

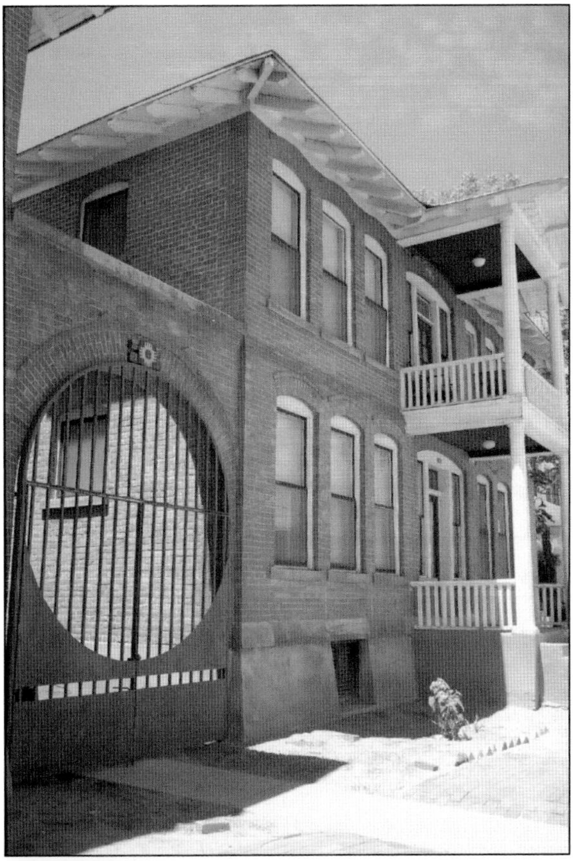

The 33-acre Raynolds Addition, between Eighth Street and Seventeenth Street to the south of Central Avenue, was platted in 1912, while much of the neighboring Huning lands closer to the river were becoming increasingly swampy. The Raynolds area filled in slowly with garden apartments, bungalows, Southwestern homes, and some of Albuquerque's earliest apartment buildings, such as the Washington Apartments at 1002–1008 Central Avenue SW (right photograph) and the distinctive Eller Apartments with brick pavilions and frame porches built in 1922 at 113–127 Eighth Street. (Both, courtesy of Judy Cook.)

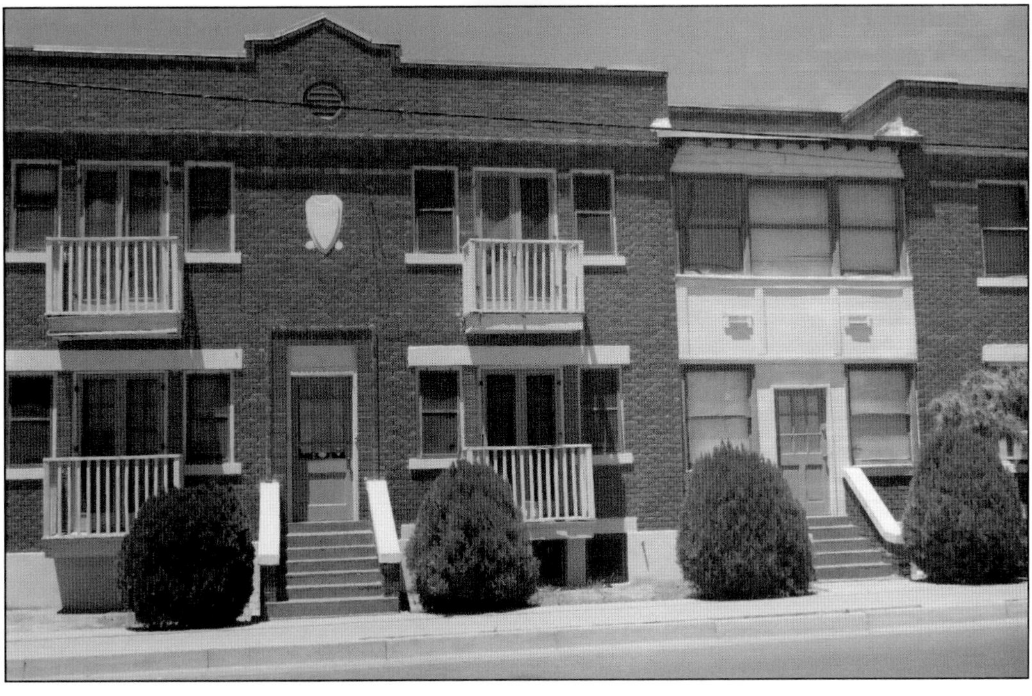

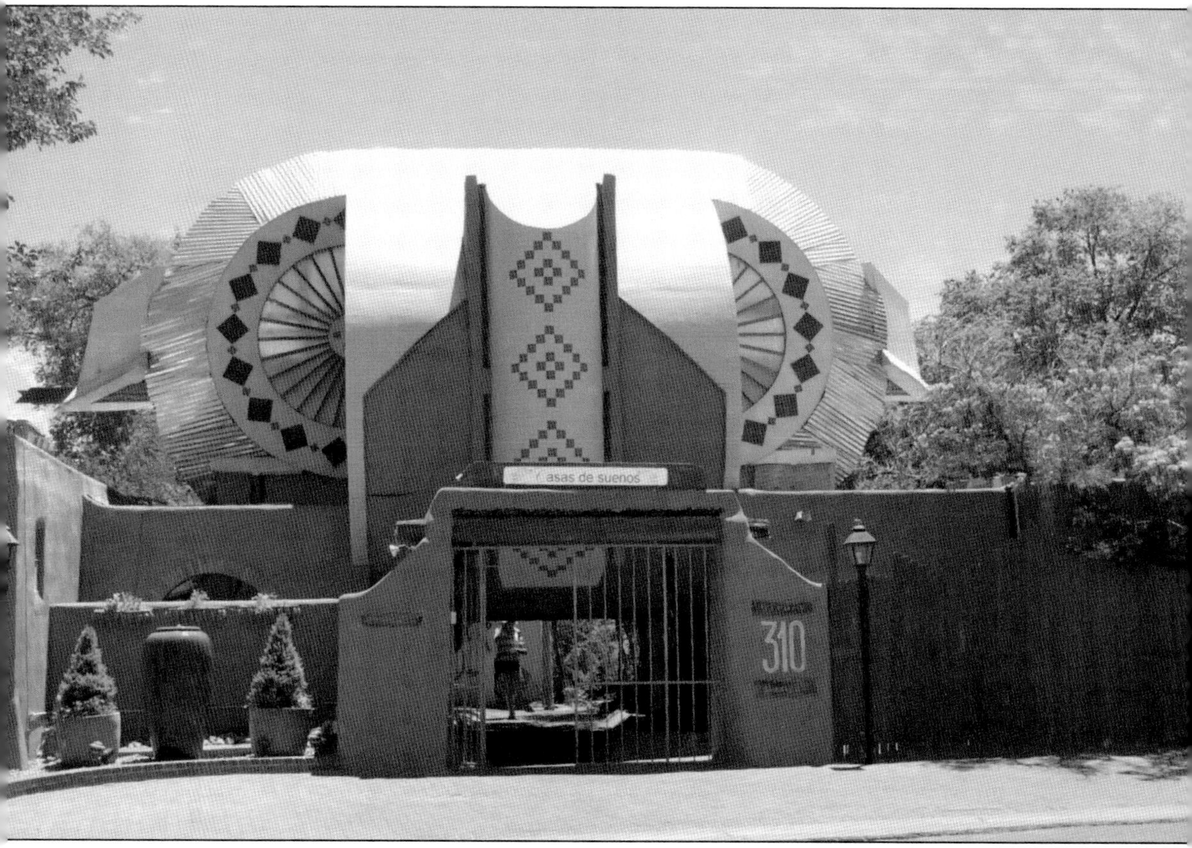

The West Park neighborhood is a small residential area sandwiched between the Albuquerque Country Club, historic Route 66, and the Rio Grande. It is an eclectic mix of single-family homes, duplexes, and courtyard apartments. It boasts of a variety of architectural styles, including bungalows, Southwest Vernacular, and Moderne. Most of the housing in this neighborhood was built in the 1930s and 1940s after the creation of the Middle Rio Grande Conservancy District. The area was platted in the late 1920s, but was not formally annexed to the City of Albuquerque until 1949. One of its most unusual buildings at 310 Rio Grande Boulevard SW is part of the former artist colony of J.R. Willis. Formerly known as La Miradora Apartments, the complex started in 1938 as Willis's home and studio, as well as casitas for other artists. Architect Bart Prince added the nautilus shape in 1978. Today, the 23 casitas have been transformed into Casas de Suenos Old Town Historic Inn, a bed-and-breakfast. (Courtesy of Judy Cook.)

Eight

Culture and Recreation

The Zoo, Albuquerque Little Theatre, and Route 66

The quiet elegant presence of the Huning Castle Addition and other neighborhoods on or near the former Huning estate are part of Albuquerque's cultural and recreational scene. Composed of several different neighborhood associations, the area is within walking distance to historic Old Town with its array of museums, shops, restaurants, and entertainment. Nearby is downtown. The proximity of the Rio Grande and the refurbished riverside parks and wetlands provide walking and bike trails. The fabled Route 66 highway forms the neighborhoods' northern boundaries. The zoo, located on property close to Franz Huning's original estate, is near enough that residents can hear an occasional lion roar.

On June 30, 1929, a joint dedication attracted an estimated 6,000 people to mark the dedication of the Albuquerque Country Club, Rio Grande Park and the Zoo, and the launch of the Huning Castle Addition development.

Albuquerque's unofficial zoo began in 1925 with two bears (Pancho and Major Hoople), two mountain lions, a porcupine, a snake, and a bobcat, all kept in cages at the water department's main pumping station. The Rio Grande Zoo moved to its present location in 1927 after the establishment of the Rio Grande Park and was formally dedicated in 1929.

The construction of the Albuquerque Little Theatre at 224 San Pasquale Avenue SW as a federal Works Progress Administration (WPA) project was approved after the playhouse company had already been in business at the KiMo Theatre in downtown for more than five years. Dedicated in 1936, the theater was designed by John Gaw Meem on land that was donated by Huning Castle Addition developers William A. Keleher and A.R. Hebenstreit.

Route 66 has been part of Central Avenue's legacy since it was designated a main arterial of the beloved Mother Road in 1937. Dozens of the city's interesting, but mostly deteriorating, motor courts and neon signage can be found along this corridor.

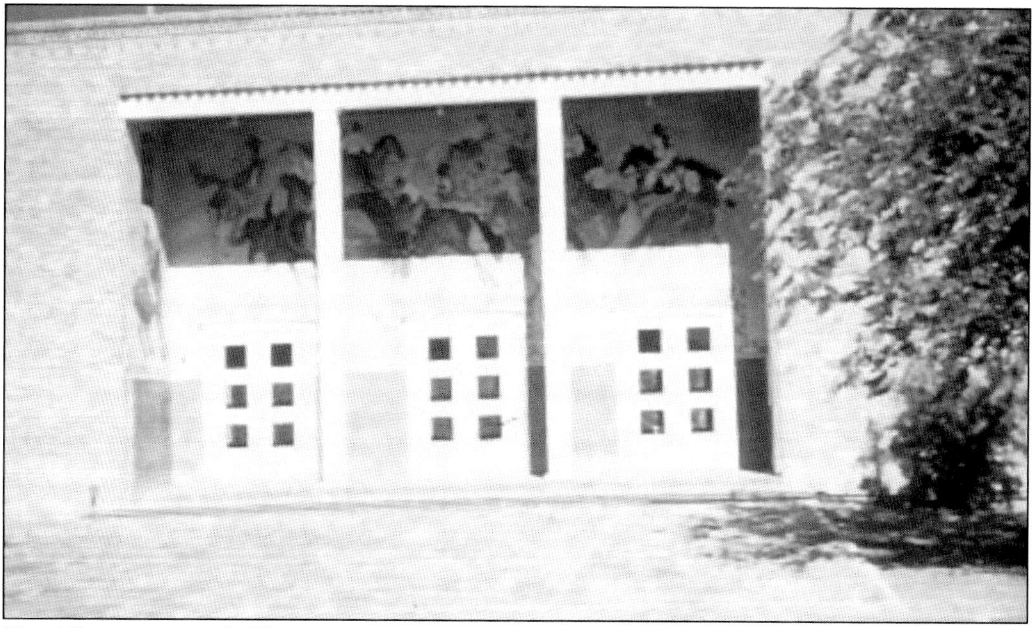

The Albuquerque Little Theatre, a community institution since 1930, was known as the Community Playhouse even after the company moved into its new theater designed by John Gaw Meem at 224 San Pasquale Avenue SW in 1936. The original entry featured a fresco by Dorothy N. Stewart depicting *Los Moros y Cristianos*, the first play presented by Spanish colonists. The murals were destroyed when the theater lobby was expanded. (Courtesy of Albuquerque Little Theatre.)

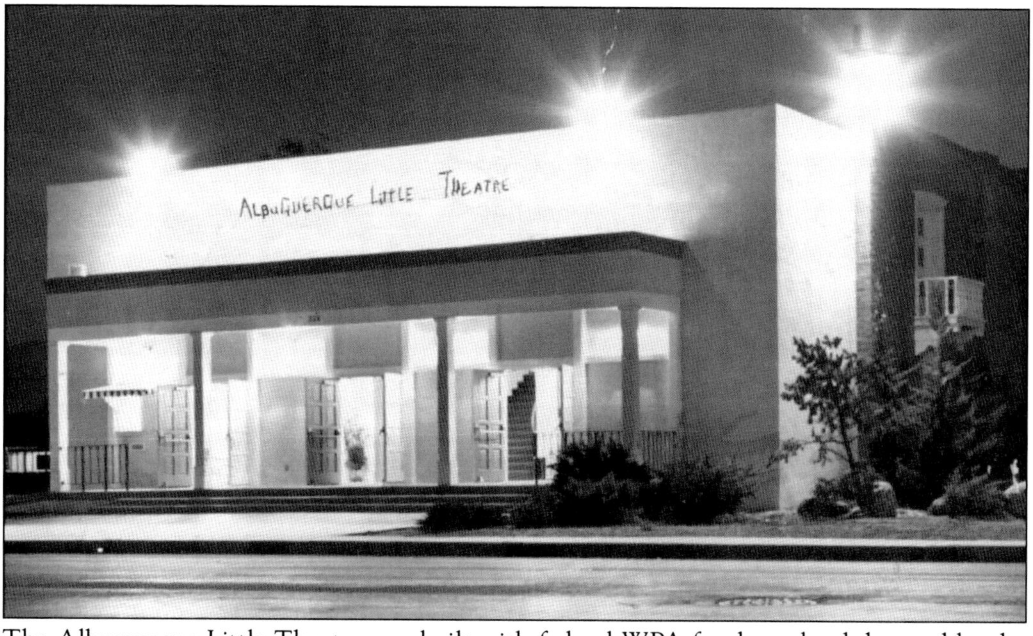

The Albuquerque Little Theatre was built with federal WPA funds on land donated by the developers of the Hunting Castle Addition. Later renovations changed its Territorial styling. A brick addition, two foyer enlargements, the loss of the murals, and the addition of a balcony pleased some theatergoers but were considered undesirable changes by others. (Courtesy of Albuquerque Little Theatre.)

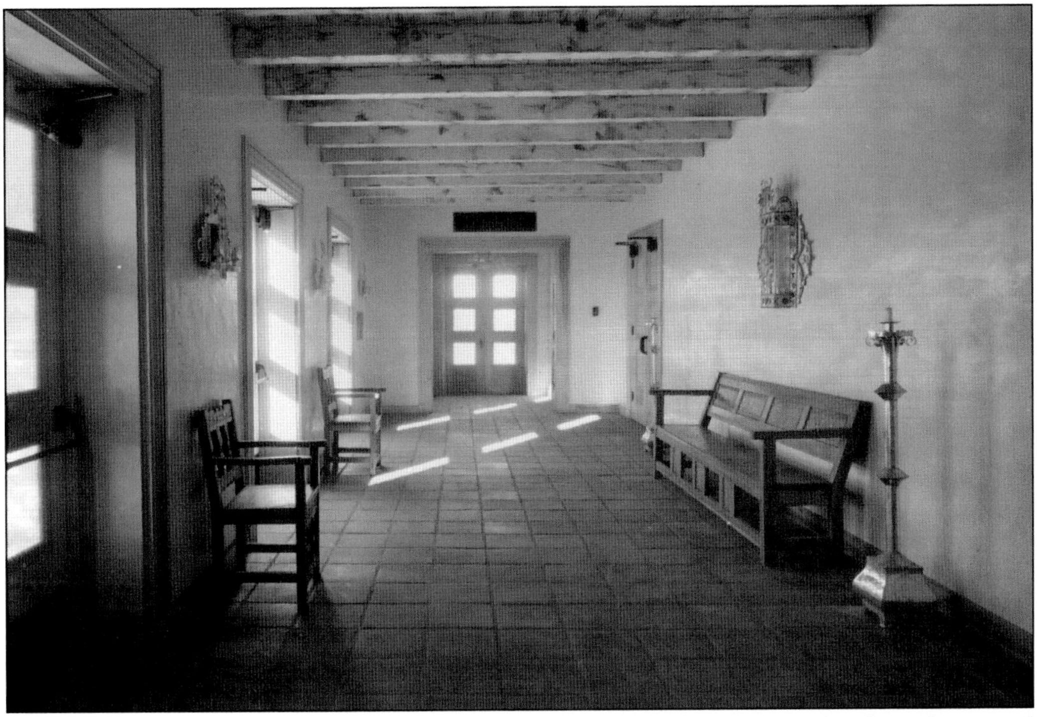

The original narrow foyer of the Little Theatre was traditional Territorial style with squared beams, plastered walls, and handcrafted Spanish Colonial–style chairs and benches made by craftsmen working with WPA funding. Some of the hand-carved furniture is still used in the original foyer. (Courtesy of Nancy Tucker.)

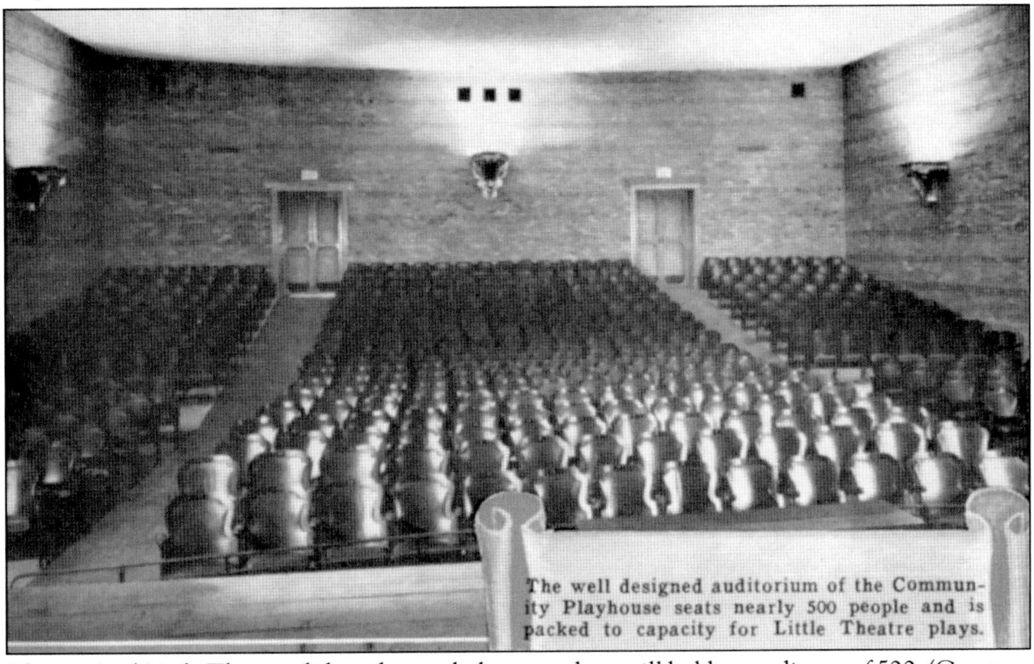

The original Little Theatre did not have a balcony and yet still held an audience of 500. (Courtesy of *Albuquerque Progress*.)

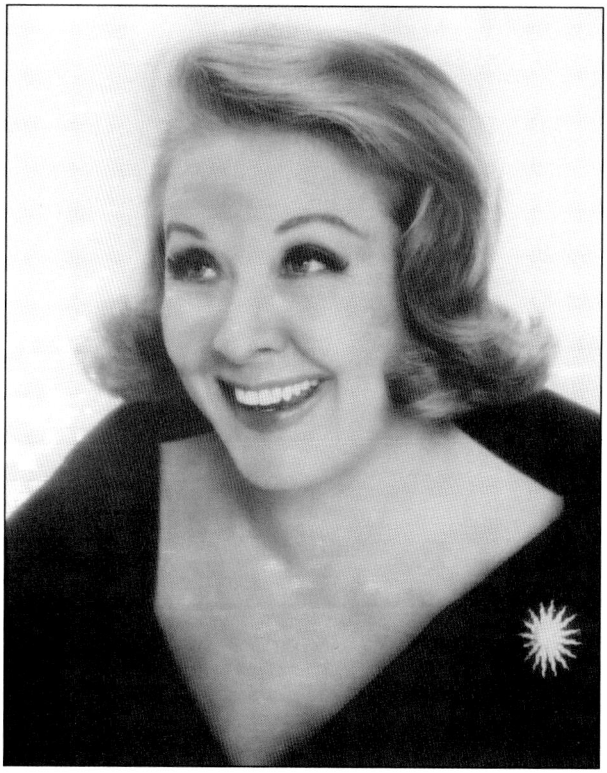

Actress Vivian Vance (1909–1979) began her acting career at the Albuquerque Little Theatre. The actress, pictured at left in 1967, moved away from Albuquerque and went on to star as Lucille Ball's neighbor, Ethel Mertz, in the *I Love Lucy* television series of the 1950s. She was the first person to win an Emmy Award for Best Supporting Actress. The Emmy is on display at the Little Theatre. Many famous actors made appearances at the Little Theatre. Among the favorites were Bill Daley (below left) and Don Knotts (below right). (Both, courtesy of Albuquerque Little Theatre and John/Carolyn Hogan.)

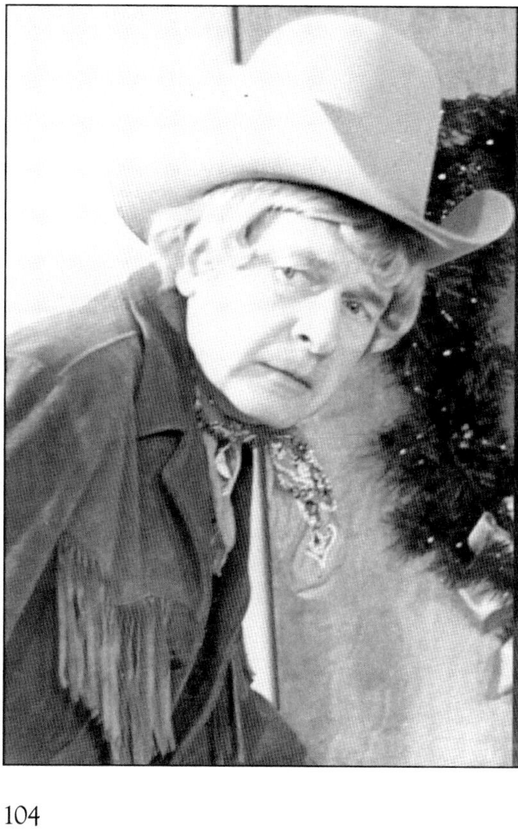

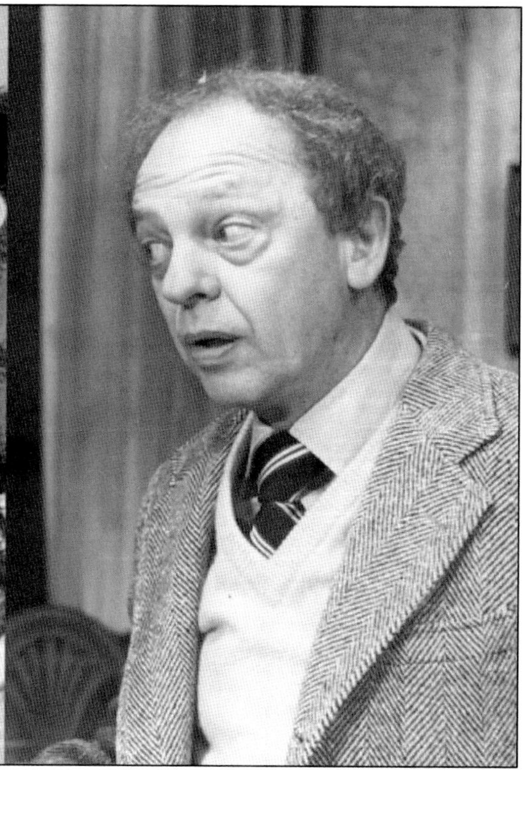

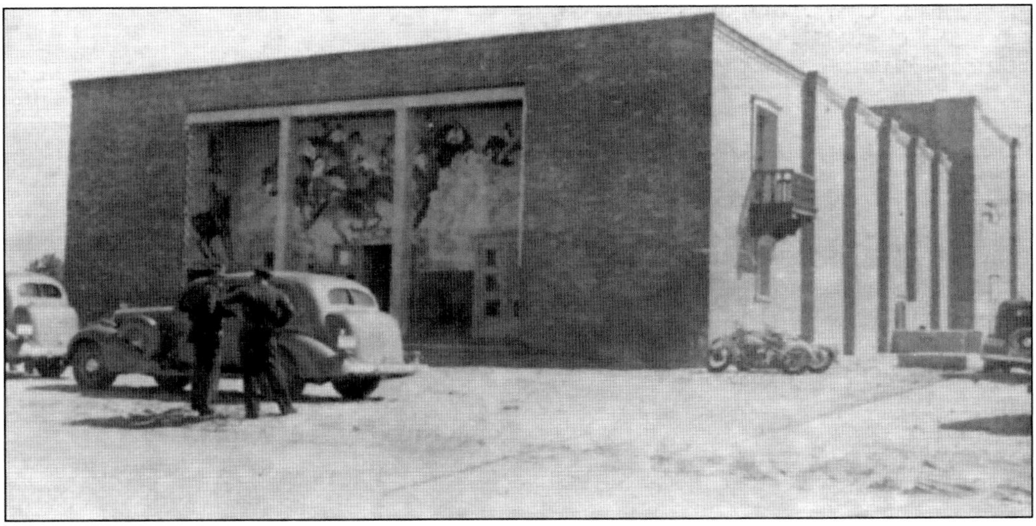

The Albuquerque Little Theatre looks different today than when it opened in 1936. Stuccoed additions covered the original brick entry facade, and subsequent additions provided space for the new entryway and equipment and wardrobe storage. The original design by John Gaw Meem is so altered that many would not recognize the architect's hand in the project. (Courtesy of *Albuquerque Progress.*)

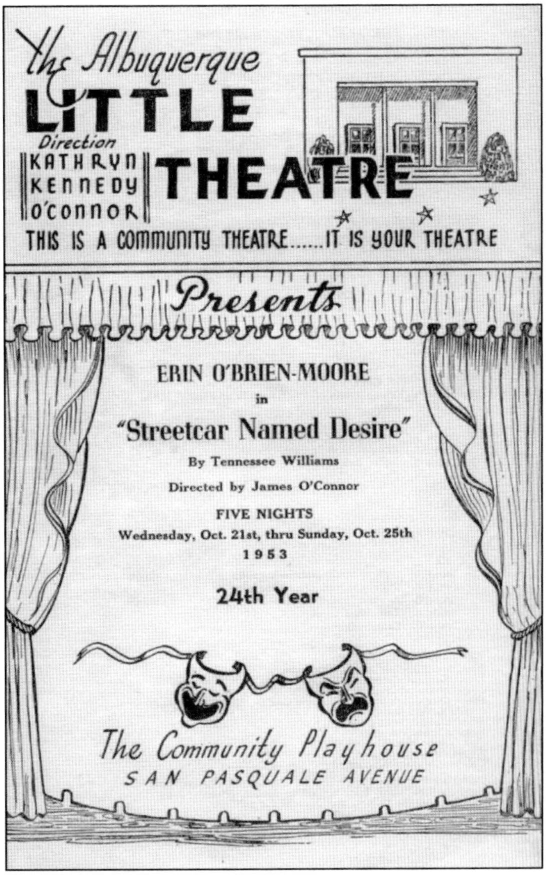

Marking the Little Theatre's 24th year was the presentation of *Streetcar Named Desire* by Tennessee Williams. The show starred Erin O'Brien-Moore and was directed by James O'Connor. (Courtesy of Albuquerque Little Theatre.)

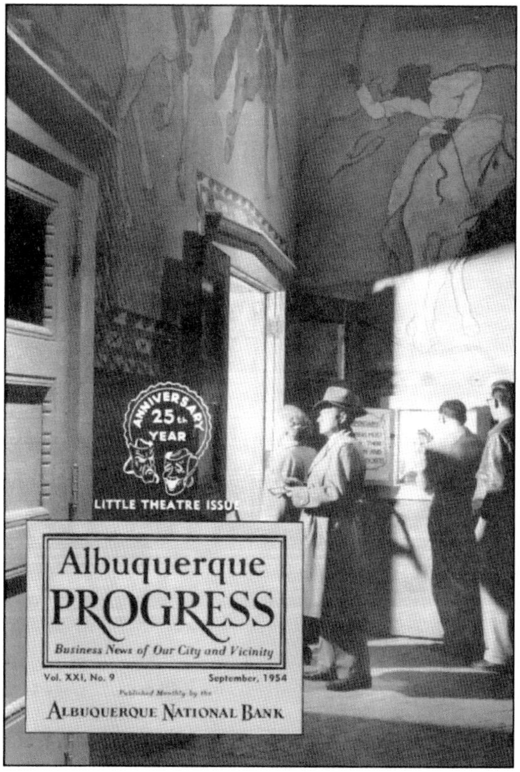

Albuquerque Progress magazine marked the 25th year of the Community Playhouse with a cover story in September 1954. This photograph shows an outdoor box office at the Little Theatre. (Courtesy of Albuquerque Little Theatre.)

Kathryn Kennedy O'Connor, a professional actress from Broadway who moved to the Southwest to recover from tuberculosis in 1930, organized the Community Playhouse (later Albuquerque Little Theatre) with the support of prominent citizens. The first plays were presented in the KiMo Theatre. Kennedy O'Connor served as the theater's longtime artistic director. (Courtesy of Albuquerque Little Theatre.)

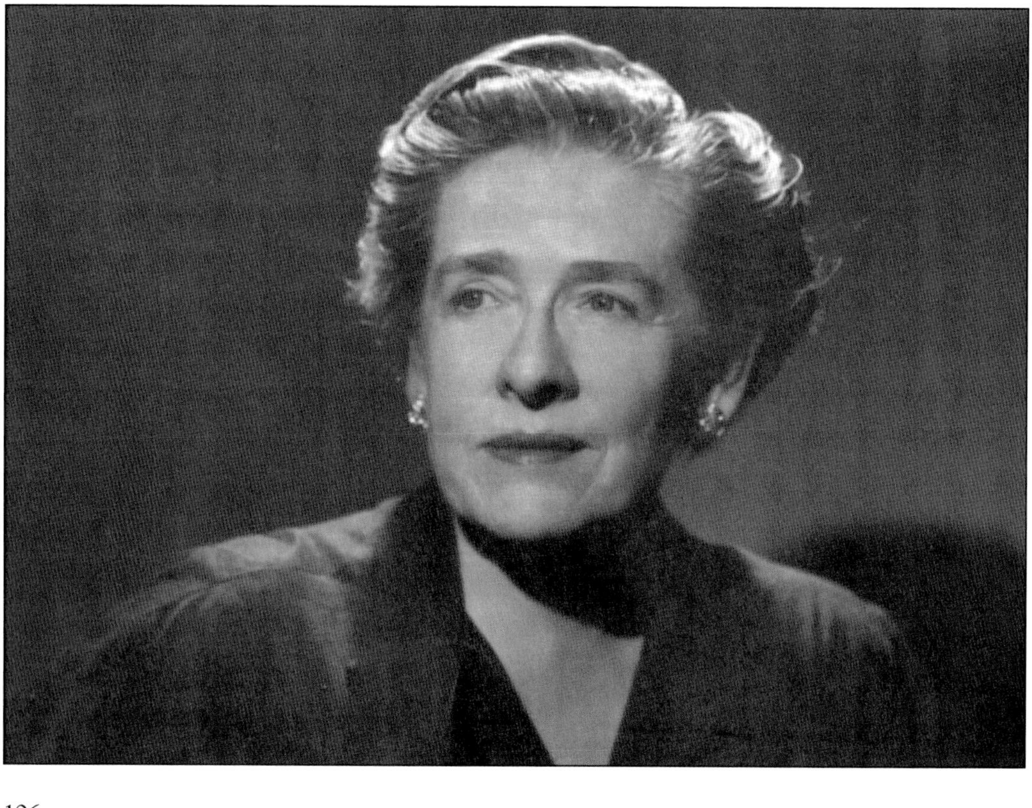

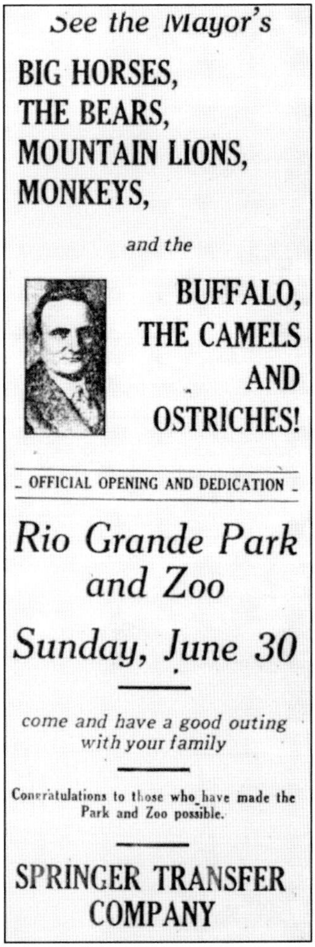

See the Mayor's

BIG HORSES,
THE BEARS,
MOUNTAIN LIONS,
MONKEYS,

and the

BUFFALO,
THE CAMELS
AND
OSTRICHES!

OFFICIAL OPENING AND DEDICATION

Rio Grande Park
and Zoo

Sunday, June 30

come and have a good outing
with your family

Congratulations to those who have made the
Park and Zoo possible.

SPRINGER TRANSFER
COMPANY

Newspaper advertisements, like this one in the *New Mexico State Tribune*, promoted a grand city celebration on June 30, 1929. More than 6,000 visitors showed up for the joint dedication of the Rio Grande Park and new zoo, the founding of the Huning Castle Addition, and the new clubhouse for the Albuquerque Country Club. (Courtesy of *New Mexico State Tribune* archives.)

The beginning of the modern-day Rio Grande Zoo began with the caging of a few native animals at one of the city's few parks prior to the 1927 acquisition of the Rio Grande Park. This photograph of undetermined date may be even older. Conservationist Aldo Leopold was a positive voice for the construction of a humane zoo. (Courtesy of Nancy Tucker.)

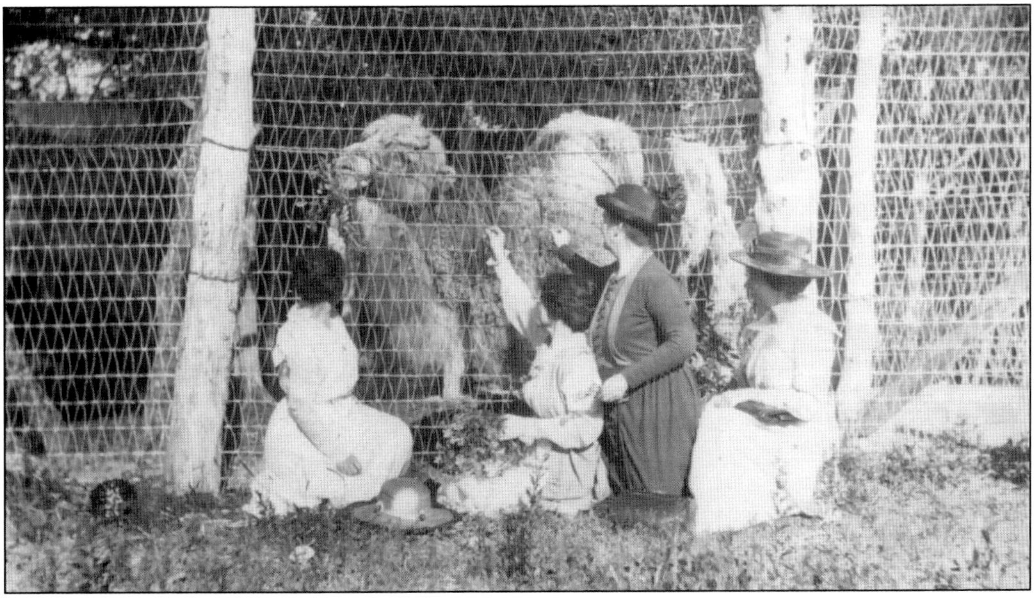

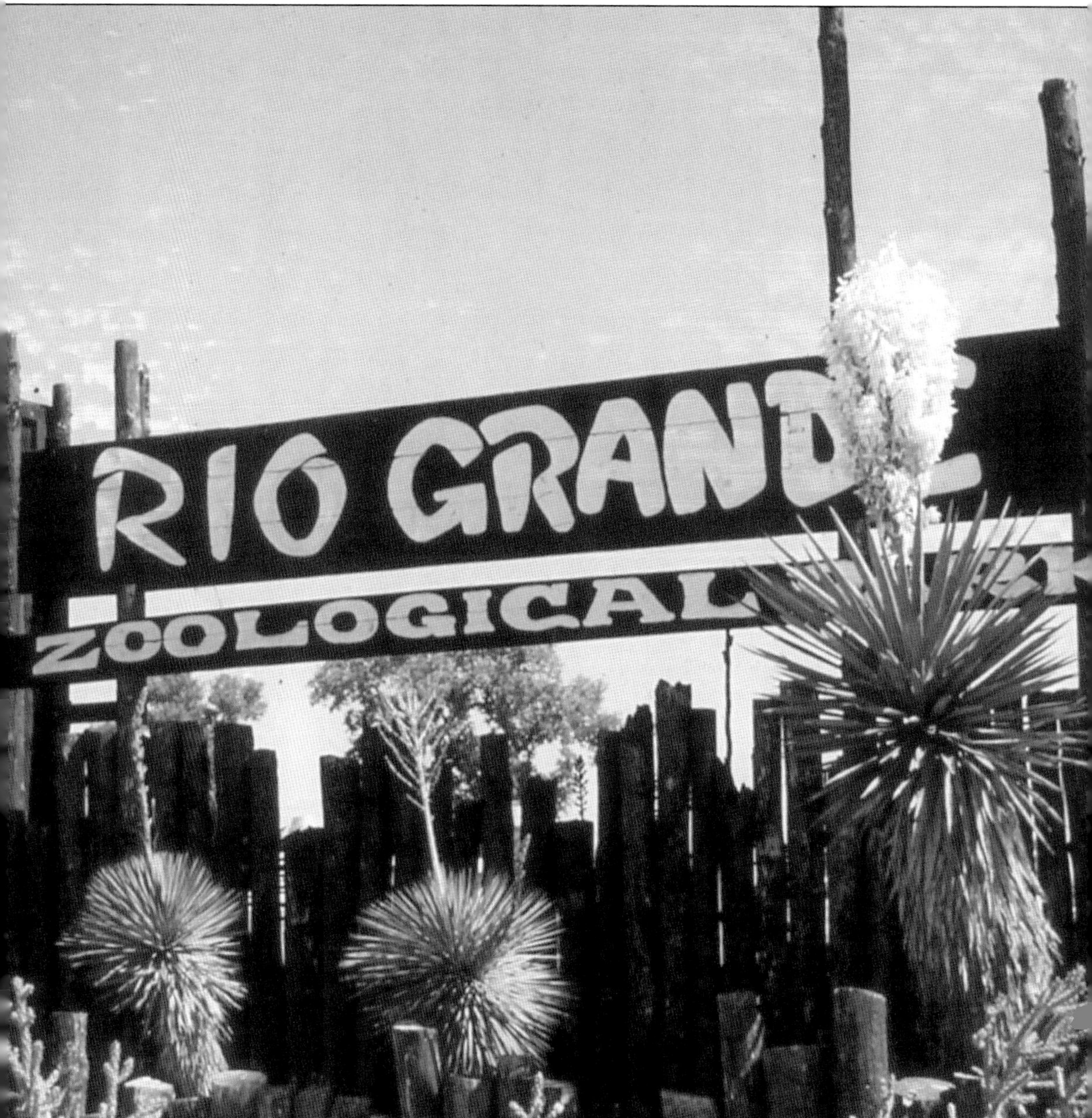

The old entryway for the Rio Grande Zoological Park came down in a remodeling phase in 1982. Some of the zoo's first animals included two bears named Pancho and Major Hoople, a porcupine, a snake, a bobcat, several coyotes, and two wolves. (Photograph by Letitia Pierce, courtesy of New Mexico BioPark Society.)

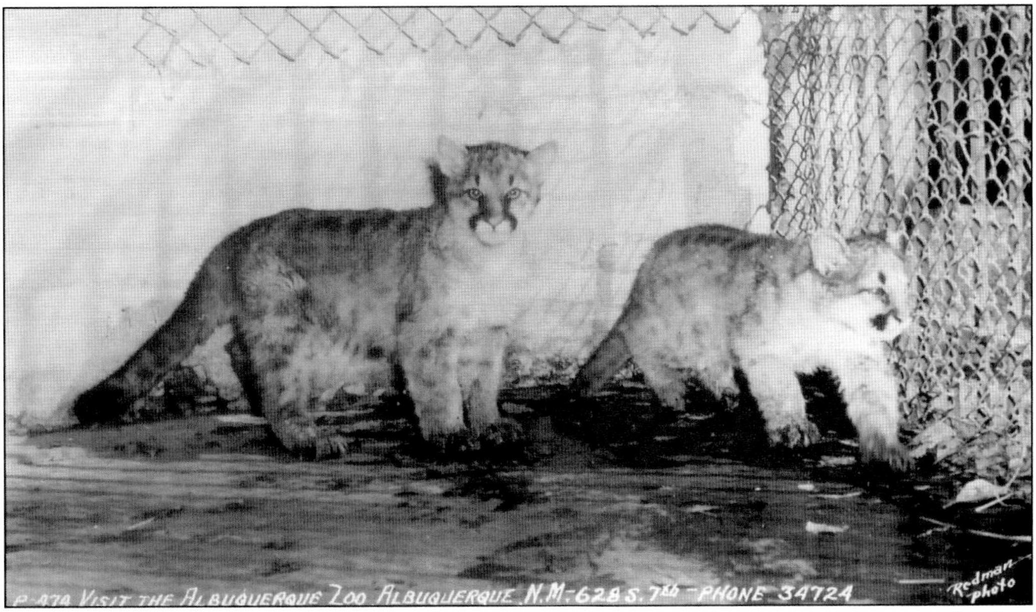

Two of the zoo's earliest animals were a donated pair of mountain lions in 1923. Reportedly, they were housed in wire cages at the corner of Broadway and Tijeras Avenue. A photograph collage in *Albuquerque Progress* shows the less-than-ideal cage for the lion. The zoo's present-day 200 species enjoy better quarters today. (Above, courtesy of New Mexico BioPark Society; below, courtesy of *Albuquerque Progress*.)

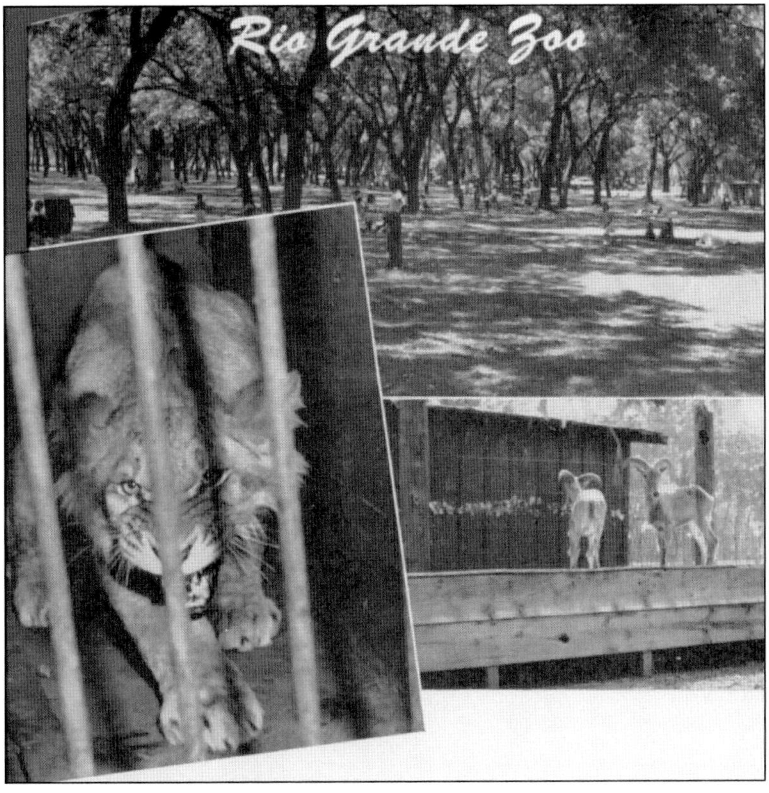

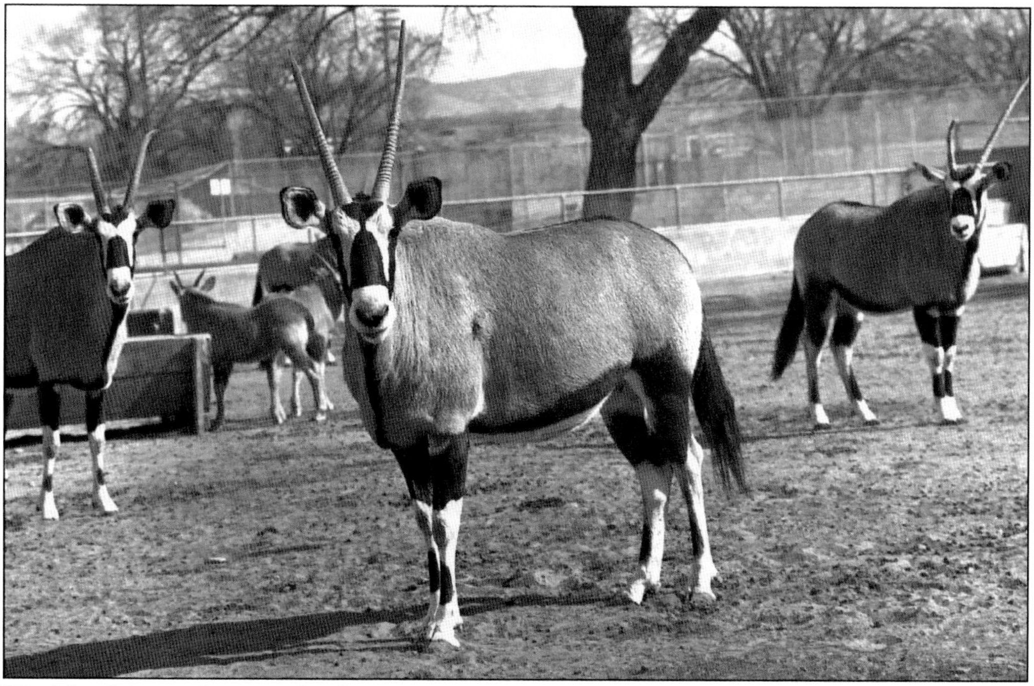

The New Mexico Game and Fish Department imported breeding herds of both ibex and oryx in the early 1960s. Federal law dictated that the imports be confined to the zoo, but the offspring could be set free. The descendants of the oryx (gemsbock) in the photograph above can still be found in the White Sands area. The ibexes in the photograph below did not thrive on their own. Other African donations ranging from tortoises to a python were contributed to the zoo by former governor Tom Bolack, a big-game hunter. (Both, courtesy of New Mexico Game and Fish Department.)

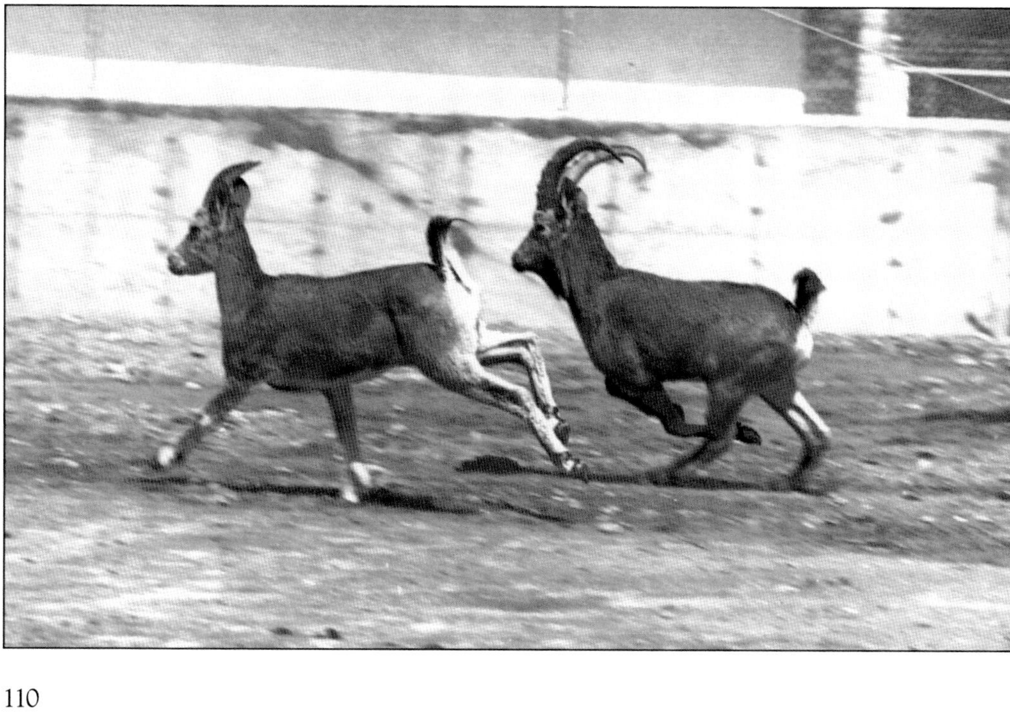

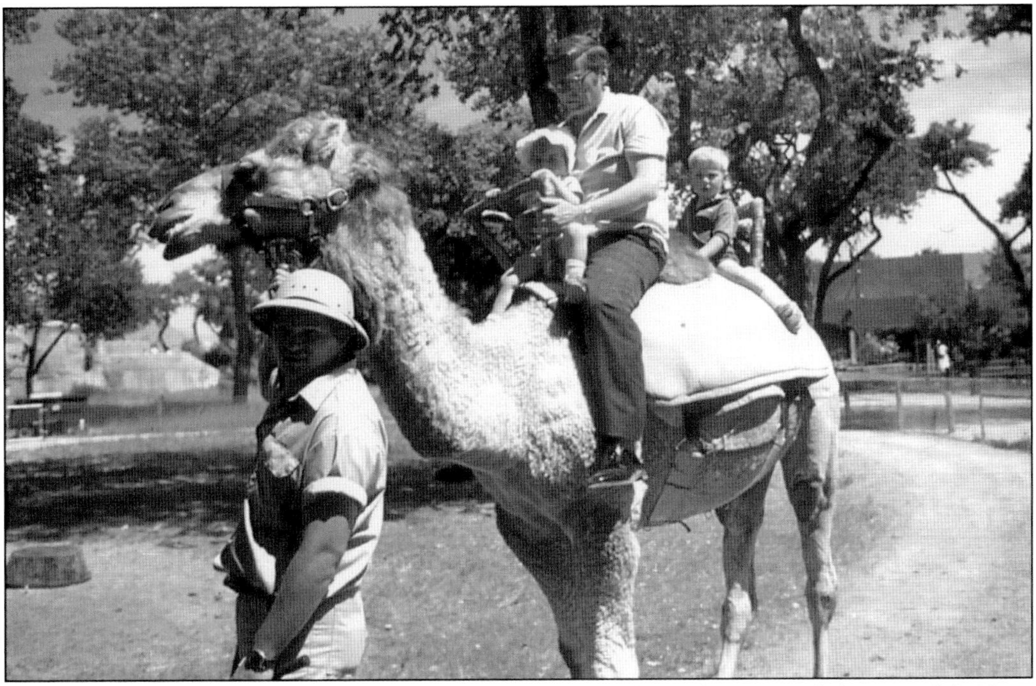

New Mexico senator Pete V. Domenici takes a camel ride at the zoo with his grandchildren Nate and Antonia Gorence about 1985. (Photograph by Letitia Pierce, courtesy of New Mexico BioPark Society.)

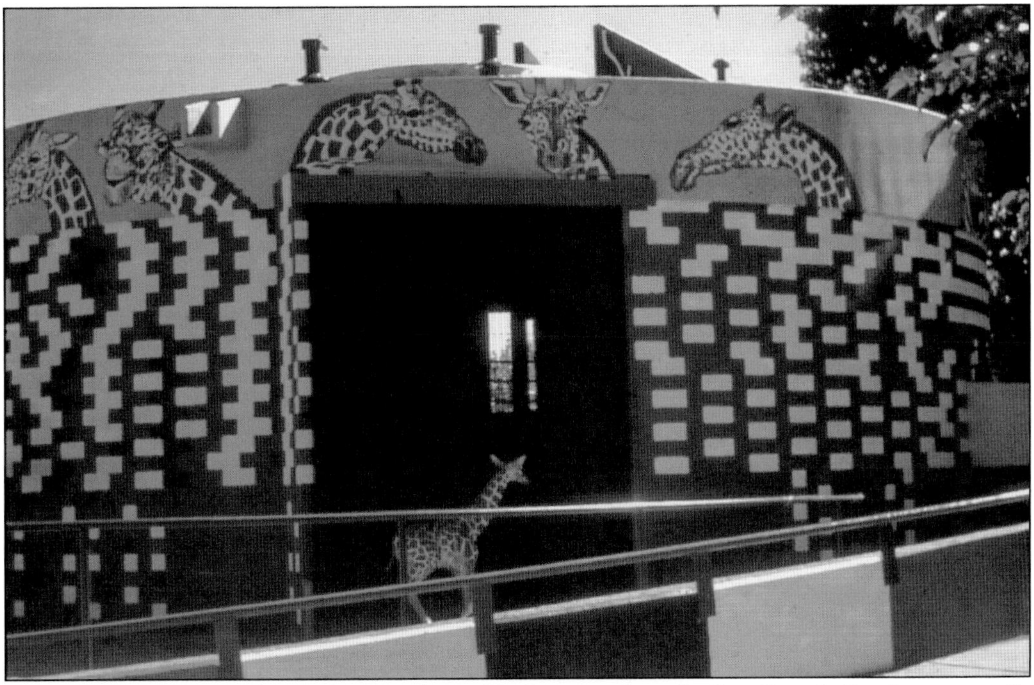

The colorful old giraffe house from in this 1977 photograph at the Rio Grande Zoo has not really disappeared. While the giraffes have increased grounds to roam, their old round home still is used as a holding pen. (Photograph by Letitia Pierce, courtesy of New Mexico BioPark Society.)

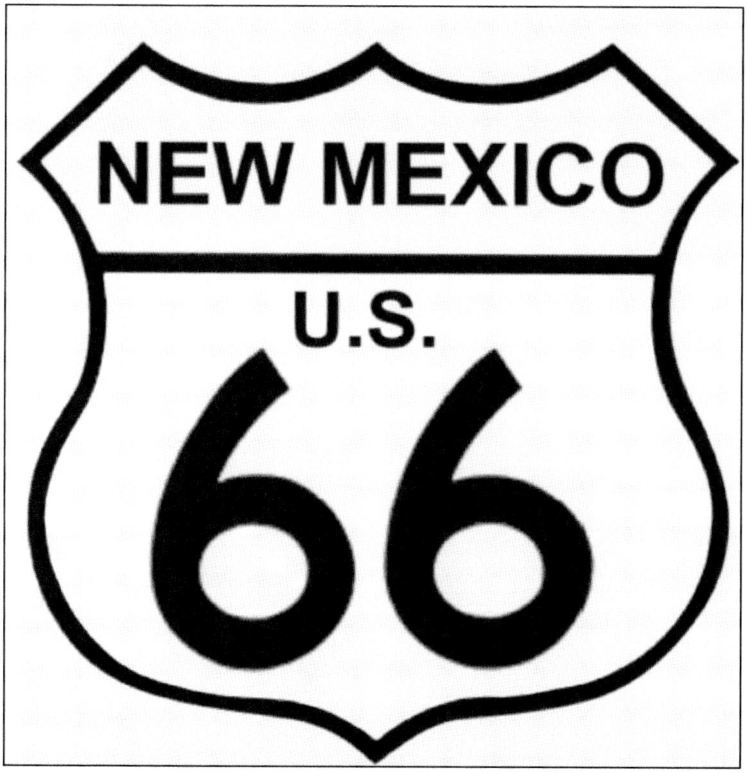

The New Mexico Route 66 emblem still lures visitors from around the world to take a drive on the old roadway once known as the "Mother Road." Through Albuquerque, the Route 66 highway is known as Central Avenue. (Left, courtesy of New Mexico Route 66 Association; below, courtesy of Nancy Tucker.)

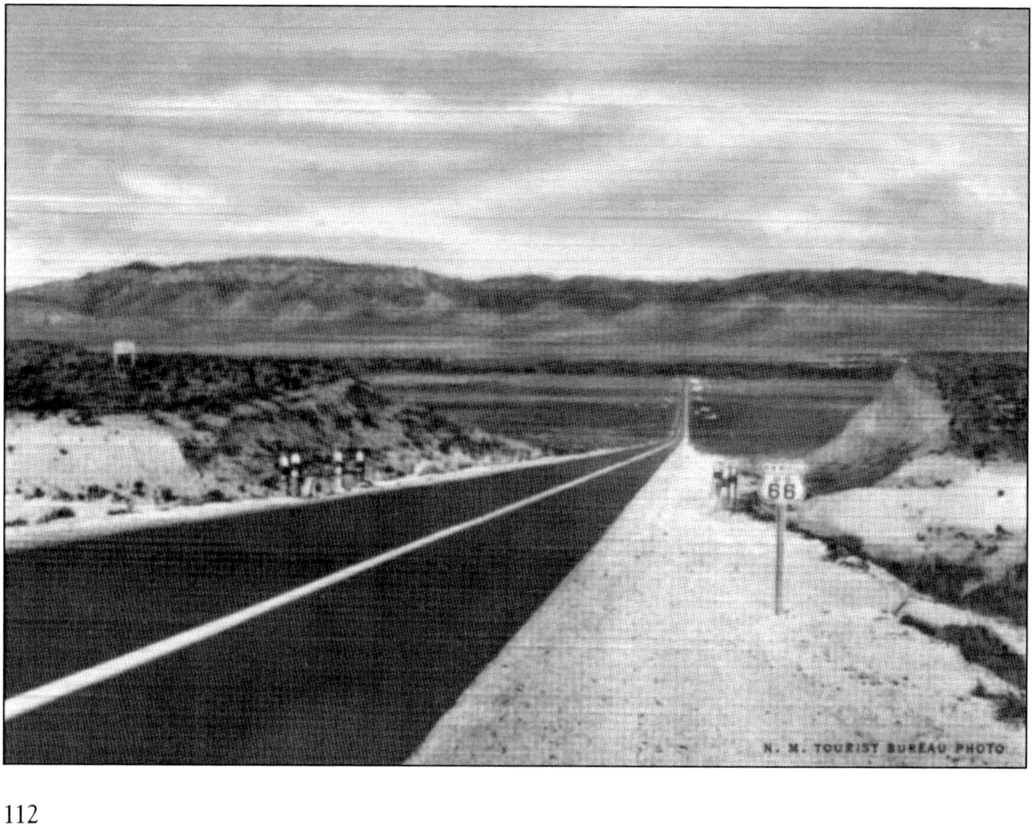

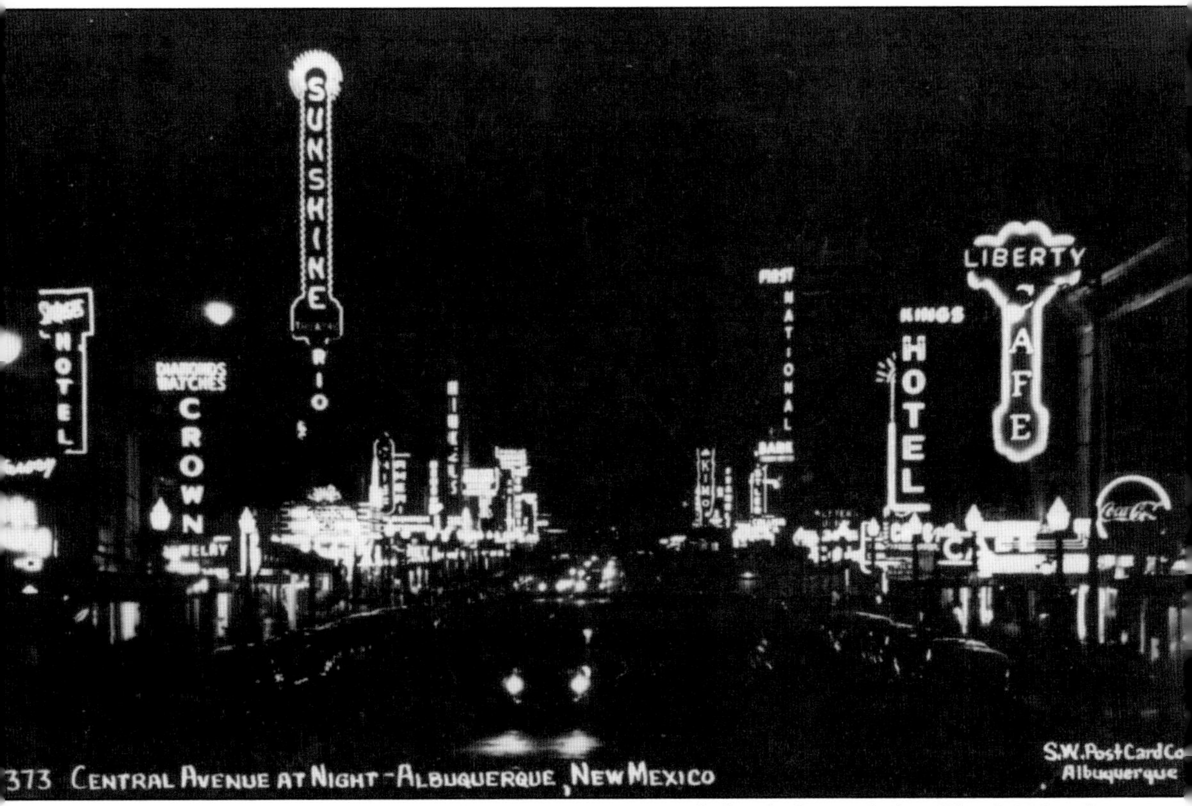

A drive along Route 66 through Albuquerque was a wonderland of neon lights. The 2,400-mile automobile trek connected Chicago to Santa Monica, California, and passed in front of the Huning Castle. The Central Avenue portion of the highway was added to the road network in 1937. (Courtesy of Nancy Tucker.)

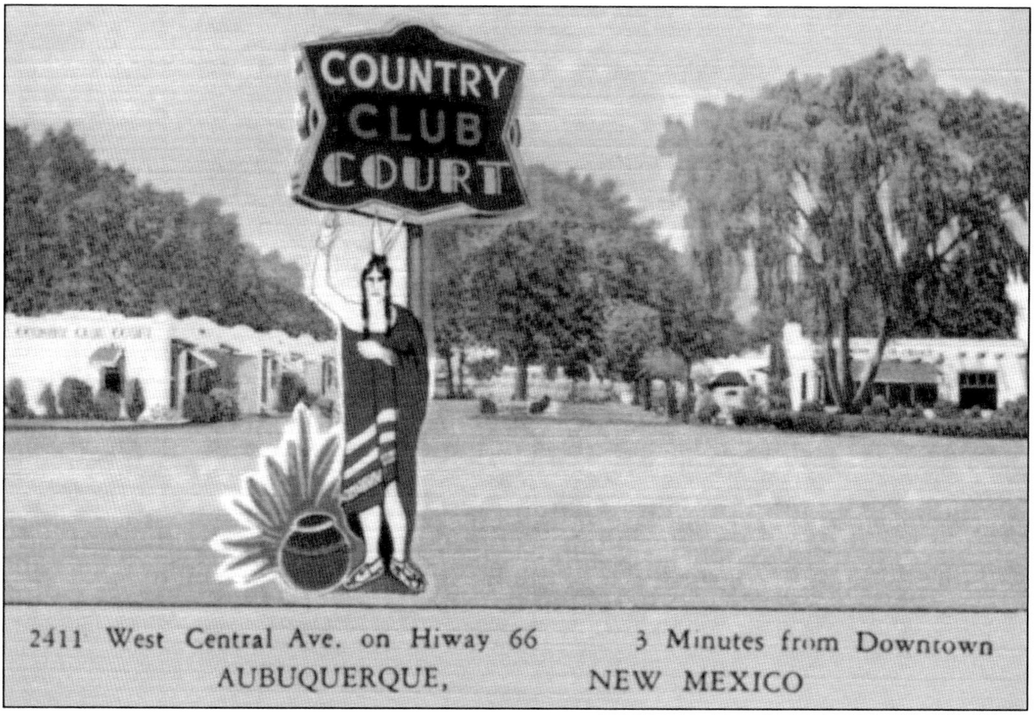

The Country Club Court offered shade trees and grass lawns for weary drivers. At 2351 West Central Avenue, the motor court offered a lovely Pueblo Revival style where tourists could see vigas and other authentic Southwestern architectural features. Signage advertised that downtown was only three minutes away. (Courtesy of Nancy Tucker.)

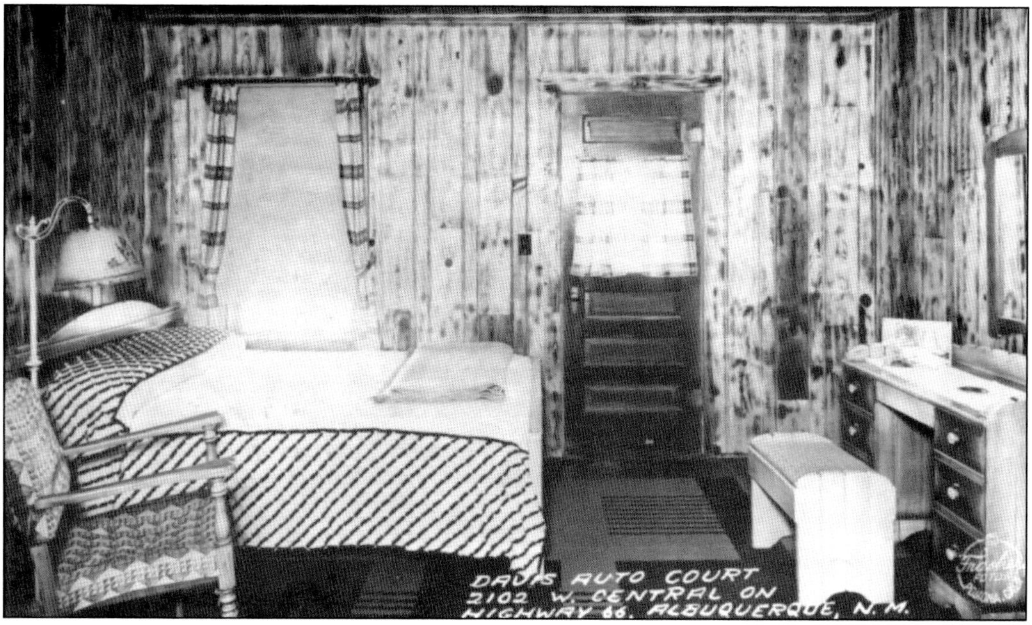

This postcard shows the interior of a room at the Davis Auto Court at 2102 W Central Avenue on Route 66. Some motor courts provided garages or swimming pools. (Courtesy of Nancy Tucker.)

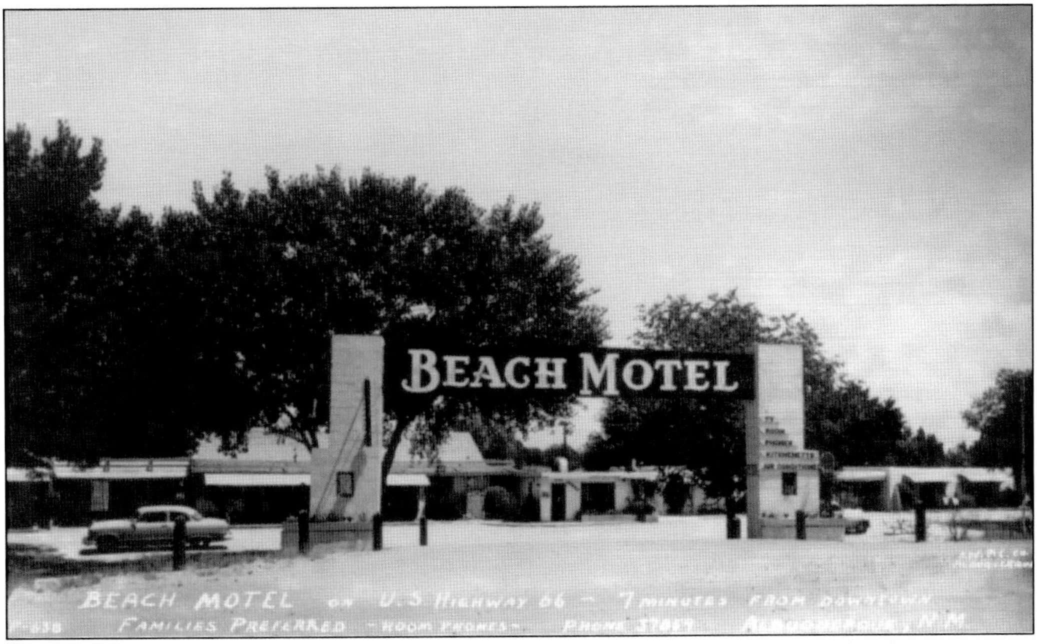

The Beach Motel was named for its proximity to Tingley Beach. For many families, a trip on Route 66 was an adventure of a lifetime. (Courtesy of Nancy Tucker.)

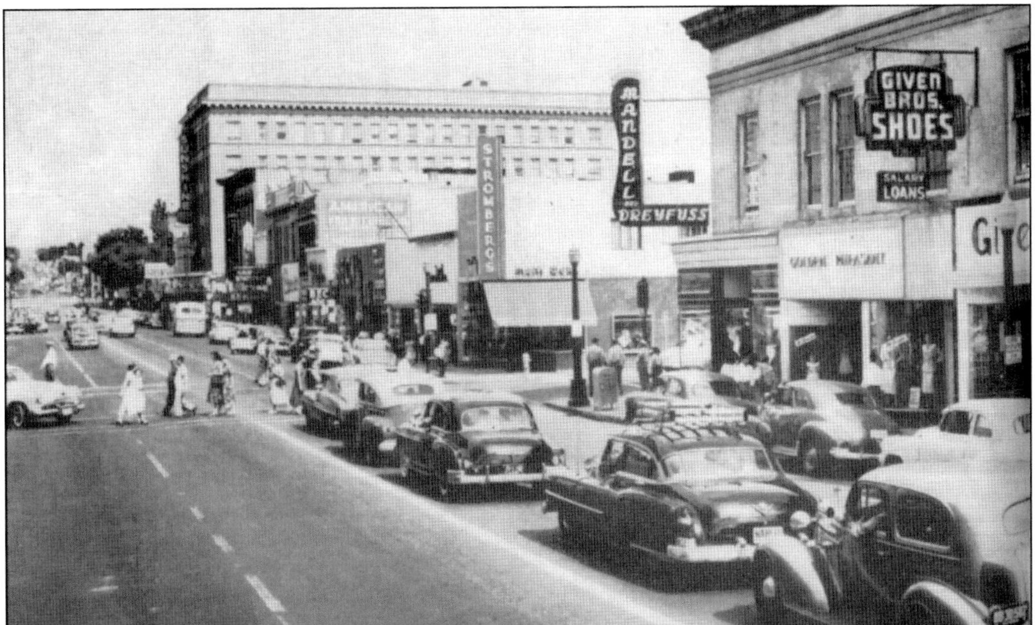

The sidewalks of Downtown Albuquerque provided a grand seat to watch automobiles in the glory days of Route 66. (Courtesy of *Progressive Magazine*.)

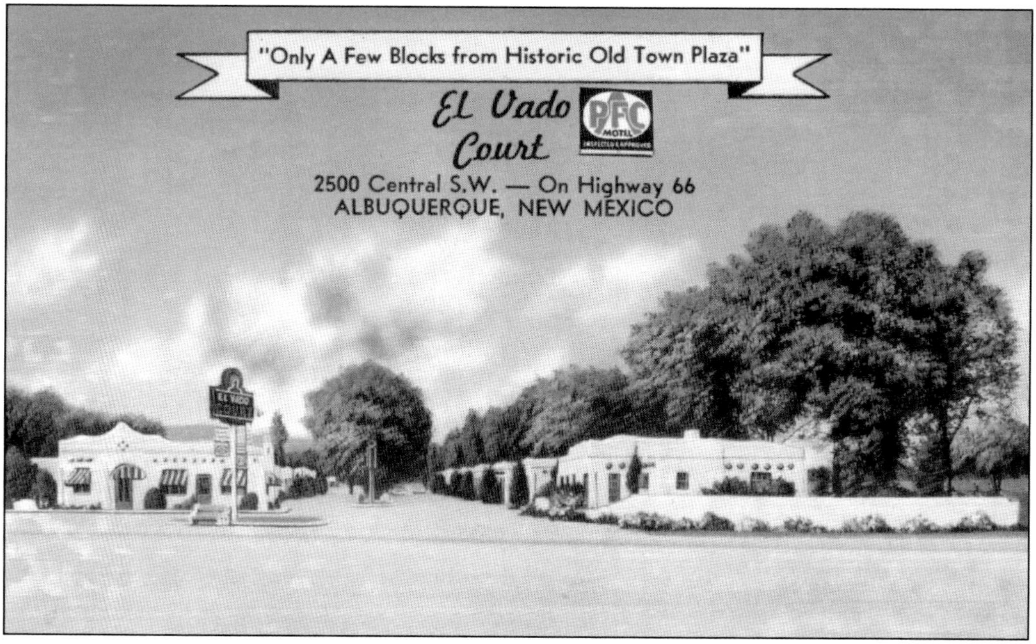

Two popular motor courts near the Huning Castle neighborhood were the El Vado Court and the Tower Court. The El Vado Court at 2500 Central Avenue SW was easily recognizable by its classic Pueblo Revival style and flashing neon sign depicting an Indian in full headdress. At the center of a battle to save these slices of American history, the El Vado is now boarded and closed. The streamlined Tower Court at 2210 Central Avenue SW no longer uses that name, but does advertise monthly apartment rates. Dozens of the old motor courts along Route 66 have been torn down. (Both, courtesy of Nancy Tucker.)

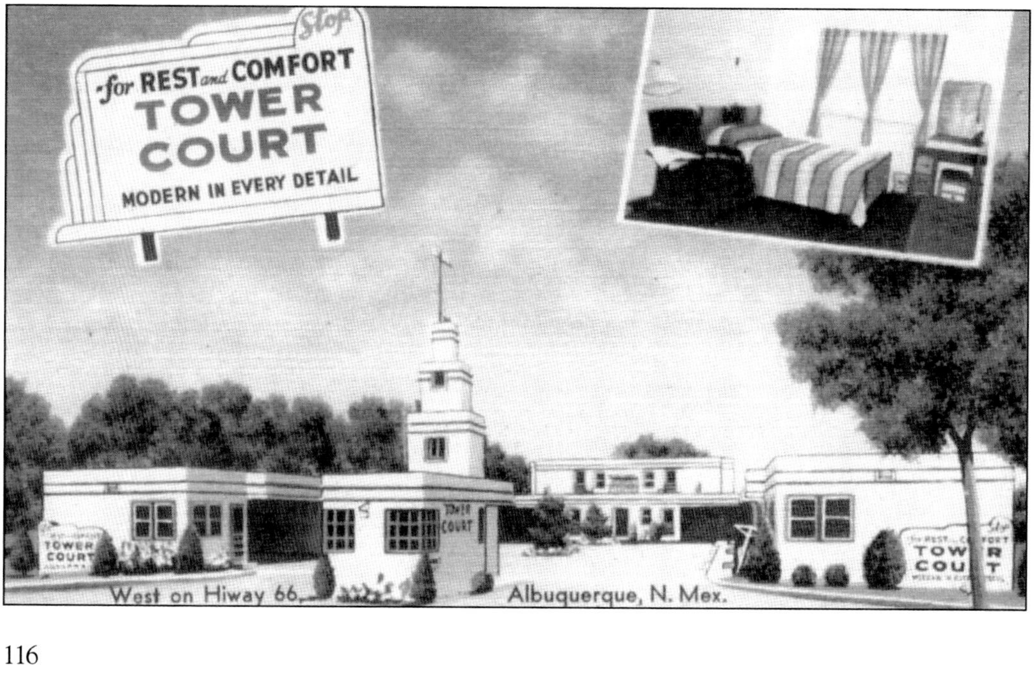

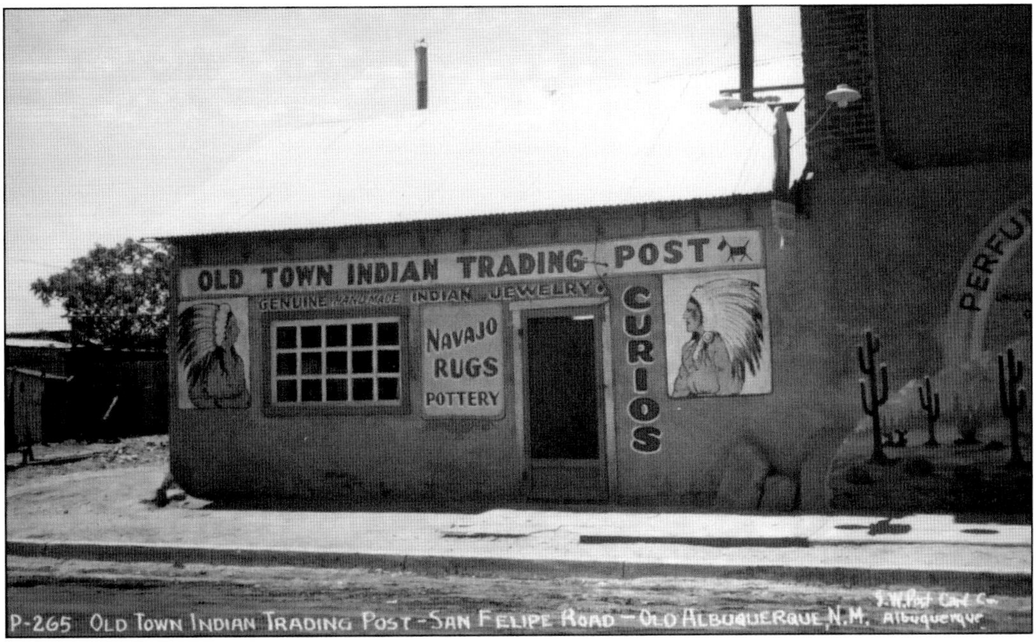

Along with the motor courts of Route 66 came the souvenir shops and trading posts along the way. The Old Town Trading Post on San Felipe Road and the La Tienda in Old Town advertised Indian curios ranging from pottery and jewelry to Navajo rugs. (Both, courtesy of Nancy Tucker.)

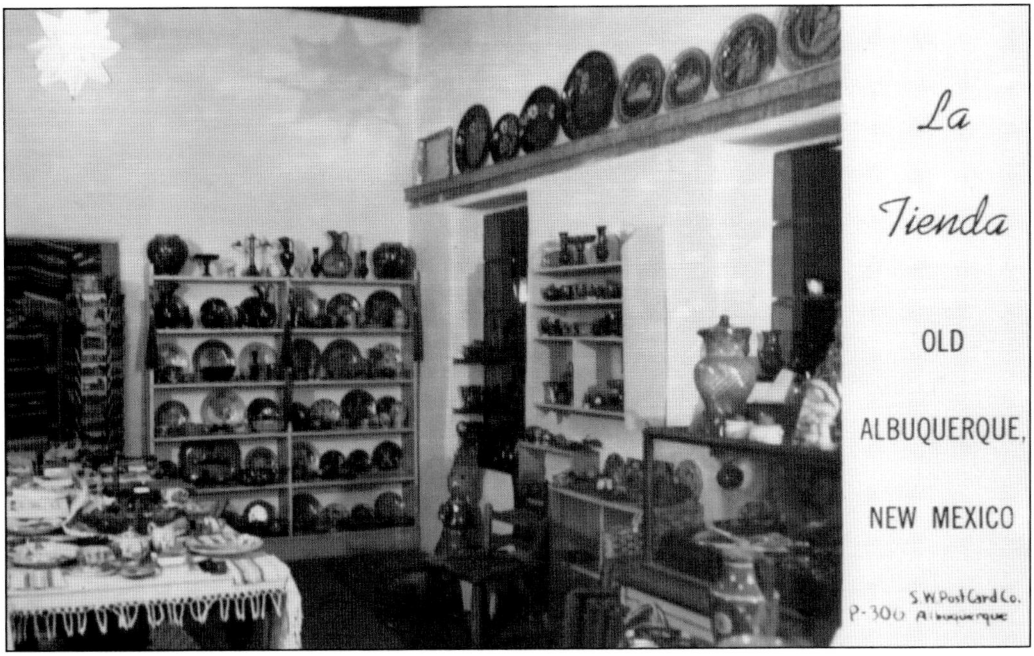

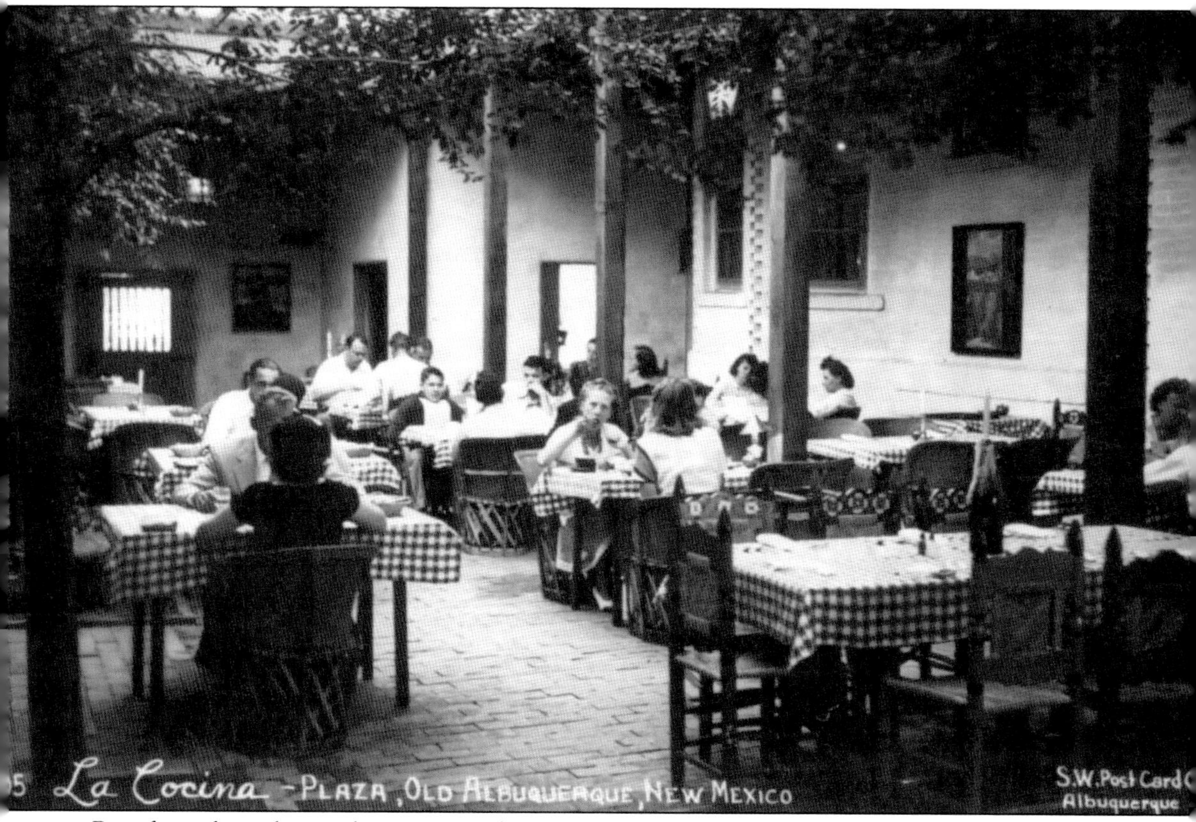

Benefiting from the nearby presence of Route 66, Old Town had a resurgence of business activity in the 1940s and 1950s. A popular restaurant on the south side of the plaza was La Cocina. (Courtesy of Nancy Tucker.)

Nine

Still Thriving
A Neighborhood between Old Town and Downtown

With the expansion of Albuquerque to the mesas on the West Side and the foothills on the East Side, the Huning Castle neighborhoods have become a centralized location in Albuquerque, a city of more than 600,000 residents in 2012. The growth makes it all the more remarkable that homeowners in this area can still easily walk or bike to downtown and Old Town, as well as the many museums and parks in the area. Within a two-mile area is the city's BioPark encompassing the Rio Grande Zoo, the Albuquerque Aquarium, and Botanic Garden and a newly restored Tingley Beach with fishing ponds and wetlands. A bike trail now parallels the Rio Grande.

Shops, galleries, and courtyards are nearby at Old Town with its historic church and plaza still intact. Downtown bustles with a movie theater complex, a lively nightclub scene, and a light-rail system that carries commuters and day-trippers from Belen to Santa Fe. Despite their proximity to commercial and cultural outlets, however, the neighborhoods in the Huning Castle area—more often called the Albuquerque Country Club area now—have maintained their distinction of well-kept homes and landscaping. The neighborhoods' tug on heartstrings is evident in the renovated homes and longtime families that still live in the area. Walk shady streets during lunch breaks or evenings and experience a neighborhood of friendly pedestrians.

Tradition is important here, and none is quite so lovely as the Christmas Eve luminarias that twinkle in rows of sand-filled bags at dusk. Venture outdoors for a late walk after the bus tours have ceased and do not be surprised if a neighbor invites one in for a holiday drink. Remember to toast the remarkable pioneer Franz Huning who first appreciated this area more than 160 years ago, and whose spirit surely remains today.

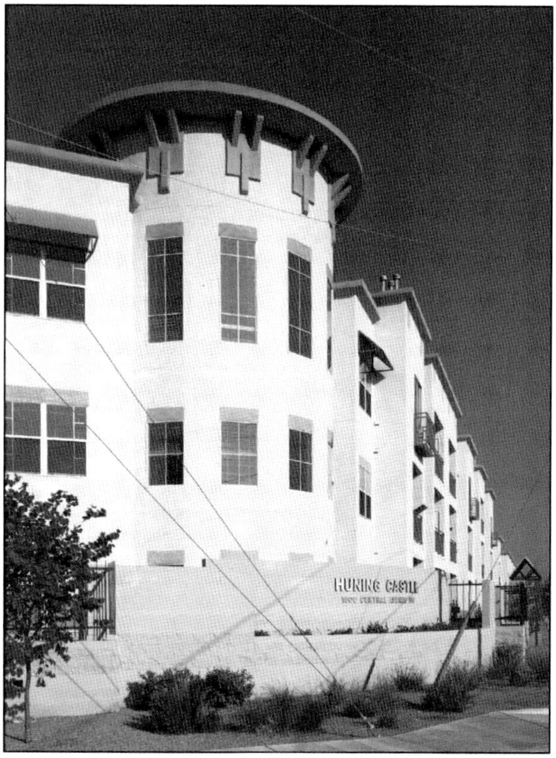

After Huning Castle was torn down in 1955, more than a half century passed before the property became anything but a vacant lot. The entire Central Avenue block between Fifteenth Street and Laguna Boulevard is now the Huning Castle Apartments, a project that generated controversy among the neighbors and opposition from some. The building was designed to honor the flair of the older castle with its tower shape. Franz Huning's original fountain has been reinstalled. (Left, photograph by Kirk Gittings; below, photograph by the author.)

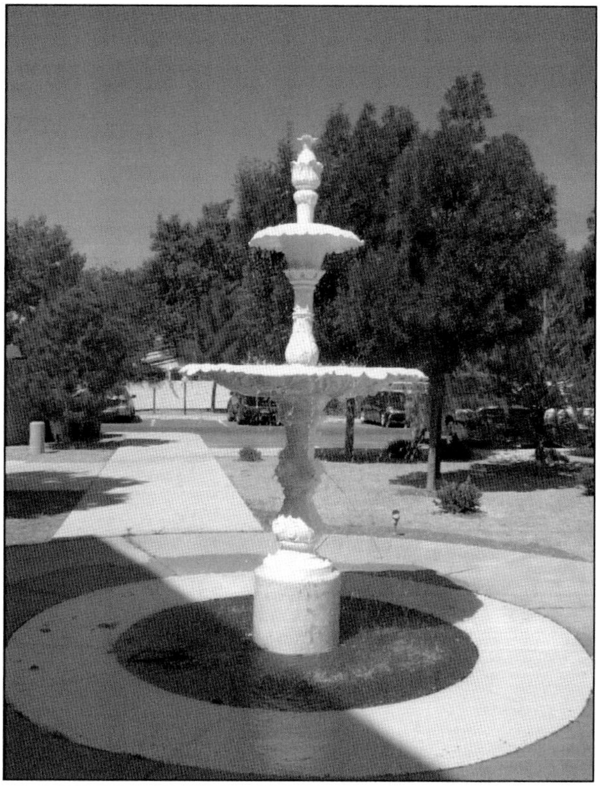

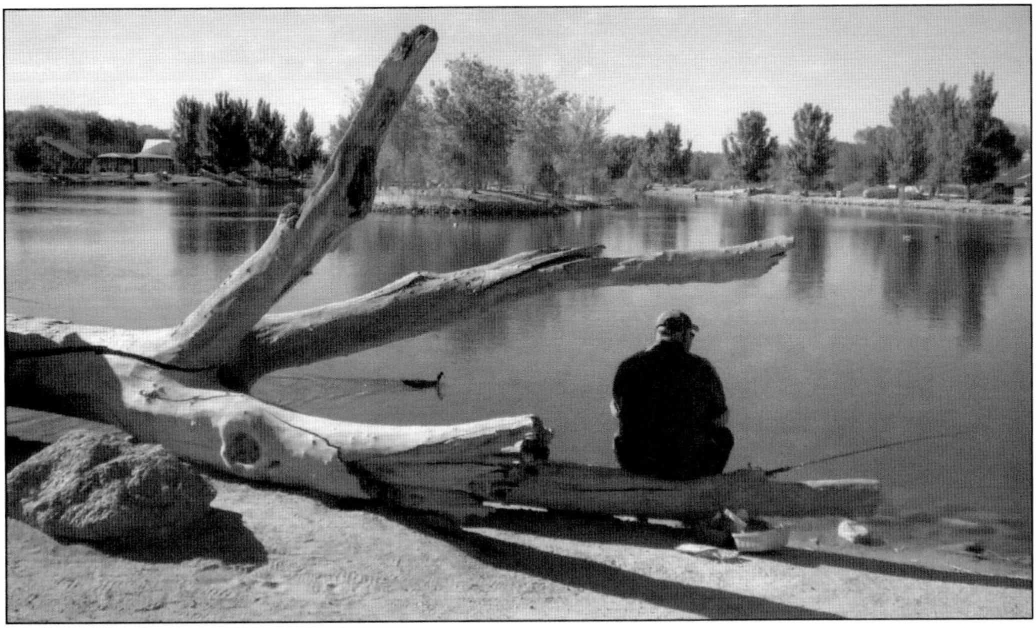

Although swimming is no longer allowed, Tingley Beach underwent a new renovation in 1994–1995. Trees, walking trails, and artwork surround several fishing ponds. Pictured is an unidentified angler perched on a log with his line cast. Tingley improvement projects have also occurred along the river's edge. Many nonnative, water-thirsty plants have been removed, and wetlands areas have been developed to attract birds and animals. (Photograph by the author.)

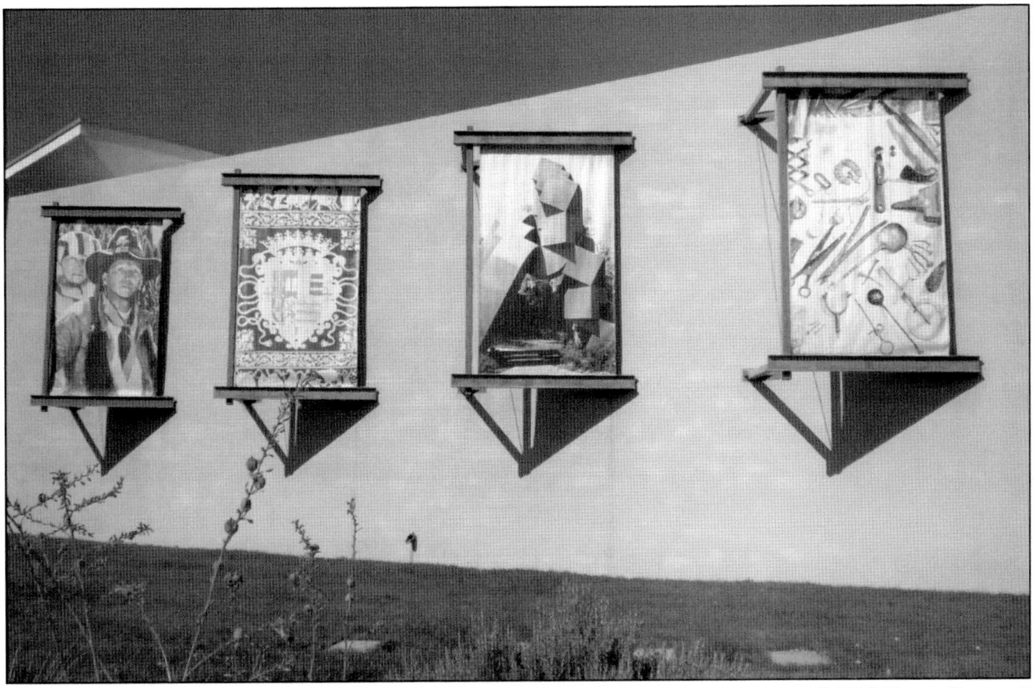

The Old Town area still resonates with shoppers, but many museums now call Old Town "home," as well. These banners provide an enticing welcome to the Albuquerque Museum of Art and History. (Photograph by the author.)

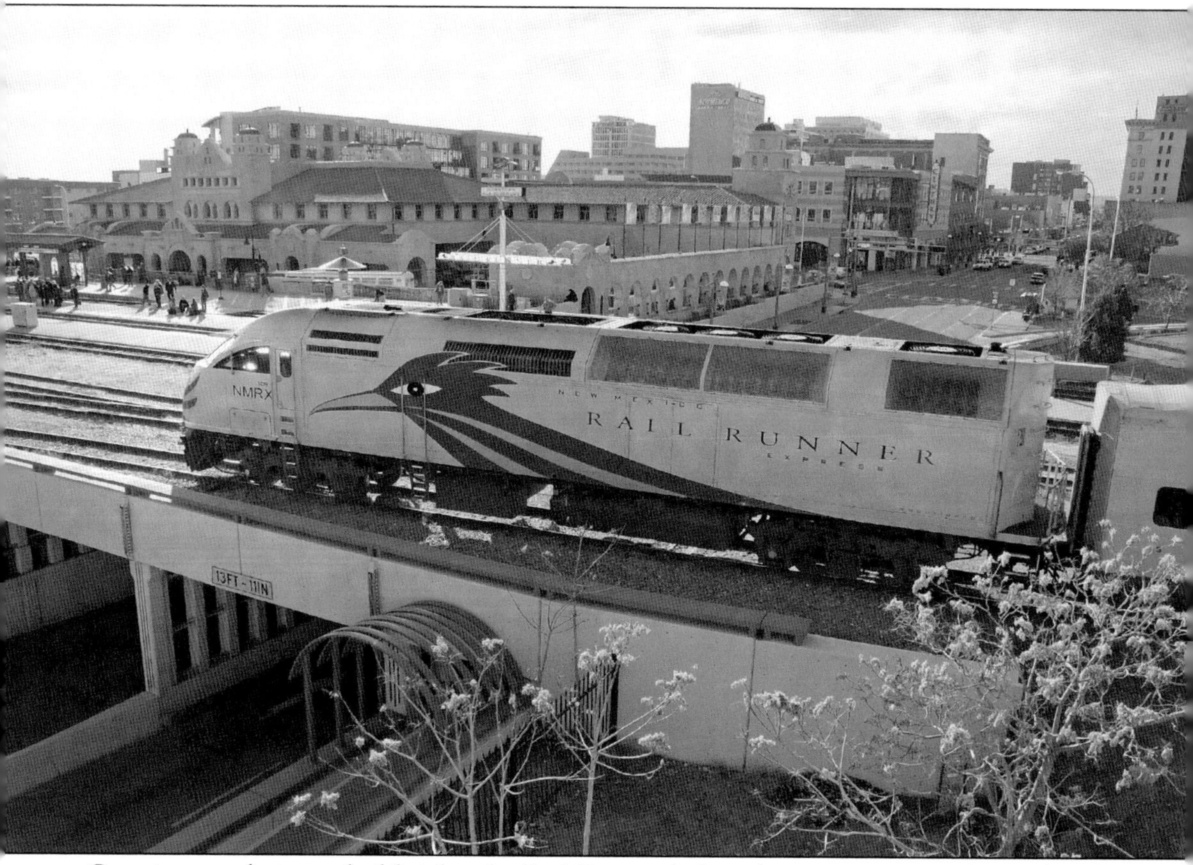

Carrying people instead of freight, the Rail Runner light-rail commuter train shares the old AT&SF tracks on daily runs for business people, tourists, and townsfolk between Belen and Santa Fe. The Alvarado Transportation Center to the rear is a respectful nod to the original design of the cherished but demolished Fred Harvey Alvarado. (Photograph by Ernie Montoya, courtesy of Rio Metro Regional Transit District.)

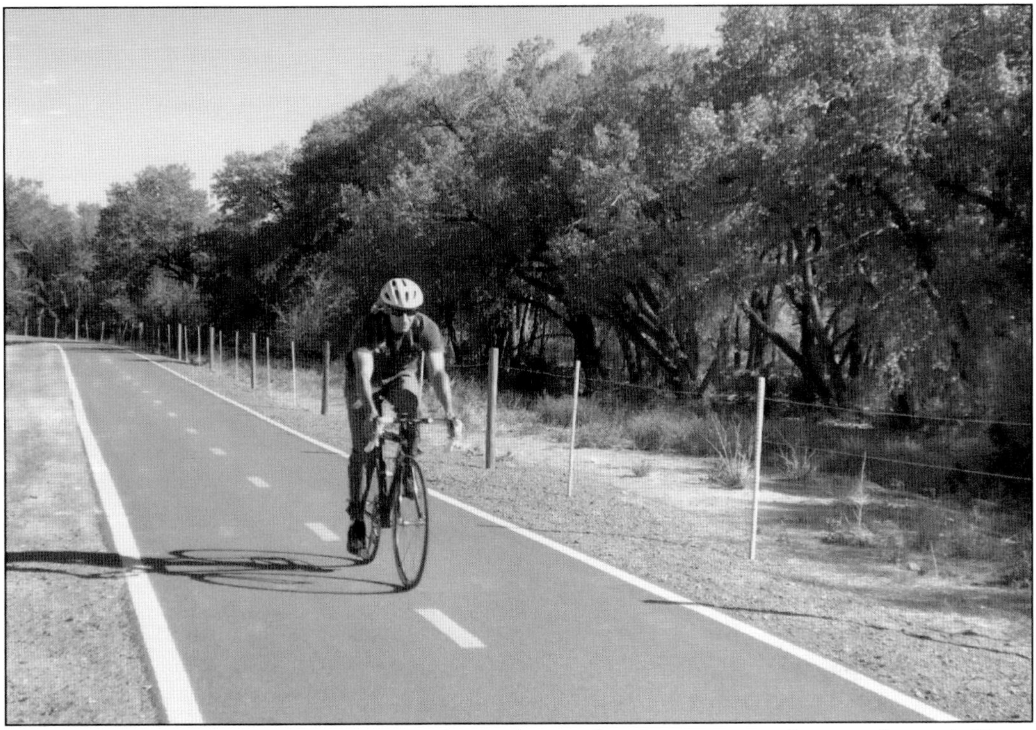

A paved bike trail parallels the Rio Grande nearly 16 miles. One portion of it runs alongside Franz Huning's former estate. The pathway connects with other trails throughout the city. (Photograph by the author.)

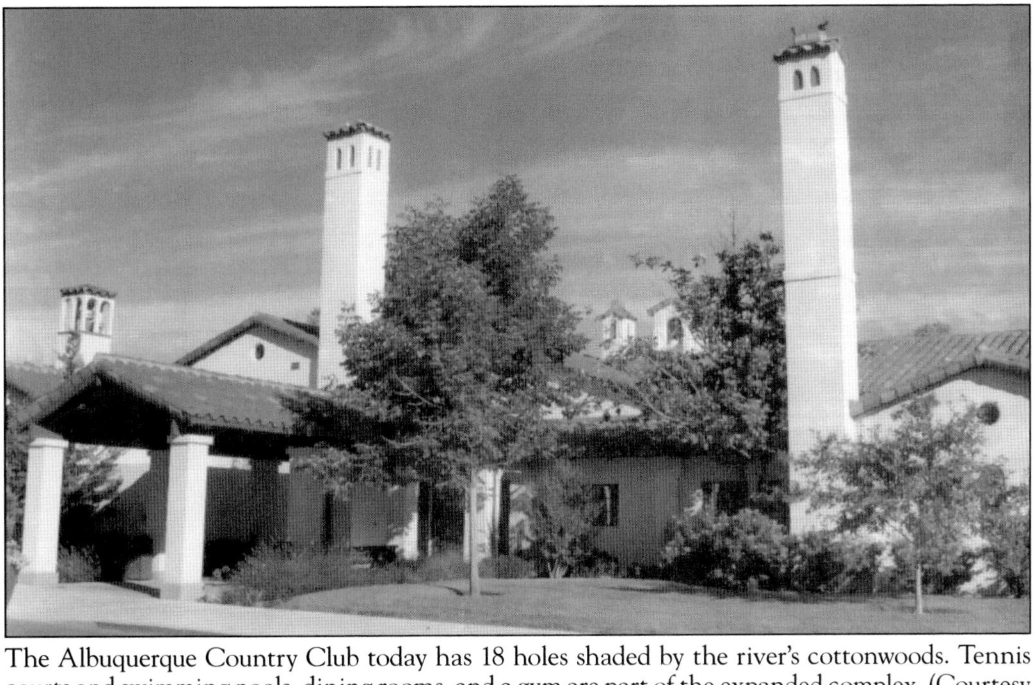

The Albuquerque Country Club today has 18 holes shaded by the river's cottonwoods. Tennis courts and swimming pools, dining rooms, and a gym are part of the expanded complex. (Courtesy of the Albuquerque Country Club.)

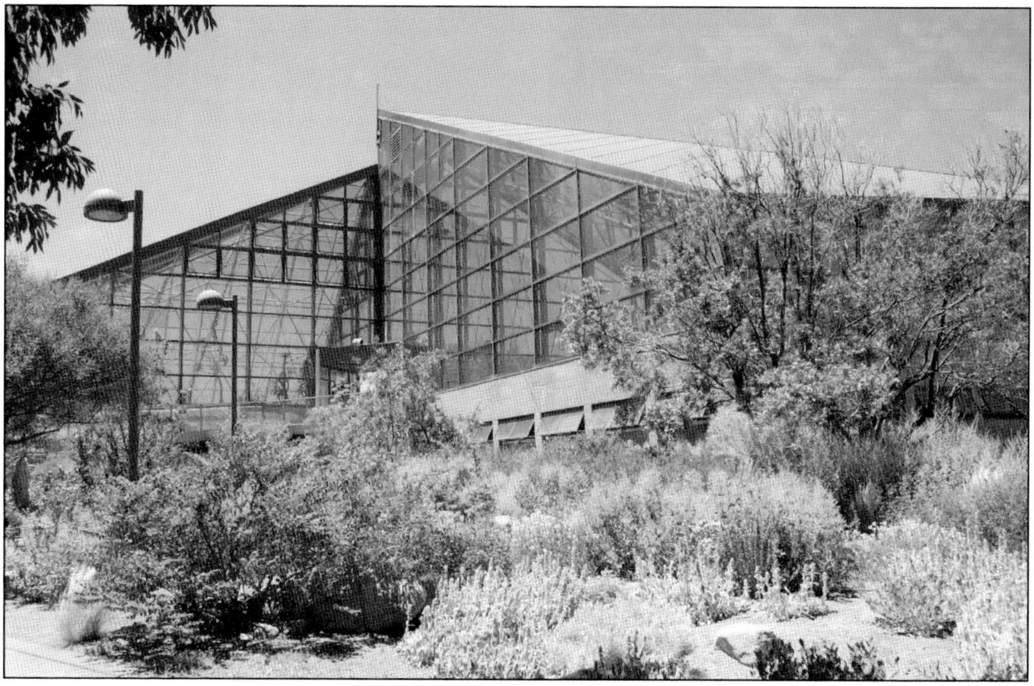

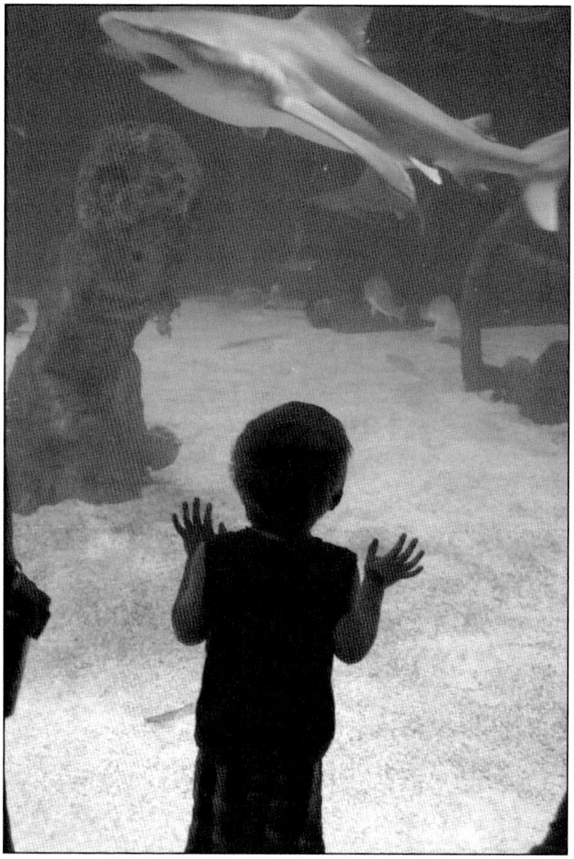

The Rio Grande Botanic Garden, located at 2601 Central Avenue NW, is part of the city's BioPark. It is a year-round destination with 36 acres of gardens and conservatories where visitors can admire blooms, attend summer concerts, or walk through the largest holiday electric light display in the state. This photograph shows the glass-enclosed Mediterranean greenhouse. (Courtesy of Judy Cook.)

The Albuquerque Aquarium, found at 2601 Central Avenue NW, is part of the BioPark's Botanic Garden. It has become a favorite with adults and kids such as this young boy fascinated by the sharks in the viewing aquarium. (Courtesy of Judy Cook.)

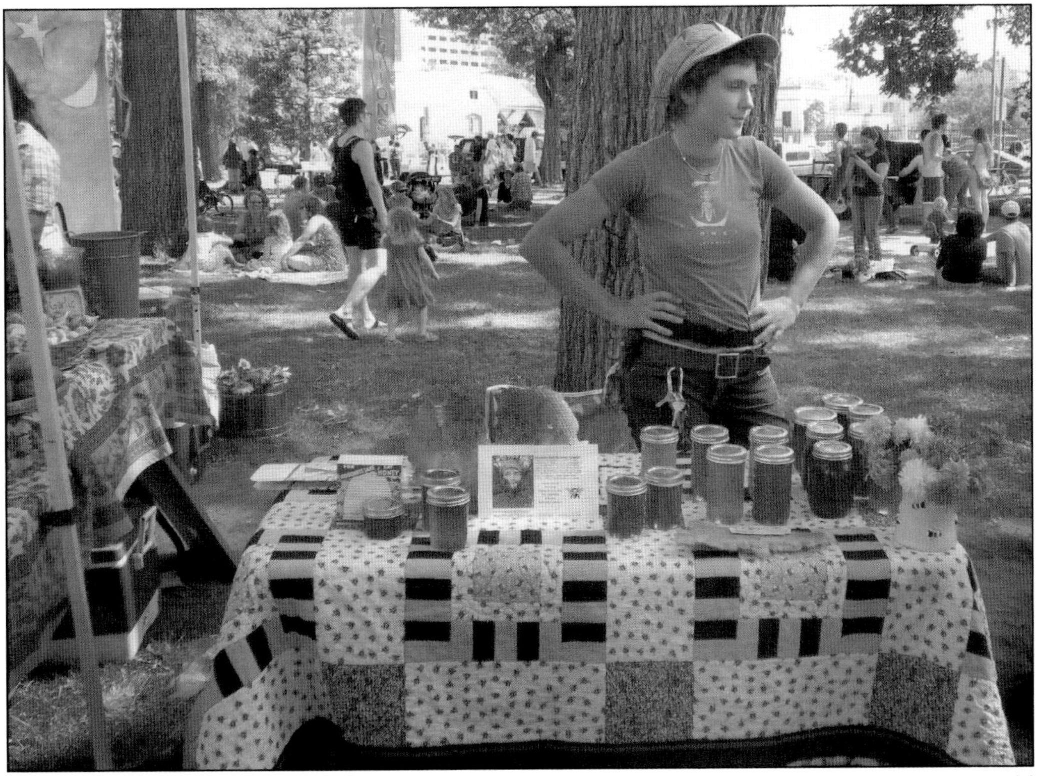

A popular park since it was founded in 1880 as Albuquerque's first public park outside the Old Town Plaza, Robinson Park near Tenth Street and Central Avenue still hums with activity today. A summer growers' market attracts shoppers from throughout the Huning Castle and other downtown neighborhoods on Saturday mornings. Musicians, artists, and food vendors mingle while the public buys fresh organic goods. Here, Megan Mahoney sells honey. (Above, photograph by the author; below, courtesy of Nancy Tucker.)

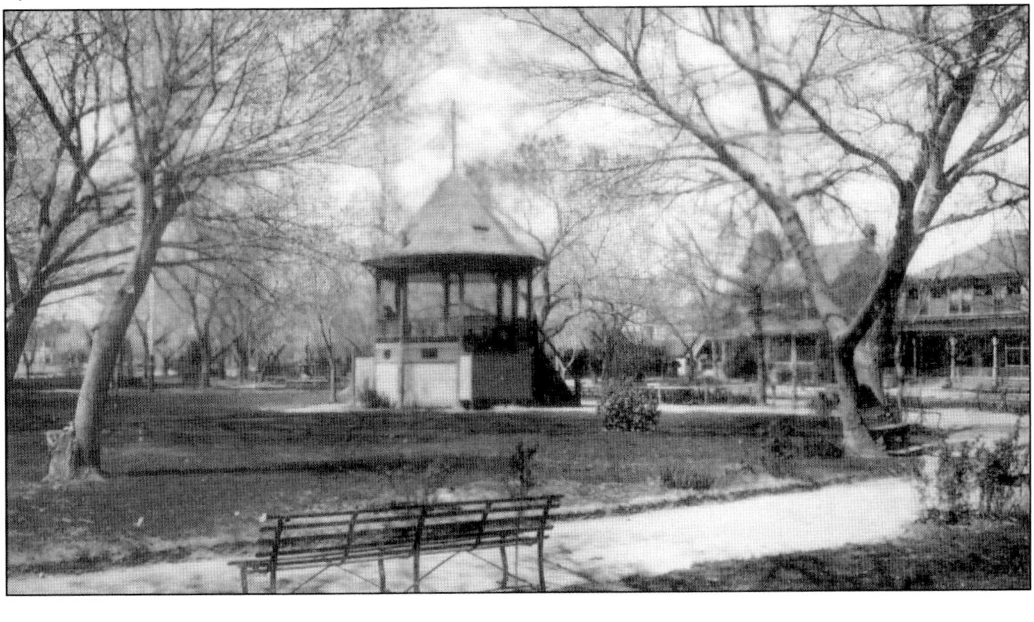

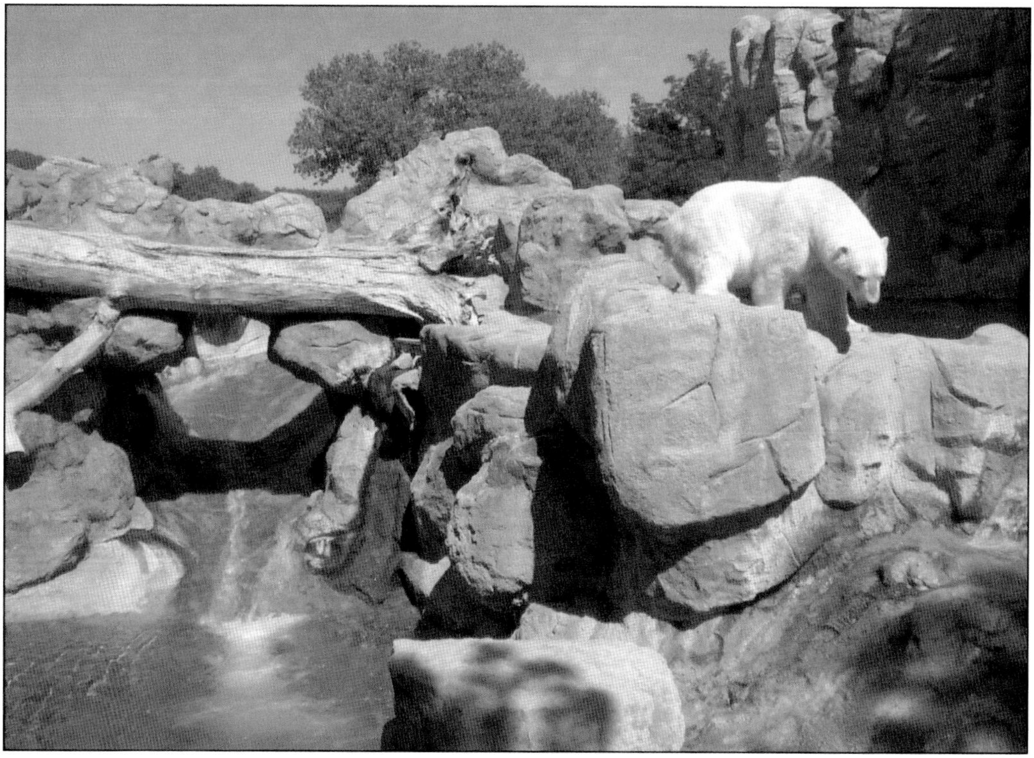

The Rio Grande Zoo with 200 species of animals is shaded under sprawling cottonwoods in a park-like setting along the Rio Grande. Animal habitats continually improve as shown in these photographs of the new and old polar bear home. The old polar bear home pictured below will be transformed into a penguin exhibit. (Above, photograph by the author; below, photograph by Leticia Price, courtesy of New Mexico BioPark Society.)

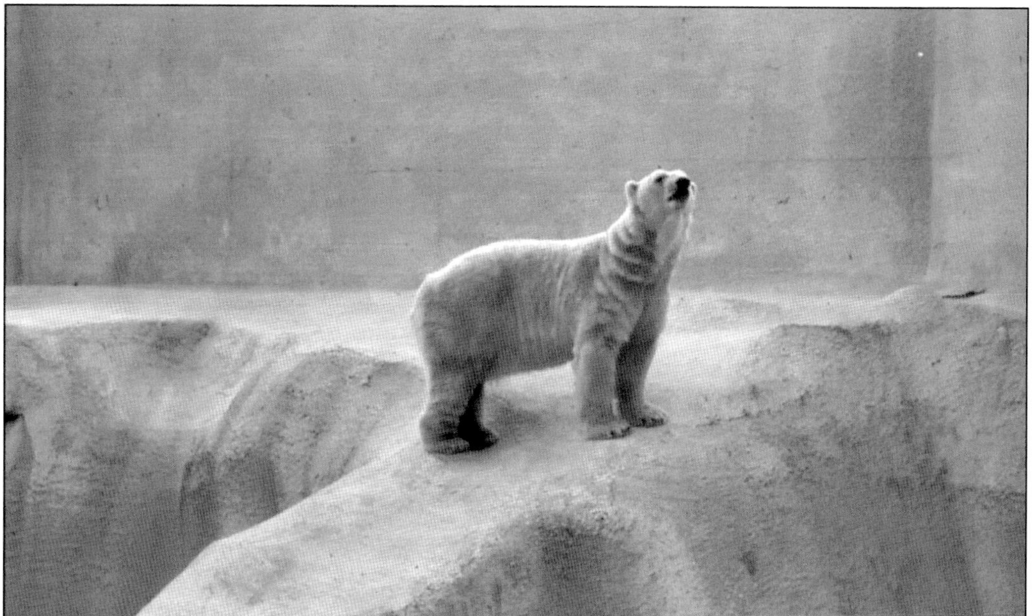

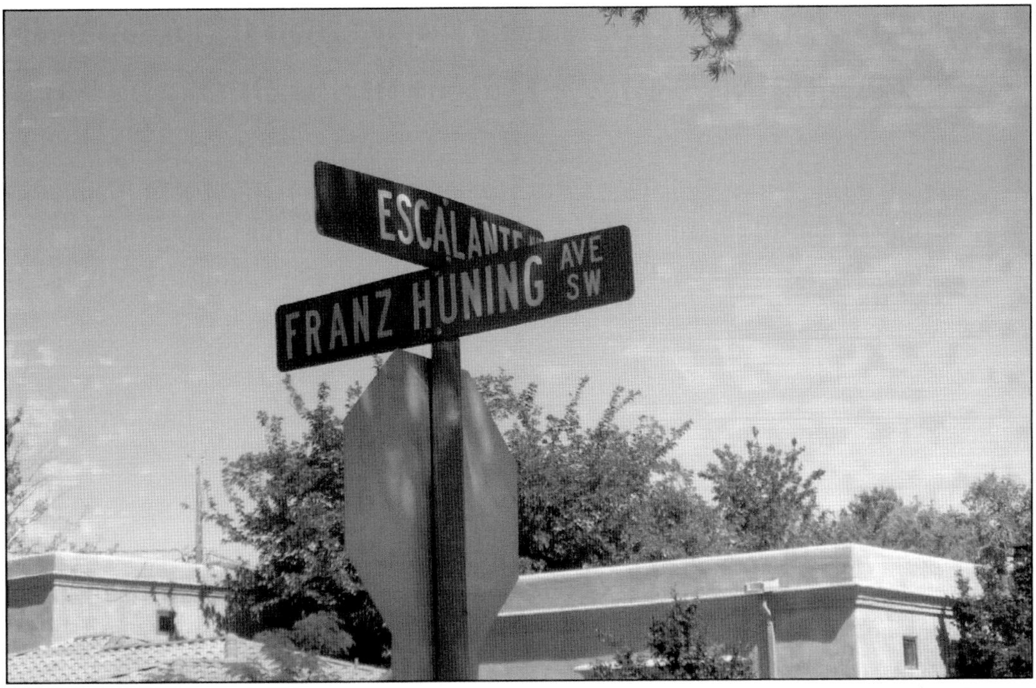

Franz Huning is still remembered everyday by the residents who live on "his" street in the Huning Castle Addition. (Photograph by the author.)

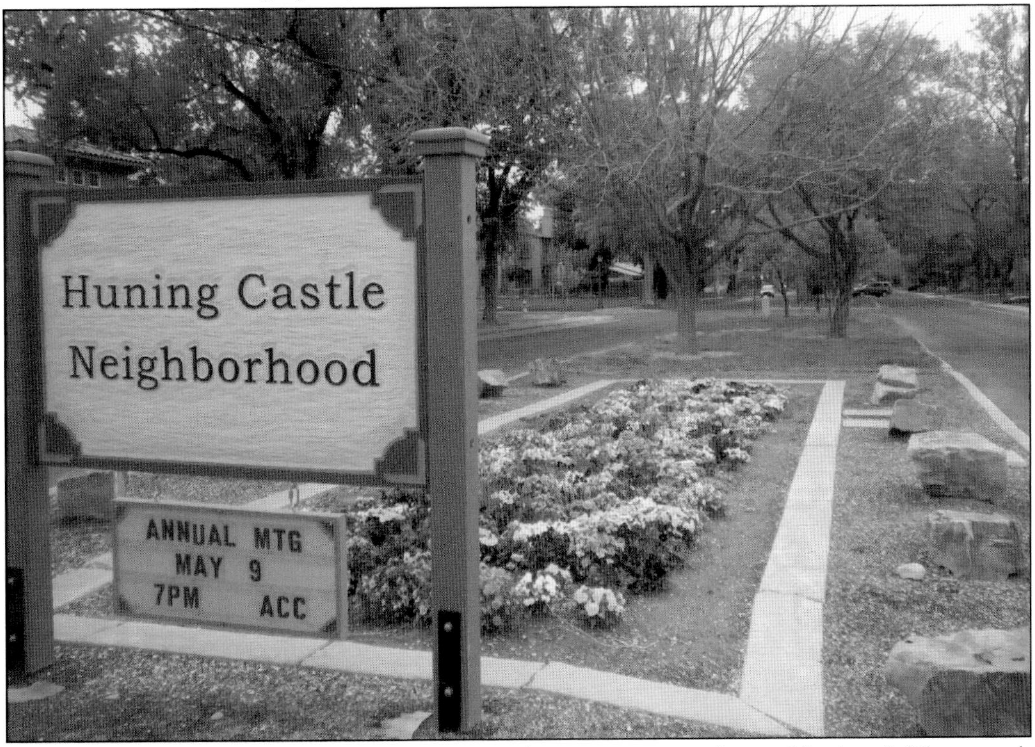

The Huning Castle Neighborhood Association welcomes visitors to the neighborhood. (Photograph by the author.)

Discover Thousands of Local History Books Featuring Millions of Vintage Images

Arcadia Publishing, the leading local history publisher in the United States, is committed to making history accessible and meaningful through publishing books that celebrate and preserve the heritage of America's people and places.

Find more books like this at
www.arcadiapublishing.com

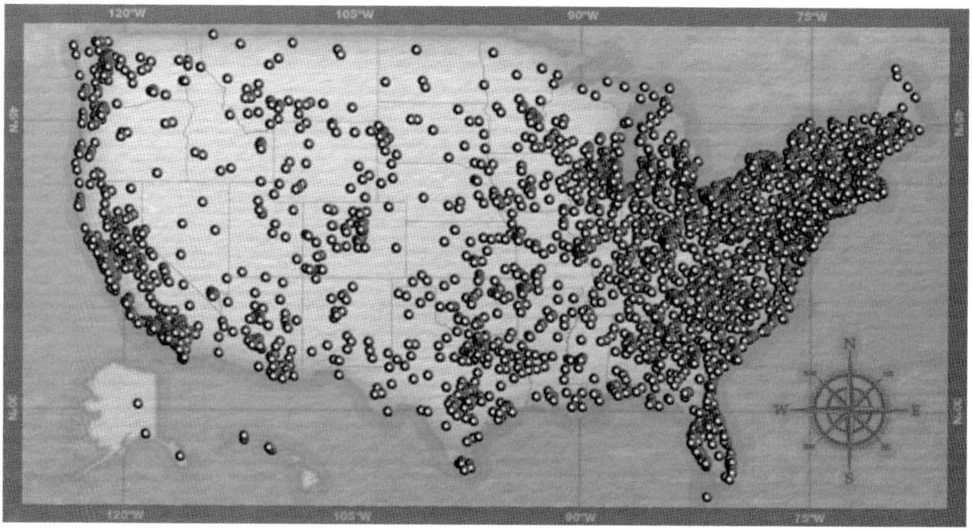

Search for your hometown history, your old stomping grounds, and even your favorite sports team.

Consistent with our mission to preserve history on a local level, this book was printed in South Carolina on American-made paper and manufactured entirely in the United States. Products carrying the accredited Forest Stewardship Council (FSC) label are printed on 100 percent FSC-certified paper.

MADE IN THE USA